M000316815

GREAT
EULOGIES
THROUGHOUT
HISTORY

GREAT
EULOGIES
THROUGHOUT
HISTORY

EDITED BY JAMES DALEY

DOVER PUBLICATIONS, INC.
MINEOLA, NEW YORK

Acknowledgments: See page xii.

Copyright

Copyright © 2016 by Dover Publications, Inc.
All rights reserved.

Bibliographical Note

Great Eulogies Throughout History is a new compilation, first published by Dover Publications, Inc., in 2016. James Daley has selected and arranged the eulogies and provided all the introductory material. Some selections in this book have been reprinted exactly as they were previously published in an effort to preserve the consistency of the original documents and their historical context, which may include archaic terminology and spelling.

Library of Congress Cataloging-in-Publication Data

Names: Daley, James, 1979–, editor.
Title: Great eulogies throughout history / edited by James Daley.
Description: Mineola, New York: Dover Publications, Inc., 2016.
Identifiers: LCCN 2016010793| ISBN 9780486805320 | ISBN 0486805328
Subjects: LCSH: Eulogies. | Biography—Miscellanea. | History—Miscellanea.
Classification: LCC CT105 .G723 2016 | DDC 920.02—dc23 LC record
available at https://lccn.loc.gov/2016010793

Manufactured in the United States by RR Donnelley
80532801 2016
www.doverpublications.com

Note

THROUGHOUT ALL OF recorded history, people of every race and culture have gathered together to honor the dead with words of praise, love, and remembrance. Whether their words are delivered at the funeral service itself, or years later at a public memorial, these writings and speeches address the loss of an entire community by remembering the life of the deceased, and speaking to their impact on friends, family, and the world in which they lived.

While ceremonies honoring the dead go back to humanity's earliest days, the modern concept of the eulogy traces its history back to the funeral orations (*epitaphios logos*) of ancient Greece, in which a prominent orator would praise a deceased citizen's virtues at a public burial ceremony. While the majority of the eulogies contained in this anthology were delivered during the last 200 years, Pericles' classic Funeral Oration is included to provide an example of these roots in antiquity.

After Pericles, the earliest eulogies contained in this collection are those given for the nation's founding fathers. These include Henry Lee's eulogy of George Washington, Harrison Otis's eulogy of Alexander Hamilton, and Daniel Webster's incredible eulogy of both Thomas Jefferson and John Adams, which he delivered in Boston one month after they both died on the Fourth of July, 1826—the 50th anniversary of the Declaration of Independence.

Some of the greatest eulogies contained in this volume are the ones in which a great artist or writer is honored by one of his or her contemporaries. Most notable among these are William Makepeace Thackeray's eulogy of Charlotte Brontë, Ralph Waldo Emerson's eulogy of Henry David Thoreau, Robert Ingersoll's eulogy of Walt Whitman, and Stephen Spender's remarks in honor of W. H. Auden, delivered in 1974, when Auden's name was added to Westminster Abbey's illustrious Poets' Corner.

On the other side of the coin, there is something singularly inspirational about a eulogy delivered not for a speaker's contemporary or friend, but for one of their personal heroes. In Bob Costas's eulogy of Mickey Mantle, the famed sportscaster reflects the impact that the legendary ballplayer had on a nation of fans, and on his own childhood love for baseball. Similarly, Victor Hugo eulogizes Voltaire on the one-hundredth anniversary of Voltaire's death, expounding on the depth and breadth of his influence on a century of writers who had never ceased reading and idolizing his work.

Perhaps the most profound eulogies are those delivered in honor of history's great humanitarians. In these, we find not only the remembrance of an individual's life, but examples of how one life can do so much to transform and shape the world for the better. Some of these include Abraham Lincoln's eulogy by Frederick Douglass, Susan B. Anthony's eulogy by Anna Howard Shaw, Martin Luther King Jr.'s eulogy by Benjamin Mays, Coretta Scott King's eulogy by Maya Angelou, and Nelson Mandela's eulogy by President Barack Obama.

While it is certainly inspiring to read the eulogies of great historic figures, delivered by impassioned orators, some of the most touching eulogies are those that spring from a deep personal relationship between the speaker and the deceased. For example, Albert Einstein's eulogy is delivered by his great friend and long-time colleague Ernst Straus; Emily Dickinson is remembered by her sister-in-law Susan Gilbert Dickinson; T. S. Eliot is eulogized by his dear friend Sir Rupert Hart-Davis; and at the end of one of literature's most famous relationships, Henry Miller delivered the eulogy for Anaïs Nin.

While reflecting on the life of Nelson Mandela in the final speech of this anthology, President Barack Obama confessed, "It is hard to eulogize any man—to capture in words not just the facts and the dates that make a life, but the essential truth of a person—their private joys and sorrows; the quiet moments and unique qualities that illuminate someone's soul." If anything, this is an understatement, as no one speech or essay can hope to encapsulate an entire life and its impact on the world and the people it touched. Nonetheless, it is the aim of this anthology to offer some of the greatest attempts at this herculean task, and in doing so to provide a unique viewpoint on some of history's most prominent figures through the remembrances of those who honored their lives.

—JAMES DALEY

Contents

Acknowledgments

W. H. Auden: *New Collected Poems by Stephen Spender* © 2004. Reprinted by kind permission of the Estate of Stephen Spender.

Albert Einstein: Reprinted by permission of Daniel Straus.

T. S. Eliot: Reprinted by permission of Duff and Adam Hart-Davis.

Coretta Scott King: "Eulogy of Coretta Scott King" by Maya Angelou. Copyright © 2006 by Maya Angelou. Used by permission of Caged Bird Legacy, LLC.

Martin Luther King Jr.: from *Born to Rebel*, Appendix C, by Benjamin E. Mays, University of Georgia Press, Copyright © 2003 by the University of Georgia Press, Athens, Georgia.

Mickey Mantle: Reprinted by permission of Bob Costas.

Anaïs Nin: Reprinted by permission of Henry Miller Estate.

FUNERAL ORATION

by Pericles (431 BC)

Pericles (495–429 BC) was an eminent politician and military leader who served as general of Athens during the Persian and Peloponnesian Wars. In this eulogy, delivered at a public funeral after the first year of the Peloponnesian War, Pericles honors the Athenian soldiers who died in battle.

MOST OF THOSE who have spoken here before me have commended the lawgiver who added this oration to our other funeral customs. It seemed to them a worthy thing that such an honor should be given at their burial to the dead who have fallen on the field of battle. But I should have preferred that, when men's deeds have been brave, they should be honored in deed only, and with such an honor as this public funeral, which you are now witnessing. Then the reputation of many would not have been imperiled on the eloquence or want of eloquence of one, and their virtues believed or not as he spoke well or ill. For it is difficult to say neither too little nor too much; and even moderation is apt not to give the impression of truthfulness. The friend of the dead who knows the facts is likely to think that the words of the speaker fall short of his knowledge and of his wishes; another who is not so well informed, when he hears of anything which surpasses his own powers, will be envious and will suspect exaggeration. Mankind are tolerant of the praises of others so long as each hearer thinks that he can do as well or nearly as well himself, but, when the speaker rises above him, jealousy is aroused and he begins to be incredulous. However, since our ancestors have set the seal of their approval upon the practice, I must obey, and to the

1

utmost of my power shall endeavor to satisfy the wishes and beliefs of all who hear me.

I will speak first of our ancestors, for it is right and seemly that now, when we are lamenting the dead, a tribute should be paid to their memory. There has never been a time when they did not inhabit this land, which by their valor they will have handed down from generation to generation, and we have received from them a free state. But if they were worthy of praise, still more were our fathers, who added to their inheritance, and after many a struggle transmitted to us their sons this great empire. And we ourselves assembled here today, who are still most of us in the vigor of life, have carried the work of improvement further, and have richly endowed our city with all things, so that she is sufficient for herself both in peace and war. Of the military exploits by which our various possessions were acquired, or of the energy with which we or our fathers drove back the tide of war, Hellenic or Barbarian, I will not speak; for the tale would be long and is familiar to you. But before I praise the dead, I should like to point out by what principles of action we rose to power, and under what institutions and through what manner of life our empire became great. For I conceive that such thoughts are not unsuited to the occasion, and that this numerous assembly of citizens and strangers may profitably listen to them.

Our form of government does not enter into rivalry with the institutions of others. Our government does not copy our neighbors', but is an example to them. It is true that we are called a democracy, for the administration is in the hands of the many and not of the few. But while there exists equal justice to all and alike in their private disputes, the claim of excellence is also recognized; and when a citizen is in any way distinguished, he is preferred to the public service, not as a matter of privilege, but as the reward of merit. Neither is poverty an obstacle, but a man may benefit his country whatever the obscurity of his condition. There is no exclusiveness in our public life, and in our private business we are not suspicious of one another, nor angry with our neighbor if he does what he likes; we do not put on sour looks at him which, though harmless, are not pleasant. While we are thus unconstrained in our private business, a spirit of reverence pervades our public acts; we are prevented from doing wrong by respect for the authorities and for the laws, having a particular regard to those which are ordained for the protection of the injured as well as those unwritten laws which bring upon the transgressor of them the reprobation of the general sentiment.

And we have not forgotten to provide for our weary spirits many relaxations from toil; we have regular games and sacrifices throughout the year; our homes are beautiful and elegant; and the delight which we daily feel in all these things helps to banish sorrow. Because of the greatness of our city the fruits of the whole earth flow in upon us, so that we enjoy the goods of other countries as freely as our own.

Then, again, our military training is in many respects superior to that of our adversaries. Our city is thrown open to the world, though, and we never expel a foreigner and prevent him from seeing or learning anything of which the secret if revealed to an enemy might profit him. We rely not upon management or trickery, but upon our own hearts and hands. And in the matter of education, whereas they from early youth are always undergoing laborious exercises which are to make them brave, we live at ease, and yet are equally ready to face the perils which they face. And here is the proof: The Lacedaemonians come into Athenian territory not by themselves, but with their whole confederacy following; we go alone into a neighbor's country; and although our opponents are fighting for their homes and we on a foreign soil, we have seldom any difficulty in overcoming them. Our enemies have never yet felt our united strength, the care of a navy divides our attention, and on land we are obliged to send our own citizens everywhere. But they, if they meet and defeat a part of our army, are as proud as if they had routed us all, and when defeated they pretend to have been vanquished by us all.

If then we prefer to meet danger with a light heart but without laborious training, and with a courage which is gained by habit and not enforced by law, are we not greatly the better for it? Since we do not anticipate the pain, although, when the hour comes, we can be as brave as those who never allow themselves to rest; thus our city is equally admirable in peace and in war. For we are lovers of the beautiful in our tastes and our strength lies, in our opinion, not in deliberation and discussion, but that knowledge which is gained by discussion preparatory to action. For we have a peculiar power of thinking before we act, and of acting, too, whereas other men are courageous from ignorance but hesitate upon reflection. And they are surely to be esteemed the bravest spirits who, having the clearest sense both of the pains and pleasures of life, do not on that account shrink from danger. In doing good, again, we are unlike others; we make our friends by conferring, not by receiving favors. Now he who confers a favor is the firmer friend, because he would rather by kindness keep alive the memory of an obligation; but the recipient is colder in his feelings, because he knows that in requiting another's generosity he will not be winning gratitude but only paying a debt. We alone do good to our neighbors not upon a calculation of interest, but in the confidence of freedom and in a frank and fearless spirit. To sum up: I say that Athens is the school of Hellas, and that the individual Athenian in his own person seems to have the power of adapting himself to the most varied forms of action with the utmost versatility and grace. This is no passing and idle word, but truth and fact; and the assertion is verified by the position to which these qualities have raised the state. For in the hour of trial Athens alone among her contemporaries is superior to the report of her. No enemy who comes against her is indignant at the reverses which he sustains at the hands of such a city; no subject complains that his masters are unworthy of him. And we shall assuredly not be without witnesses; there are mighty monuments of our power which will make us the wonder of this and of succeeding ages; we shall not need the praises of Homer or of any other panegyrist whose poetry may please for the moment, although his representation of the facts will not bear the light of day. For we have compelled every land and every sea to open a path for our valor, and have everywhere planted eternal memorials of our friendship and of our enmity. Such is the city for whose sake these men nobly fought and died; they could not bear the thought that she might be taken from them; and every one of us who survive should gladly toil on her behalf.

I have dwelt upon the greatness of Athens because I want to show you that we are contending for a higher prize than those who enjoy none of these privileges, and to establish by manifest proof the merit of these men whom I am now commemorating. Their loftiest praise has been already spoken. For in magnifying the city I have magnified them, and men like them whose virtues made her glorious. And of how few Hellenes can it be said as of them, that their deeds when weighed in the balance have been found equal to their fame! I believe that a death such as theirs has been the true measure of a man's worth; it may be the first revelation of his virtues, but is at any rate their final seal. For even those who come short in other ways may justly plead the valor with which they have fought for their country; they have blotted out the evil with the good, and have benefited the state more by their public services than they have injured her by their private actions. None of these men were enervated by wealth or hesitated to resign the pleasures of life; none of them put off the evil day in the hope, natural to poverty, that a man, though poor, may one day become rich. But, deeming that the punishment of their enemies was sweeter than any of these things, and that they could fall in no nobler cause, they determined at the hazard of their lives to be honorably avenged, and to leave the rest. They resigned to hope their unknown chance of happiness; but in the face of death they resolved to rely upon themselves alone. And when the moment came they were minded to resist and suffer, rather than to fly and save their lives; they ran away from the word of dishonor, but on the battlefield their feet stood fast, and in an instant, at the height of their fortune, they passed away from the scene, not of their fear, but of their glory.

Such was the end of these men; they were worthy of Athens, and the living need not desire to have a more heroic spirit, although they may pray for a less fatal issue. The value of such a spirit is not to be expressed in words. Any one can discourse to you for ever about the advantages of a brave defense, which you know already. But instead of listening to him I would have you day by day fix your eyes upon the greatness of Athens, until you become filled with the love of her; and when you are impressed by the spectacle of her glory, reflect that this empire has been acquired by men who knew their duty and had the courage to do it, who in the hour of conflict had the fear of dishonor always present to them, and who, if ever they failed in an enterprise, would not allow their virtues to be lost to their country, but freely gave their lives to her as the fairest offering which they could present at her feast. The sacrifice which they collectively made was individually repaid to them; for they received again each one for himself a praise which grows not old, and the noblest of all tombs, I speak not of that in which their remains are laid, but of that in which their glory survives, and is proclaimed always and on every fitting occasion both in word and deed. For the whole earth is the tomb of famous men; not only are they commemorated by columns and inscriptions in their own country, but in foreign lands there dwells also an unwritten memorial of them, graven not on stone but in the hearts of men. Make them your examples, and, esteeming courage to be freedom and freedom to be happiness, do not weigh too nicely the perils of war. The unfortunate who has no hope of a change for the better has less reason to throw away his life than the prosperous who, if he survive, is always liable to a change for the worse, and to whom any accidental fall makes the most serious difference. To a man of spirit, cowardice and disaster coming together are far more bitter than death striking him unperceived at a time when he is full of courage and animated by the general hope.

Wherefore I do not now pity the parents of the dead who stand here; I would rather comfort them. You know that your dead have passed away amid manifold vicissitudes; and that they may be deemed fortunate who have gained their utmost honor, whether an honorable death like theirs, or an honorable sorrow like yours, and whose share of happiness has been so ordered that the term of their happiness is likewise the term of their life. I know how hard it is to make you feel this, when the good fortune of others will too often remind you of the gladness which once lightened your hearts. And sorrow is felt at the want of those blessings, not which a man never knew, but which were a part of his life before they were taken from him. Some of you are of an age at which they may hope to have other children, and they ought to bear their sorrow better; not only will the children who may hereafter be born make them forget their own lost ones, but the city will be doubly a gainer. She will not be left desolate, and she will be safer. For a man's counsel cannot have equal weight or worth, when he alone has no children to risk in the general danger. To those of you who have passed their prime, I say: "Congratulate yourselves that you have been happy during the greater part of your days; remember that your life of sorrow will not last long, and be comforted by the glory of those who are gone. For the love of honor alone is ever young, and not riches, as some say, but honor is the delight of men when they are old and useless.

To you who are the sons and brothers of the departed, I see that the struggle to emulate them will be an arduous one. For all men praise the dead, and, however preeminent your virtue may be, I do not say even to approach them, and avoid living their rivals and detractors, but when a man is out of the way, the honor and goodwill which he receives is unalloyed. And, if I am to speak of womanly virtues to those of you who will henceforth be widows, let me sum them up in one short admonition: To a woman not to show more weakness than is natural to her sex is a great glory, and not to be talked about for good or for evil among men.

I have paid the required tribute, in obedience to the law, making use of such fitting words as I had. The tribute of deeds has been paid in part; for the dead have them in deeds, and it remains only that their children should be maintained at the public charge until they are grown up: this is the solid prize with which, as with a garland, Athens crowns her sons living and dead, after a struggle like theirs. For where the rewards of virtue are greatest, there the noblest citizens are enlisted in the service of the state. And now, when you have duly lamented, every one his own dead, you may depart.

GEORGE WASHINGTON (1732–1799)

by Major General Henry Lee (1799)

George Washington was the first President of the United States, serving in office from 1789 through 1797. Henry Lee, father of Confederate General Robert E. Lee, was an early American statesman and patriot who fought alongside Washington before going on to become the ninth Governor of Virginia. This eulogy was delivered at Washington's Funeral on December 26, 1799.

IN OBEDIENCE TO your* will, I rise your humble organ, with the hope of executing a part of the system of public mourning which you have been pleased to adopt, commemorative of the death of the most illustrious and most beloved personage this country has ever produced; and which, while it transmits to posterity your sense of the awful event, faintly represents your knowledge of the consummate excellence you so cordially honour.

Desperate, indeed, is any attempt on earth to meet correspondently this dispensation of Heaven; for, while with pious resignation we submit to the will of an all-gracious Providence, we can never cease lamenting, in our finite view of Omnipotent Wisdom, the heart-rending privation for which our nation weeps. When the civilized world shakes to its centre; when every moment gives birth to strange and momentous changes; when our peaceful quarter of the globe, exempt as it happily has been from any share in the slaughter of the human race, may yet be compelled to abandon her pacific policy, and to risk the doleful casualties of war; what limit is there to the

---

* The two Houses of Congress.

8

extent of our loss? None within the reach of my words to express; none which your feelings will not disavow.

The founder of our federate republic—our bulwark in war, our guide in peace, is no more! O that this were but questionable! Hope, the comforter of the wretched, would pour into our agonizing hearts its balmy dew. But, alas! there is no hope for us; our WASHINGTON is removed forever! Possessing the stoutest frame and purest mind, he had passed nearly to his sixty-eighth year, in the enjoyment of high health, when, habituated by his care of us to neglect himself, a slight cold, disregarded, became inconvenient on Friday, oppressive on Saturday, and, defying every medical interposition, before the morning of Sunday put an end to the best of men. An end, did I say? His fame survives! bounded only by the limits of the earth, and by the extent of the human mind. He survives in our hearts—in the growing knowledge of our children—in the affection of the good throughout the world. And when our monuments shall be done away; when nations now existing shall be no more; when even our young and far-spreading empire shall have perished; still will our WASHINGTON's glory unfaded shine, and die not, until love of virtue cease on earth, or earth itself sinks into chaos!

How, my fellow-citizens, shall I single to your grateful hearts his pre-eminent worth? Where shall I begin, in opening to your view a character throughout sublime? Shall I speak of his warlike achievements, all springing from obedience to his country's will, all directed to his country's good?

Will you go with me to the banks of the Monongahela, to see your youthful WASHINGTON supporting, in the dismal hour of Indian victory, the ill-fated Braddock, and saving, by his judgment and by his valour, the remains of a defeated army, pressed by the conquering savage foe? or when, oppressed America nobly resolving to risk her all in defence of her violated rights, he was elevated by the unanimous voice of Congress to the command of her armies? Will you follow him to the high grounds of Boston, where, to an undisciplined, courageous and virtuous yeomanry, his presence gave the stability of system, and infused the invincibility of love of country? Or shall I carry you to the painful scenes of Long-Island, York-Island and New-Jersey, when, combating superior and gallant armies, aided by powerful fleets, and led by chiefs high in the roll of fame, he stood the bulwark of our safety, undismayed by disaster, unchanged by change of fortune? Or will you view him in the precarious fields of

Trenton, where deep gloom, unnerving every arm, reigned trium-phant through our thinned, worn down, unaided ranks—himself unmoved? Dreadful was the night. It was about this time of winter. The storm raged. The Delaware, rolling furiously with floating ice, forbad the approach of man. WASHINGTON, self-collected, viewed the tremendous scene. His country called. Unappalled by surround-ing dangers, he passed to the hostile shore; he fought; he conquered. The morning sun cheered the American world. Our country rose on the event; and her dauntless Chief, pursuing his blow, completed in the lawns of Princeton, what his vast soul had conceived on the shores of Delaware.

Thence to the strong grounds of Morristown he led his small but gallant band; and through an eventful winter, by the high efforts of his genius, whose matchless force was measurable only by the growth of difficulties, he held in check formidable hostile legions, conducted by a chief experienced in the art of war, and famed for his valour on the ever memorable heights of Abraham, where fell Wolfe, Montcalm, and since, our much lamented Montgomery; all covered with glory. In this fortunate interval, produced by his masterly conduct, our fathers, ourselves, animated by his resistless example, rallied around our country's standard, and continued to follow her beloved Chief through the various and trying scenes to which the destinies of our Union led.

Who is there that has forgotten the vales of Brandywine, the fields of Germantown, or the plains of Monmouth? Every where present, wants of every kind obstructing, numerous and valiant armies encoun-tering, himself a host, he assuaged our sufferings, limited our priva-tions, and upheld our tottering republic. Shall I display to you the spread of the fire of his soul, by rehearsing the praises of the hero of Saratoga, and his much loved compeer of the Carolinas? No: our WASHINGTON wears not borrowed glory. To Gates, to Greene, he gave without reserve the applause due to their eminent merit; and long may the chiefs of Saratoga and of Eutaws, receive the grateful respect of a grateful people.

Moving in his own orbit, he imparted heat and light to his most distant satellites; and combining the physical and moral force of all within his sphere, with irresistible weight he took his course, com-miserating folly, disdaining vice, dismaying treason, and invigorat-ing despondency; until the auspicious hour arrived, when, united with the intrepid forces of a potent and magnanimous ally, he brought to submission the since conqueror of India; thus finishing his long career of military glory with a lustre corresponding to his great name, and, in this his last act of war, affixing the seal of fate to our nation's birth.

To the horrid din of battle sweet peace succeeded; and our virtuous Chief, mindful only of the common good, in a moment tempting personal aggrandizement, hushed the discontents of growing sedition, and, surrendering his power into the hands from which he had received it, converted his sword into a ploughshare; teaching an admiring world, that to be truly great you must be truly good.

Were I to stop here, the picture would be incomplete, and the task imposed unfinished. Great as was our WASHINGTON in war, and as much as did that greatness contribute to produce the American republic, it is not in war alone his pre-eminence stands conspicuous. His various talents, combining all the capacities of a statesman with those of a soldier, fitted him alike to guide the councils and the armies of our nation: Scarcely had he rested from his martial toils, while his invaluable parental advice was still sounding in our ears, when he, who had been our shield and our sword, was called forth to act a less splendid, but more important part.

Possessing a clear and penetrating mind, a strong and sound judgment, calmness and temper for deliberation, with invincible firmness and perseverance in resolutions maturely formed; drawing information from all; acting from himself, with incorruptible integrity and unvarying patriotism; his own superiority and the public confidence alike marked him as the man designed by Heaven to lead in the great political as well as military events which have distinguished the era of his life.

The finger of an over-ruling Providence, pointing at WASHINGTON, was neither mistaken nor unobserved, when, to realize the vast hopes to which our revolution had given birth, a change of political system became indispensable.

How novel, how grand the spectacle! Independent States stretched over an immense territory, and known only by common difficulty, clinging to their union as the rock of their safety; deciding, by frank comparison of their relative condition, to rear on that rock, under the guidance of reason, a common government; through whose commanding protection, liberty and order, with their long train of blessings, should be safe to themselves, and the sure inheritance of their posterity.

This arduous task devolved on citizens selected by the people, from knowledge of their wisdom and confidence in their virtue. In this august assembly of sages and of patriots, WASHINGTON of course was found; and, as if acknowledged to be most wise where all were wise, with one voice he was declared their Chief. How well he merited this rare distinction, how faithful were the labours of himself and his compatriots, the work of their hands, and our union, strength and prosperity, the fruits of that work, best attest.

But to have essentially aided in presenting to his country this consummation of her hopes, neither satisfied the claims of his fellow-citizens on his talents, nor those duties which the possession of those talents imposed. Heaven had not infused into his mind such an uncommon share of its ethereal spirit to remain unemployed, nor bestowed on him his genius unaccompanied with the corresponding duty of devoting it to the common good. To have framed a Constitution, was shewing only, without realizing, the general happiness. This great work remained to be done; and America, stedfast in her preference, with one voice summoned her beloved WASHINGTON, unpractised as he was in the duties of civil administration, to execute this last act in the completion of the national felicity. Obedient to her call, he assumed the high office with that self-distrust peculiar to his innate modesty, the constant attendant of pre-eminent virtue. What was the burst of joy through our anxious land on this exhilarating event, is known to us all. The aged, the young, the brave, the fair, rivalled each other in demonstrations of their gratitude; and this high-wrought, delightful scene was heightened in its effect, by the singular contest between the zeal of the bestowers and the avoidance of the receiver of the honours bestowed.

Commencing his administration, what heart is not charmed with the recollection of the pure and wise principles announced by himself, as the basis of his political life? He best understood the indissoluble union between virtue and happiness, between duty and advantage, between the genuine maxims of an honest and magnanimous policy, and the solid rewards of public prosperity and individual felicity. Watching with an equal and comprehensive eye over this great assemblage of communities and interests, he laid the foundations of our national policy in the unerring, immutable principles of morality, based on religion, exemplifying the pre-eminence of a free government by all the attributes which win the affections of its citizens, or command the respect of the world.

"O fortunatos nimium, sua si bona norint!"

Leading through the complicated difficulties produced by previous obligations and conflicting interests, seconded by succeeding Houses of Congress, enlightened and patriotic, he surmounted all original obstruction, and brightened the path of our national felicity.

The presidential term expiring, his solicitude to exchange exaltation for humility returned with a force increased with increase of age; and he had prepared his Farewell Address to his countrymen, proclaiming his intention, when the united interposition of all around him, enforced by the eventful prospects of the epoch, produced a further sacrifice of inclination to duty. The election of President followed; and Washington, by the unanimous vote of the nation, was called to resume the Chief Magistracy. What a wonderful fixture of confidence! Which attracts most our admiration, a people so correct, or a citizen combining an assemblage of talents forbidding rivalry, and stifling even envy itself? Such a nation ought to be happy; such a Chief must be for ever revered.

War, long menaced by the Indian tribes, now broke out; and the terrible conflict, deluging Europe with blood, began to shed its baneful influence over our happy land. To the first, out-stretching his invincible arm, under the orders of the gallant Wayne, the American eagle soared triumphant through distant forests. Peace followed victory; and the melioration of the condition of the enemy followed peace. Godlike virtue! which uplifts even the subdued savage.

To the second he opposed himself. New and delicate was the conjuncture, and great was the stake. Soon did his penetrating mind discern and seize the only course, continuing to us all the felicity enjoyed. He issued his proclamation of neutrality. This index to his whole subsequent conduct, was sanctioned by the approbation of both Houses of Congress, and by the approving voice of the people.

To this sublime policy he inviolably adhered, unmoved by foreign intrusion, unshaken by domestic turbulence.

> "Justum et tenacem propositi virum,
> Non civium ardor prava jubentium,
> Non vultus instantis tyranni,
> Mente quatit solida."

Maintaining his pacific system at the expense of no duty, America, faithful to herself, and unstained in her honour, continued to enjoy the delights of peace, while afflicted Europe mourns in every quarter under the accumulated miseries of an unexampled war; miseries in which our happy country must have shared, had not our pre-eminent WASHINGTON been as firm in council as he was brave in the field.

Pursuing stedfastly his course, he held safe the public happiness, preventing foreign war, and quelling internal discord, till the revolving period of a third election approached, when he executed his interrupted, but inextinguishable desire of returning to the humble walks of private life.

The promulgation of his fixed resolution stopped the anxious wishes of an affectionate people from adding a third unanimous testimonial of their unabated confidence in the man so long enthroned in their hearts. When before was affection like this exhibited on earth? Turn over the records of ancient Greece; review the annals of mighty Rome; examine the volumes of modern Europe—you search in vain. AMERICA and her WASHINGTON only afford the dignified exemplification.

The illustrious personage called by the national voice in succession to the arduous office of guiding a free people, had new difficulties to encounter. The amicable effort of settling our difficulties with France, begun by WASHINGTON, and pursued by his successor in virtue as in station, proving abortive, America took measures of self-defence. No sooner was the public mind roused by a prospect of danger, than every eye was turned to the friend of all, though secluded from public view, and grey in public service. The virtuous veteran, following his plough,* received the unexpected summons with mingled emotions of indignation at the unmerited ill treatment of his country, and of a determination once more to risk his all in her defence.

The annunciation of these feelings in his affecting letter to the President, accepting the command of the army, concludes his official conduct.

First in war, first in peace, and first in the hearts of his countrymen, he was second to none in the humble and endearing scenes of private life. Pious, just, humane, temperate and sincere; uniform, dignified and commanding, his example was as edifying to all around him, as were the effects of that example lasting.

---

* General WASHINGTON, though opulent, gave much of his time to practical agriculture.

To his equals he was condescending, to his inferiors kind, and to the dear object of his affections exemplarily tender. Correct throughout, vice shuddered in his presence, and virtue always felt his fostering hand. The purity of his private character gave effulgence to his public virtues.

His last scene comported with the whole tenor of his life. Although in extreme pain, not a sigh, not a groan escaped him; and with undisturbed serenity he closed his well-spent life. Such was the man America has lost! Such was the man for whom our nation mourns!

Methinks I see his august image, and hear, falling from his venerable lips, these deep sinking words:

"Cease, Sons of America, lamenting our separation. Go on, and confirm by your wisdom the fruits of our joint councils, joint efforts, and common dangers. Reverence religion; diffuse knowledge throughout your land; patronize the arts and sciences; let liberty and order be inseparable companions; control party spirit, the bane of free government; observe good faith to, and cultivate peace with all nations; shut up every avenue to foreign influence; contract rather than extend national connexion; rely on yourselves only: be American in thought and deed. Thus will you give immortality to that union, which was the constant object of my terrestrial labours: thus will you preserve undisturbed to the latest posterity, the felicity of a people to me most dear; and thus will you supply (if my happiness is now aught to you) the only vacancy in the round of pure bliss high Heaven bestows."

ALEXANDER HAMILTON (1755–1804)

by Harrison G. Otis (1804)

Alexander Hamilton served as the first Secretary of the Treasury to the United States, though he is most remembered for his efforts to promote the U.S. Constitution through his contributions to the Federalist Papers. He is eulogized here by Harrison Otis, a prominent member of the Federalist Party and longtime colleague of Alexander Hamilton.

WE ARE CONVENED, afflicted Fellow-Citizens, to perform the only duties which our republics acknowledge or fulfil to their illustrious dead. To present to departed excellence an oblation of gratitude and respect; to inscribe its virtues on the urn which contains its ashes, and to consecrate its example by the tears and sympathy of an affectionate people.

MUST we then realize that HAMILTON is no more! Must the sod, not yet cemented on the tomb of WASHINGTON, still moist with our tears, be so soon disturbed to admit the beloved companion of WASHINGTON, the partner of his dangers, the object of his confidence, the disciple who leaned upon his bosom! Insatiable Death! will not the heroes and statesmen whom mad ambition has sent from the crimsoned fields of Europe, suffice to people thy dreary dominions! Thy dismal avenues have been thronged with princely martyrs and illustrious victims. Crowns and sceptres, the spoils of royalty are among thy recent trophies, and the blood of innocence and valour has flowed in torrents at thy inexorable command. Such have been thy ravages in the old world. And in our infant country how small was the remnant of our revolutionary heroes which had been spared from thy fatal grasp! Could not our WARREN, our MONTGOMERY, our MERCER, our GREENE, our WASHINGTON appease

16

thy vengeance for a few short years! Shall none of our early patriots be permitted to behold the perfection of their own work in the stability of our government and the maturity of our institutions! Or hast thou predetermined, dread King of Terrors! to blast the world's best hope, and by depriving us of all the conductors of our glorious revolution, compel us to bury our liberties in their tombs! O HAMILTON! great would be the relief of my mind, were I permitted to exchange the arduous duty of attempting to portray the varied excellence of thy character, for the privilege of venting the deep and unavailing sorrow which swells my bosom, at the remembrance of the gentleness of thy nature, of thy splendid talents and placid virtues! But, my respected friends, an indulgence of these feelings would be inconsistent with that deliberate recital of the services and qualities of this great man, which is required by impartial justice and your expectations.

In governments which recognize the distinctions of splendid birth and titles, the details of illustrious lineage and connections become interesting to those who are accustomed to value those advantages. But in the man whose loss we deplore, the interval between manhood and death was so uniformly filled by a display of the energies of his mighty mind, that the world has scarcely paused to enquire into the story of his infant or puerile years. He was a planet, the dawn of which was not perceived; which rose with full splendor, and emitted a constant stream of glorious light, until the hour of its sudden and portentous eclipse.

At the age of eighteen, while cultivating his mind at Columbia College, he was roused from the leisure and delights of scientific groves by the din of war. He entered the American army as an officer of artillery, and at that early period familiarized himself to wield both his sword and his pen in the service of his country. He developed at once the qualities which command precedency, and the modesty which conceals its pretensions. Frank, affable, intelligent and brave, young HAMILTON became the favourite of his fellow-soldiers. His intuitive perception and correct judgment rendered him a rapid proficient in military science, and his merit silenced the envy which it excited.

A most honourable distinction now awaited him. He attracted the attention of the Commander in Chief, who appointed him an aid, and honoured him with his confidence and friendship. This domestic relation afforded to both, frequent means of comparing their opinions upon the policy and destinies of our country, upon the sources of its future prosperity and grandeur, upon the imperfection of its existing establishments; and to digest those principles, which in happier times might be interwoven into a more perfect model of government. Hence probably originated that filial veneration for WASHINGTON and adherence to his maxims, which were ever conspicuous in the deportment of HAMILTON; and hence the exalted esteem and predilection uniformly displayed by the magnanimous patron to the faithful and affectionate pupil.

While the disasters of the American army, and the perseverance of the British ministry, presented the gloomy prospect of protracted warfare, young HAMILTON appeared to be content in his station, and with the opportunities which he had of fighting by the side, and executing the orders of his beloved Chief. But the investment of the army of CORNWALLIS suddenly changed the aspect of affairs, and rendered it probable that this campaign, if successful, would be the most brilliant and decisive of any that was likely to occur. It now appeared that his heart had long panted for an occasion to signalize his intrepidity and devotion to the service of his country. He obtained by earnest entreaties the command of a detachment destined to storm the works of Yorktown. It is well known with what undaunted courage he pressed on to the assault with unloaded arms, presented his bosom to the dangers of the bayonet, carried the fort, and thus eminently contributed to decide the fate of the battle and of his country. But even here the impetuosity of the youthful conqueror was restrained by the clemency of the benevolent man,—The butchery of the American garrison at New-London would have justified and seemed to demand an exercise of the rigours of retaliation. This was strongly intimated to Col. HAMILTON, but we find in his report to his commanding officer, in his own words, that, "incapable of imitating examples of barbarity, and forgetting recent provocations, be spared every man who ceased to resist."

Having soon afterwards terminated his military career, he returned to New-York, and qualified himself to commence practice as a counsellor at law. But the duties and emoluments of his profession were not then permitted to stifle his solicitude to give a correct tone to public opinion by the propagation of principles worthy of adoption, by a people who had just undertaken to govern themselves. He found the minds of men chafed and irritated by the recollection of their recent sufferings and dangers. The city of New-York, so long a garrison, presented scenes and incidents which naturally aggravated these dispositions, and too many were inclined to fan the flame of

discord, and mar the enjoyment and advantages of peace, by foment-
ing the animosities engendered by the collisions of war. To sooth
these angry passions—to heal these wounds—to demonstrate the
folly and inexpediency of scattering the bitter tares of national prejudice and private rancour among the seeds of public prosperity, were
objects worthy of the heart and head of HAMILTON. To these he
applied himself, and by a luminous pamphlet, assuaged the public
resentment against those, whose sentiments had led them to oppose
the revolution; and thus preserved from exile many valuable citizens,
who have supported the laws and increased the opulence of their
native State.

From this period he appears to have devoted himself principally
to professional occupations, which were multiplied by his increasing
celebrity; until he became a member of the Convention, which
met at Annapolis, merely for the purpose of devising a mode of levy-
ing and collecting a general impost. Although the object of this
Convention was thus limited, yet so manifold in his view were the
defects of the old Confederation, that a reform in one particular
would be ineffectual; *he therefore first suggested the proposal of attempting
a radical change in its principles;* and the address to the people of the
United States, recommending a general Convention with more
extensive powers, which was adopted by that assembly, was the work
of his pen.[*]

To the second Convention which framed the Constitution he was
also deputed as a delegate from the State of New-York.

In that assemblage of the brightest jewels of America, the genius
of HAMILTON sparkled with pre-eminent lustre. The best of our orators were improved by the example of his eloquence. The most
experienced of our statesmen were instructed by the solidity of his
sentiments, and all were convinced of the utility and extent of his
agency in framing the Constitution.

When the instrument was presented to the people for their rati-
fication; the obstacles incident to every attempt to combine the
interests, views and opinions of the various states, threatened in some
of them to frustrate the hopes and exertions of its friends. The fears
of the timid; the jealousies of the ignorant; the arts of the designing;
and the sincere conviction of the superficial, were arrayed into a
formidable alliance, in opposition to the system. But the magic pen

---

[*] This information is derived from a respectable member of that Convention
from the State of New-York.

of HAMILTON dissolved this league. Animated by the magnitude of
his object, he enriched the daily papers with the researches of a mind
teeming with political information. In these rapid essays, written
amid the avocations of business, and under the pressure of the occasion, it would be natural to expect that much would require revision
and correction. But in the mind of HAMILTON nothing was superficial but resentment of injuries; nothing fugitive, but those transient
emotions which sometimes lead virtue astray. These productions of
his pen are now considered as a standard commentary upon the nature
of our government; and he lived to hear them quoted by his friends
and adversaries, as high authority, in the tribunals of justice, and in
the legislature of the nation.

When the Constitution was adopted, and WASHINGTON was called
to the Presidency by his grateful country, our departed friend was
appointed to the charge of the treasury department, and of consequence became a confidential member of the administration. In this
new sphere of action, he displayed a ductility and extent of genius,
a fertility in expedients, a faculty of arrangement, an industry in
application to business, and a promptitude in dispatch, but beyond
all, a purity of public virtue and disinterestedness, which are too
mighty for the grasp of my feeble powers of description. Indeed the
public character of HAMILTON, and his measures from this period,
are so intimately connected with the history of our country, that it
is impossible to do justice to one without devoting a volume to the
other. The treasury of the United States, at the time of his entrance
upon the duties of his office, was literally a creature of the imagination, and existed only in name, unless folios of unsettled balances,
and bundles of reproachful claims were deserving of the name of a
treasury. Money there was none; and of public credit scarcely a
shadow remained. No national system for raising and collecting a
revenue had been attempted, and no estimate could be formed from
the experiments of the different states, of the probable result of any
project of deriving it from commerce. The national debt was not
only unpaid, but its amount was a subject of uncertainty and con-
jecture. Such was the chaos from which the Secretary was called
upon to elicit the elements of a regular system, adequate to the
immediate exigencies of a new and expensive establishment, and to
an honourable provision for the public debt. His arduous duty was
not to reform abuses, but to create resources; not to improve upon
precedent, but to invent a model. In an ocean of experiment, he had

neither chart nor compass but those of his own invention. Yet such was the comprehensive vigour of his mind, that his original projects possessed the hardihood of settled regulations. His sketches were little short of the perfection of finished pictures. In the first session of Congress, he produced a plan for the organization of the treasury department, and for the collection of a national revenue; and in the second, a report of a system for funding the national debt. Great objections were urged against the expediency of the principles assumed by him for the basis of his system; but no doubt remained of their effect. A dormant capital was revived, and with it commerce and agriculture awoke as from the sleep of death. By the enchantment of this "mighty magician," the beauteous fabric of public credit rose in full majesty upon the ruins of the old Confederation; and men gazed with astonishment upon a youthful prodigy, who at the age of thirty-three, having already been the ornament of the camp, the forum and the senate, was now suddenly transformed into an accomplished financier, and a self-taught adept not only in the general principles, but the intricate details, of his new department.

It is not wonderful that such resplendent powers of doing right should have exposed him to the suspicion of doing wrong. He was suspected and accused. His political adversaries were his judges. Their investigation of his conduct and honourable acquittal added new lustre to his fame, and confirmed the national sentiment, that in his public character he was indeed "a man without fear and without reproach."

To his exertions in this department we are indebted for many important institutions. Among others, the plan for redeeming the public debt, and of a national bank to facilitate the operations of government, were matured and adopted under his auspices; and so complete were his arrangements, that his successors, though men of undoubted talents, and one of them a political opponent, have found nothing susceptible of material improvement.

But the obligations of his country during this period were not confined to his merit as a financier.

The flame of insurrection was kindled in the Western Counties of Pennsylvania, and raged with such violence, that large detachments of military force were marched to the scene of the disturbance, and the presence of the great WASHINGTON was judged necessary to quell the increasing spirit of revolt. He ordered the Secretary to quit the duties of his department, and attend him on the expedition.

His versatile powers were immediately and efficaciously applied to restore the authority of the laws. The principal burden of the important civil and military arrangements requisite for this purpose devolved upon his shoulders. It was owing to his humanity, that the leaders of this rebellion escaped exemplary punishment; and the successful issue was, in public and unqualified terms, ascribed to him by those whose political relations would not have prompted them to pay him the homage of unmerited praise.

He was highly instrumental in preserving our peace and neutrality, and saving us from the ruin which has befallen the republics of the old world. Upon this topic, I am desirous of avoiding every intimation which might prove offensive to individuals of any party. God forbid that the sacred sorrow in which we all unite should be disturbed by the mixture of any unkindly emotions! I would merely do justice to this honoured shade, without arraigning the motives of those who disapproved and opposed his measures.

The dangers which menaced our infant government at the commencement of the French Revolution are no longer a subject of controversy. The principles professed by the first leaders of that revolution were so congenial to those of the American people; their pretences of aiming merely at the reformation of abuses were so plausible; the spectacle of a great people struggling to recover their "long lost liberties" was so imposing and august; while that of a combination of tyrants to conquer and subjugate, was so revolting; the services received from one of the belligerent powers, and the injuries inflicted by the other, were so recent in our minds, that the sensibility of the nation was excited to the most exquisite pitch. To this disposition, so favourable to the wishes of France, every appeal was made, which intrigue, corruption, flattery and threats could dictate. At this dangerous and dazzling crisis, there were but few men entirely exempt from the general delirium. Among that few was HAMILTON. His penetrating eye discerned, and his prophetic voice foretold, the tendency and consequence of the first revolutionary movements. He was assured that every people which should espouse the cause of France would pass under her yoke, and that the people of France, like every nation which surrenders its reason to the mercy of demagogues, would be driven by the storms of anarchy upon the shores of despotism. All this he knew was conformable to the invariable law of nature and experience of mankind. From the reach of this desolation he was anxious to save his country, and in the pursuit of his purpose, he breasted the assaults of calumny and prejudice.

"The torrent roared, and he did buffet it." Appreciating the advantages of a neutral position, he co-operated with WASHINGTON, ADAMS, and the other patriots of that day, in the means best adapted to maintain it. The rights and duties of neutrality proclaimed by the President, were explained and enforced by HAMILTON in the character of Pacificus. The attempts to corrupt and intimidate were resisted. The British treaty was justified and defended as an honourable compact with our natural friends, and pregnant with advantages, which have since been realized and acknowledged by its opponents.

BY this pacific and vigorous policy, in the whole course of which the genius and activity of HAMILTON were conspicuous, time and information were afforded to the American nation, and correct views were acquired of our situation and interests. We beheld the republics of Europe march in procession to the funeral of their own liberties, by the lurid light of the revolutionary torch. The tumult of the passions subsided, the wisdom of the administration was perceived, and America now remains a solitary monument in the desolated plains of liberty.

Having remained at the head of the treasury several years, and filled its coffers; having developed the sources of an ample revenue, and tested the advantages of his own system by his own experience; and having expended his private fortune; he found it necessary to retire from public employment, and to devote his attention to the claims of a large and dear family. What brighter instance of disinterested honour has ever been exhibited to an admiring world! That a man, upon whom devolved the task of originating a system of revenue for a nation; of devising the checks in his own department; of providing for the collection of sums, the amount of which was conjectural; that a man, who anticipated the effects of a funding system, yet a secret in his own bosom, and who was thus enabled to have secured a princely fortune, consistently with principles esteemed fair by the world; that such a man, by no means addicted to an expensive or extravagant style of living, should have retired from office destitute of means adequate to the wants of mediocrity, and have resorted to professional labour for the means of decent support, are facts which must instruct and astonish those, who in countries habituated to corruption and venality are more attentive to the gains than to the duties of official station.—Yet HAMILTON was that man. It was a fact always known to his friends, and it is now evident from his testament, made under a deep presentiment of his approaching fate. Blush then, ministers and warriors of imperial France, who have deluded your nation by pretensions to a disinterested regard for its liberties and rights! Disgorge the riches extorted from your fellow citizens, and the spoils amassed from confiscation and blood! Restore to impoverished nations the price paid by them for the privilege of slavery, and now appropriated to the refinements of luxury and corruption! Approach the tomb of HAMILTON, and compare the insignificance of your gorgeous palaces with the awful majesty of this tenement of clay!

We again accompany our friend in the walks of private life, and in the assiduous pursuit of his profession, until the aggressions of France compelled the nation to assume the attitude of defence. He was now invited by the great and enlightened statesman who had succeeded to the Presidency, and at the express request of the Commander in Chief, to accept of the second rank in the army. Though no man had manifested a greater desire to avoid war, yet it is freely confessed that when war appeared to be inevitable, his heart exulted in "the tented field," and he loved the life and occupation of a soldier. His early habits were formed amid the fascinations of the camp. And though the pacific policy of ADAMS once more rescued us from war, and shortened the existence of the army establishment, yet its duration was sufficient to secure to him the love and confidence of officers and men, to enable him to display the talents and qualities of a great general, and to justify the most favourable prognostics of his prowess in the field.

Once more this excellent man unloosed the helmet from his brow, and returned to the duties of the forum. From this time he persisted in a firm resolution to decline all civil honours and promotion, and to live a private citizen unless again summoned to the defence of his country. He became more than ever assiduous in his practice at the bar, and intent upon his plans of domestic happiness, until a nice and mistaken estimate of the claims of honour, impelled him to the fatal act which terminated his life.

While it is far from my intention to draw a veil over this last great error, or in the least measure to justify a practice, which threatens in its progress to destroy the liberty of speech and of opinion; it is but justice to the deceased, to state the circumstances which should palliate the resentment that may be excited in some good minds towards his memory. From the last sad memorial which we possess from his hand, and in which, if our tears permit, we may trace the sad presage of the impending catastrophe, it appears that his religious principles were at variance with the practice of duelling, and that he could not reconcile his benevolent heart to shed the blood of an adversary in private combat, even in his own defence. It was then from public motives that he committed this great mistake. It was for the benefit of his country that he erroneously conceived himself obliged to make the painful sacrifice of his principles, and to expose his life. The sober judgment of the man, was confounded and misdirected by the jealous honour of the soldier; and he evidently adverted to the possibility of events that might render indispensable, the esteem and confidence of soldiers as well as of citizens.

But while religion mourns for this aberration of the judgment of a great man, she derives some consolation from his testimony in her favour. If she rejects the apology, she admits the repentance; and if the good example be not an atonement, it may be an antidote for the bad. Let us then, in an age of infidelity, join, in imagination, the desolate group of wife and children and friends, who surround the dying bed of the inquisitive, the luminous, the scientific HAMILTON, and witness his attestation to the truth and comforts of our holy religion. Let us behold the lofty warrior bow his head before the Cross of the meek and lowly JESUS; and he who had so lately graced the sumptuous tables and society of the luxurious and rich, now, regardless of these meaner pleasures, and aspiring to be admitted to a sublime enjoyment with which no worldly joys can compare—to a devout and humble participation of the bread of life. The religious fervor of his last moments was not an impulse of decaying nature yielding to its fears, but the result of a firm conviction of the truths of the Gospel. I am well informed, that in early life, the evidences of the Christian religion had attracted his serious examination, and obtained his deliberate assent to their truth, and that he daily upon his knees devoted a portion of time to a compliance with one of its most important injunctions: And that however these edifying propensities might have yielded occasionally to the business and temptations of life, they always resumed their influence, and would probably have prompted him to a public profession of his faith in his Redeemer.

Such was the untimely fate of ALEXANDER HAMILTON; whose character warrants the apprehension, that, "take him for all in all, we ne'er shall look upon his like again."

Nature, even in the partial distribution of her favors, generally limits the attainments of great men within distinct and particular spheres of eminence. But he was the darling of nature, and privileged beyond the rest of her favorites. His mind caught at a glance that perfect comprehension of a subject, for which others are indebted to patient labour and investigation. In whatever department he was called to act, he discovered an intuitive knowledge of its duties, which gave him an immediate ascendency over those who had made them the study of their lives; so that after running through the circle of office, as a soldier, statesman and financier, no question remained for which he had been qualified, but only in which he had evinced the most superlative merit. He did not dissemble his attachment to a military life, nor his consciousness of possessing talents for command; yet no man more strenuously advocated the rights of the civil over the military power, nor more cheerfully abdicated command and returned to the rank of the citizen, when his country could dispense with the necessity of an army.

In his private profession, at a bar abounding with men of learning and experience, he was without a rival. He arranged with happiest facility, the materials collected in the vast store-house of his memory, surveyed his subject under all its aspects, and enforced his arguments with such powers of reasoning, that nothing was wanting to produce conviction, and generally to ensure success. His eloquence combined the nervousness and copious elegance of the Greek and Roman schools, and gave him the choice of his clients and his business. These wonderful powers were accompanied by a natural politeness and winning condescension, which forestalled the envy of his brethren. Their hearts were gained before their pride was alarmed; and they united in their approbation of a pre-eminence, which reflected honour on their fraternity.

From such talents, adorned by incorruptible honesty and boundless generosity, an immense personal influence over his political and private friends was inseparable; and by those who did not know him, and who saw the use to which ambition might apply it, he was sometimes suspected of views unpropitious to the nature of our government. The charge was inconsistent with the exertions he had made, to render that government in its present form worthy of the attachment and support of the people, and his voluntary relinquishment of the means of ambition, the purse-strings of the nation. He was indeed ambitious, *but not of power;* he was ambitious only to convince the world of the spotless integrity of his administration and character. This was the key to the finest sensibilities of his heart. He shrunk from the imputation of misconduct in public life: and if his judgment ever misled him, it was only when warped by an excessive eagerness to vindicate himself at the expense of his discretion. To calumny in every other shape he opposed the defence of dignified silence and contempt.

Had such a character been exempt from foibles and frailties, it would not have been human. Yet so small was the catalogue of these, that they would have escaped observation, but for the unparalleled frankness of his nature, which prompted him to confess them to the world. He did not consider greatness as an authority for habitual vice; and he repented with such contrition of casual error, that none remained offended but those who never had a right to complain. The virtues of his private and domestic character comprised whatever conciliates affection and begets respect. To envy he was a stranger, and of merit and talents the unaffected eulogist and admirer. The charms of his conversation, the brilliance of his wit, his regard to decorum, his ineffable good humour, which led him down from the highest range of intellect, to the level of colloquial pleasantry, will never be forgotten, perhaps never equalled.

To observe that such a man was dear to his family would be superfluous. To describe how dear, impossible. Of this we might obtain some adequate conception, could we look into the retreat which he had chosen for the solace of his future years; which, enlivened by his presence, was so lately the mansion of cheerfulness and content; but now, alas! of lamentation and wo!—

> "For him no more the blazing hearth shall burn,
> "Nor tender consort wait with anxious care;
> "No children run to lisp their sire's return,
> "Nor climb his knees, the envy'd kiss to share."

With his eye upon the eternal world, this dying Hero had been careful to prepare a testament almost for the sole purpose of bequeathing to his orphans the rich legacy of his principles; and having exhibited in his last hours to this little band the manner in which a Christian should die, he drops in his flight to heaven a summary of the principles, by which a man of honour should live.

The universal sorrow manifested in every part of the Union upon the melancholy exit of this great man, is an unequivocal testimonial of the public opinion of his worth. The place of his residence is overspread with a gloom, which bespeaks the presence of a public calamity, and the prejudices of party are absorbed in the overflowing tide of national grief.

It is indeed a subject of consolation, that diversity of political opinions has not yet extinguished the sentiment of public gratitude. There is yet a hope that events like these which bring home to our bosoms the sensation of a common loss, may yet remind us of our common interest, and of the times when with one accord we joined in the homage of respect to our living as well as to our deceased worthies.

Should those days once more return, when the people of America, united as they once were united, shall make merit the measure of their approbation and confidence, we may hope for a constant succession of patriots and heroes. But should our country be rent by factions, and the merit of the man be estimated by the zeal of the partizan, irreparable will be the loss of those few men, who, having once been esteemed by all, might again have acquired the confidence of all, and saved their country in an hour of peril, by their talents and virtues.

> "So stream the sorrows that embalm the brave;
> "The tears which virtue sheds on glory's grave."

JOHN ADAMS (1735–1826) AND THOMAS JEFFERSON (1743–1826)

by Daniel Webster (1826)

John Adams and Thomas Jefferson, respectively the second and third Presidents of the United States, both died on July 4th, 1826—on the exact day of the 50th anniversary of the signing of The Declaration of Independence. One month later, famed orator and statesman Daniel Webster delivered the following eulogy for the two Founding Fathers at Faneuil Hall in Boston.

THIS IS AN unaccustomed spectacle. For the first time, fellow citizens, badges of mourning shroud the columns and overhang the arches of this Hall. These walls, which were consecrated, so long ago, to the cause of American liberty, which witnessed her infant struggles, and rung with the shouts of her earliest victories, proclaim now that distinguished friends and champions of that great cause have fallen. It is right that it should be thus. The tears which flow, and the honors that are paid, when the Founders of the Republic die, give hope that the Republic itself may be immortal. It is fit, that by public assembly and solemn observance, by anthem and by eulogy, we commemorate the services of national benefactors, extol their virtues, and render thanks to God for eminent blessings, early given and long continued, to our favored country.

ADAMS and JEFFERSON are now no more; and we are assembled, fellow citizens, the aged, the middle aged and the young, by the spontaneous impulse of all, under the authority of the municipal government, with the presence of the chief magistrate of the Commonwealth, and others its official representatives, the university, and the learned societies, to bear our part, in those manifestations of respect and gratitude which universally pervade the land. ADAMS and JEFFERSON are no more. On our fiftieth anniversary, the great day of National Jubilee, in the very hour of public rejoicing, in the midst of echoing and re-echoing voices of thanksgiving, while their own names were on all tongues, they took their flight, together to the world of spirits.

If it be true that no one can safely be pronounced happy while he lives; if that event which terminates life can alone crown its honors and its glory, what felicity is here! The great Epic of their lives, how happily concluded! Poetry itself has hardly closed illustrious lives, and finished the career of earthly renown, by such a consummation. If we had the power, we could not wish to reverse this dispensation of the Divine Providence. The great objects of life were accomplished, the drama was ready to be closed; it has closed; our patriots have fallen; but so fallen, at such age, with such coincidence, on such a day, that we cannot rationally lament that that end has come, which we knew could not be long deferred.

Neither of these great men, fellow citizens, could have died, at any time, without leaving an immense void in our American society. They have been so intimately, and for so long a time blended with the history of the country, especially so united, in our thoughts and recollections, with the events of the Revolution, that the death of either would have touched the strings of public sympathy. We should have felt that one great link, connecting us with former times, was broken; that we had lost something more, as it were, of the presence of the Revolution itself, and of the act of independence, and were driven on, by another great remove, from the days of our country's early distinction, to meet posterity, and to mix with the future. Like the mariner, whom the ocean and the winds carry along, till the stars which have directed his course, and lighted his pathless way, descend, one by one, beneath the rising horizon, we should have felt that the stream of time had borne us onward, till another great luminary, whose light had cheered us, and whose guidance we had followed, had sunk away from our sight.

But the concurrence of their death, on the anniversary of Independence, has naturally awakened stronger emotions. Both had been presidents, both had lived to great age, both were early patriots, and both were distinguished and ever honored by their immediate agency in the act of independence. It cannot but seem striking and extraordinary, that these two should live to see the fiftieth year from the date of that act; that they should complete that year; and that then, on the day which had fast linked forever their own fame with their country's glory, the heavens should open to receive them both at once. As their lives themselves were the gifts of Providence, who is not willing to recognize in their happy termination as well as in their long continuance, proofs that our country, and its benefactors, are objects of His care?

ADAMS and JEFFERSON, I have said, are no more. As human beings indeed, they are no more. They are no more, as in 1776, bold and fearless advocates of independence; no more as on subsequent periods, the head of the government; no more as we have recently seen them, aged and venerable objects of admiration and regard. They are no more. They are dead. But how little is there, of the great and good, which can die! To their country they yet live, and live forever. They live in all that perpetuates the remembrance of men on earth; in the recorded proofs of their own great actions in the offspring of their intellect, in the deep engraved lines of public gratitude, and in the respect and homage of mankind. They live in their example; and they live, emphatically, and will live in the influence which their lives and efforts, their principles and opinions, now exercise, and will continue to exercise, on the affairs of men, not only in their own country, but throughout the civilized world. A superior and commanding human intellect, a truly great man, when Heaven vouchsafes so rare a gift, is not a temporary flame, burning bright for a while, and then expiring, giving place to returning darkness. It is rather a spark of fervent heat, as well as radiant light, with power to enkindle the common mass of human mind; so that when it glimmers, in its own decay, and finally goes out in death, no night follows; but it leaves the world all light, all on fire, from the potent contact of its own spirit. Bacon died; but the human understanding, roused by the touch of his miraculous wand, to a perception of the true philosophy, and the just mode of inquiring after truth, has kept on its course, successfully and gloriously. Newton died; yet the courses of the spheres are still known, and they yet move on, in the orbits which he saw, and described for them, in the infinity of space.

No two men now live, fellow-citizens, perhaps it may be doubted, whether any two men have ever lived, in one age, who, more than those we now commemorate, have impressed their own sentiments, in regard to politics and government, on mankind, infused their own opinions more deeply into the opinions of others, or given a more lasting direction to the current of human thought. Their work doth not perish with them. The tree which they assisted to plant, will flourish, although they water it and protect it no longer; for it has struck its roots deep, it has sent them to the very centre; no storm, not of force to burst the orb, can overturn it; its branches spread wide; they stretch their protecting arms broader and broader, and its top is destined to reach the heavens. We are not deceived. There is no delusion here. No age will come in which it will cease to be seen and felt, on either continent, that a mighty step, a great advance, not only in American affairs, but in human affairs, was made on the 4th of July, 1776. And no age will come, we trust, so ignorant or so unjust, as not to see and acknowledge the efficient agency of those we now honor, for producing that momentous event.

We are not assembled, therefore, fellow citizens, as men overwhelmed with calamity by the sudden disruption of the ties of friendship or affection, or as in despair for the Republic, by the untimely blighting of its hopes. Death has not surprised us by an unseasonable blow. We have, indeed, seen the tomb close, but it has closed only over mature years, over long protracted public service, over the weakness of age, and over life itself only when the ends of living had been fulfilled. These suns, as they rose slowly, and steadily, amidst clouds and storms, in their ascendant, so they have not rushed from their meridian, to sink suddenly in the west. Like the mildness, the serenity, the continuing benignity of a summer's day, they have gone down with slow descending, grateful, long lingering light; and now that they are beyond the visible margin of the world, good omens cheer us from "the bright track of their fiery car!"

There were many points of similarity in the lives and fortunes of these great men. They belonged to the same profession, and had pursued its studies and its practice, for unequal lengths of time indeed, but with diligence and effect. Both were learned and able lawyers. They were natives and inhabitants, respectively, of those two of the colonies, which, at the revolution, were the largest and most powerful, and which naturally had a lead in the political affairs of the times. When the colonies became, in some degree, united, by the assembling of a general congress, they were brought to act together, in its deliberations, not indeed at the same time, but both at early periods. Each had already manifested his attachment to the cause of the country, as well as his ability to maintain it, by printed addresses, public speeches, extensive correspondence, and whatever other mode could be adopted, for the purpose of exposing the encroachments of the British parliament and animating the people to a manly resistance.

Both were not only decided, but early friends of Independence. While others yet doubted, they were resolved where others hesitated, they pressed forward. They were both members of the committee for preparing the Declaration of Independence, and they constituted the sub-committee, appointed by the other members to make the draught. They left their seats in congress, being called to other public employments, at periods not remote from each other, although one of them returned to it, afterwards for a short time. Neither of them was of the assembly of great men which formed the present constitution, and neither was at any time member of congress under its provisions. Both have been public ministers abroad, both vice-presidents, and both presidents. These coincidences are now singularly crowned and completed. They have died, together and they died on the anniversary of liberty.

When many of us were last in this place, fellow citizens, it was on the day of that anniversary. We were met to enjoy the festivities belonging to the occasion, and to manifest our grateful homage to our political fathers.

We did not, we could not here, forget our venerable neighbor of Quincy. We knew that we were standing, at a time of high and palmy prosperity, when he had stood, in the hours of utmost peril; that we saw nothing but liberty and security, where he had met the frown of power; that we were enjoying everything, where he had hazarded everything; and just and sincere plaudits arose to his name, from the crowds which filled this area, and hung over these galleries. He whose grateful duty it was to speak to us, on that day, of the virtues of our fathers, had indeed admonished us that time and years were about to level his venerable frame with the dust. But he bade us hope, that "the sound of a nation's joy, rushing from our cities, ringing from our valleys, echoing from our hills, might yet break the silence of his aged ear; that the rising blessings of grateful millions might yet visit, with glad light, his decaying vision." Alas! that vision was then closing forever. Alas! the silence which was then settling on that aged ear, was an everlasting silence! For lo in the very moment of our festivities, his freed spirit ascended to God who gave it! Human aid and human solace terminate at the grave; or we would gladly have borne him upward, on a nation's outspread hands; we would have accompanied him, and with the blessings of millions and the prayers of millions, commended him to the divine favor.

While still indulging our thoughts on the coincidence of the death of this venerable man with the anniversary of independence, we learn that Jefferson, too, has fallen; and that these aged patriots, these illustrious fellow-laborers, had left our world together. May not such events raise the suggestion that they are not undesigned, and that Heaven does so order things, as sometimes to attract strongly the attention, and excite the thoughts of men? The occurrence has added new interest to our anniversary, and will be remembered in all time to come.

The occasion, fellow-citizens, requires some account of the lives and services of JOHN ADAMS and THOMAS JEFFERSON. This duty must necessarily be performed with great brevity, and in the discharge of it I shall be obliged to confine myself, principally, to those parts of their history and character which belonged to them as public men.

JOHN ADAMS was born at Quincy, then part of the ancient town of Braintree, on the 19th of October, 1735. He was a descendant of the Puritans, his ancestors having early emigrated from England, and settled in Massachusetts. Discovering early a strong love of reading and of knowledge, together with marks of great strength and activity of mind, proper care was taken by his worthy father, to provide for his education. He pursued his youthful studies in Braintree, under Mr. Marsh, a teacher whose fortune it was that Josiah Quincy, Jr., as well as the subject of these remarks, should receive from him his instruction in the rudiments of classical literature. Having been admitted, in 1751, a member of Harvard College, Mr. ADAMS was graduated, in course, 1755; and on the catalogue of that institution, his name, at the time of his death, was second among the living Alumni, being preceded only by that of the venerable Holyoke. With what degree of reputation he left the University, is not now precisely known. We know only that he was distinguished, in a class which numbered Locke and Hemenway among its members. Choosing the law for his profession, he commenced and prosecuted its studies at Worcester, under the direction of Samuel Putnam, a gentleman whom he has himself described as an acute man, an able and learned lawyer, and as in large professional practice at that time. In 1758, he was admitted to the bar, and commenced business in Braintree. He is understood to have made his first considerable effort, or to have attained his first signal success, at Plymouth, on one of those occasions which furnish the earliest opportunity for distinction to many young men of the profession, a jury trial, and a criminal cause. His business naturally grew with his reputation, and his residence in the vicinity afforded the opportunity, as his growing eminence gave the power, of entering on the larger field of practice which the capital presented. In 1766, he removed his residence to Boston, still continuing his attendance on the neighboring circuits, and not unfrequently called to remote parts of the Province. In 1770 his professional firmness was brought to a test of some severity, on the application of the British officers and soldiers to undertake their defence, on the trial of the indictments found against them on account of the transactions of the memorable 5th of March. He seems to have thought, on this occasion, that a man can no more abandon the proper duties of his profession, than he can abandon other duties. The event proved, that as he judged well for his own reputation, so he judged well, also, for the interest and permanent fame of his country. The result of that trial proved that notwithstanding the high degree of excitement then existing, in consequence of the measures of the British government, a jury of Massachusetts would not deprive the most reckless enemies, even the officers of that standing army, quartered among them, which they so perfectly abhorred, of any part of that protection which the law, in its mildest and most indulgent interpretation, afforded to persons accused of crimes.

Without pursuing MR. ADAM's professional course further, suffice it to say, that on the first establishment of the judicial tribunals under the authority of the State, in 1776, he received an offer of the high and responsible station of Chief Justice of the Supreme Court. But he was destined for another and a different career. From early life the bent of his mind was toward politics; a propensity, which the state of the times, if it did not create, doubtless, very much strengthened. Public subjects must have occupied the thoughts and filled up the conversation in the circles in which he then moved; and the interesting questions, at that time just arising, could not but seize on a mind, like his, ardent sanguine and patriotic. The letter, fortunately preserved, written by him at Worcester, so early as the 12th of October, 1755, is a proof of very comprehensive views, and uncommon depth of reflection, in a young man not yet quite twenty. In this letter he predicted the transfer of power, and the establishment of a new seat of empire in America; he predicted, also, the increase of population in the colonies; and anticipated their naval distinction, and foretold that all Europe, combined, could not subdue them. All this is said, not on a public occasion, or for effect, but in the style of sober and friendly correspondence, as the result of his own thoughts. "I sometimes retire," said he, at the close of the letter, "and laying things together, form some reflections pleasing to myself. The produce of one of these reveries you have read above." This prognostication, so early in his own life, so early in the history of the country, of independence, of vast increase of numbers, of naval force, of such augmented power as might defy all Europe, is remarkable. It is more remarkable, that its author should live to see fulfilled to the letter, what could have seemed to others, at the time, but the extravagance of youthful fancy. His earliest political feelings were thus strongly American; and from this ardent attachment to his native soil he never departed.

While still living at Quincy, and at the age of twenty-four, Mr. Adams was present, in this town, on the argument before the Supreme Court, respecting *Writs of Assistance,* and heard the celebrated and patriotic speech of JAMES OTIS. Unquestionably that was a masterly performance. No flighty declamation about liberty, no superficial discussion of popular topics, it was learned, penetrating, convincing, constitutional argument, expressed in a strain of high and resolute patriotism. He grasped the question, then pending between England and her Colonies, with the strength of a lion; and if he sometimes sported, it was only because the lion himself is sometimes playful. Its success appears to have been as great as its merits, and its impression was widely felt. Mr. Adams himself seems never to have lost the feeling it produced, and to have entertained constantly the fullest conviction of its important effects. "I do say," he observes, "in the most solemn manner, that Mr. Otis's Oration against Writs of Assistance, breathed into this nation the breath of life."

In 1765 Mr. Adams laid before the public, what I suppose to be his first printed performance, except essays for the periodical press, a Dissertation on the Canon and Feudal Law. The object of this work was to show that our New England ancestors, in consenting to exile themselves from their native land, were actuated, mainly, by the desire of delivering themselves from the power of the hierarchy, and from the monarchial and aristocratical political systems of the other continent; and to make this truth bear, with effect on the politics of the times. Its tone is uncommonly bold and animated, for that period. He calls on the people, not only to defend, but to study and under-stand their rights and privileges; urges earnestly the necessity of dif-fusing general knowledge, invokes the clergy and the bar, the colleges and academies, and all others who have the ability and the means, to expose the insidious designs of arbitrary power, to resist its approaches, and to be persuaded that there is a settled design on foot to enslave all America. "Be it remembered," says the author, "that liberty must, at all hazards, be supported. We have a right to it derived from our Maker. But if we had not, our fathers have earned it, and bought it for us, at the expense of their ease, their estate, their pleasure and their blood. And liberty cannot be preserved without a general knowledge among the people, who have a right, from the frame of their nature, to knowledge, as their great Creator, who does nothing in vain, has given them understandings, and a desire to know; but besides this, they have a right, an indisputable, unalienable, indefeasible right to that most dreaded and envied kind of knowledge, I mean of the character and conduct of their rulers. Rulers are no more than attorneys, agents, and trustees of the people; and if the cause, the interest and trust, is insidiously betrayed, or wantonly trifled away, the people have a right to revoke the authority, that they themselves have deputed, and to constitute other and better agents, attorneys and trustees."

The citizens of this town conferred on Mr. Adams his first political distinction, and clothed him with his first political trust, by electing him one of their representatives, in 1770. Before this time he had become extensively known throughout the province, as well by the part he had acted in relation to public affairs, as by the exercise of his professional ability. He was among those who took the deepest interest in the controversy with England, and whether in or out of the Legislature, his time and talents were alike devoted to the cause. In the years 1773 and 1774 he was chosen a counsellor, by the members of the General Court, but rejected by Governor Hutchinson, in the former of those years, and by Governor Gage in the latter.

The time was now at hand, however, when the affairs of the colonies urgently demanded united councils. An open rupture with the parent State appeared inevitable, and it was but the dictate of prudence, that those who were united by a common interest and a common danger, should protect that interest and guard against that danger, by united efforts. A general Congress of Delegates from all the colonies, having been proposed and agreed to, the House of Representatives, on the 17th of June, 1774, elected JAMES BOWDOIN, THOMAS CUSHING, SAMUEL ADAMS, JOHN ADAMS, and ROBERT TREAT PAINE, delegates from Massachusetts. This appointment was made at Salem, where the General Court had been convened by Governor Gage, in the last hour of the existence of a House of Representatives under the provincial Charter. While engaged in this important business, the governor having been informed of what was passing, sent his secretary with a message dissolving the General Court. The secretary finding the door locked, directed the messenger to go in and inform the speaker that the secretary was at the door with a message from the governor. The messenger returned, and informed the secretary that the orders of the House were that the doors should be kept fast; whereupon the secretary soon after read a proclamation, dissolving the General Court upon the stairs. Thus terminated, forever, the actual exercise of the political power of England in or over Massachusetts. The four last named delegates accepted their appointments, and took their seats in Congress, the first day of its meeting, September 5, 1774, in Philadelphia.

The proceedings of the first Congress are well known, and have been universally admired. It is in vain that we would look for superior proofs of wisdom, talent, and patriotism. Lord Chatham said, that for himself, he must declare, that he had studied and admired the free states of antiquity, the master states of the world, but that for solidity of reasoning, force of sagacity, and wisdom of conclusion, no body of men could stand in preference to this Congress. It is hardly inferior praise to say, that no production of that great man himself can be pronounced superior to several of the papers published as the proceedings of this most able, most firm, most patriotic assembly. There is, indeed, nothing superior to them in the range of political disquisition. They not only embrace, illustrate, and enforce everything which political philosophy, the love of liberty, and the spirit of free inquiry had antecedently produced, but they add new and striking views of their own, and apply the whole, with irresistible force, in support of the cause which had drawn them together.

Mr. Adams was a constant attendant on the deliberations of this body, and bore an active part in its important measures. He was of the committee to state the rights of the colonies, and of that also which reported the address to the king.

As it was in the continental Congress, fellow-citizens, that those whose deaths have given rise to this occasion, were first brought together, and called on to unite their industry and their ability, in the service of the country, let us now turn to the other of these distinguished men, and take a brief notice of his life, up to the period when he appeared within the walls of Congress.

THOMAS JEFFERSON, descended from ancestors who had been settled in Virginia for some generations, was born near the spot on which he died, in the county of Albermale, on the 2d of April, 1743.

His youthful studies were pursued in the neighborhood of his father's residence, until he was removed to the college of William and Mary, the highest honors of which, he in due time received. Having left the college with reputation, he applied himself to the study of law, under the tuition of George Wythe, one of the highest judicial names of which that State can boast. At an early age he was elected a member of the Legislature, in which he had no sooner appeared than he distinguished himself, by knowledge capacity, and promptitude.

Mr. Jefferson appears to have been imbued with an early love of letters and science, and to have cherished a strong disposition to pursue these objects. To the physical sciences, especially, and to ancient classic literature, he is understood to have had a warm attachment, and never entirely to have lost sight of them, in the midst of the busiest occupations. But the times were times for action, rather than for contemplation. The country was to be defended, and to be saved before it could be enjoyed. Philosophic leisure and literary pursuits, and even the objects of professional attention, were all necessarily postponed to the urgent calls of the public service. The exigency of the country made the same demand on Mr. Jefferson that it made on others who had the ability and the disposition to serve it; and he obeyed the call; thinking and feeling, in this respect, with the great Roman orator: *Quis enim est tam cupidus in perspicienda cognoscendaque rerum natura, ut, si ei tractanta contemplantique res cognitione dignissimas subito sit allatum periculum discrimenque patriæ, cui subvenire opitularique possit, non illa omnia relinquat atque abjiciat, etiam si dinumerare se stellas, aut metira mundi magnitudinem posse arbitretur?*

Entering, with all his heart, into the cause of liberty, his ability, patriotism, and power with the pen, naturally drew upon him a large participation in the most important concerns. Wherever he was, there was found a soul devoted to the cause, power to defend and maintain it, and willingness to incur all its hazards. In 1774 he published a Summary View of the Rights of British America, a valuable production among those intended to show the dangers which threatened the liberties of the country, and to encourage the people in their defence. In June 1775 he was elected a member of the Continental Congress, as successor to PEYTON RANDOLPH, who had retired on account of ill health, and took his seat in that body on the 21st of the same month.

And now, fellow citizens, without pursuing the biography of these illustrious men further, for the present, let us turn our attention to the most prominent act of their lives, their participation in the DECLARATION OF INDEPENDENCE.

Preparatory to the introduction of that important measure, a committee, at the head of which was Mr. Adams, had reported a resolution, which Congress adopted the 10th of May, recommending in substance, to all the colonies which had not already established governments suited to the exigencies of their affairs, *to adopt such government, as would, in the opinion of the representatives of the people, best conduce to the happiness and safety of their constituents in particular, and America in general.*

This significant vote was soon followed by the direct proposition, which RICHARD HENRY LEE had the honor to submit to Congress, by resolution, on the 7th day of June. The published journal does not expressly state it, but there is no doubt, I suppose, that this resolution was in the same words, when originally submitted by Mr. Lee, as when finally passed. Having been discussed, on Saturday the 8th, and Monday the 10th of June, this resolution was on the last mentioned day postponed, for further consideration, to the first day of July; and, at the same time it was voted, that a committee be appointed to prepare a DECLARATION, to the effect of the resolution. This committee was elected by ballot, on the following day, and consisted of THOMAS JEFFERSON, JOHN ADAMS, BENJAMIN FRANKLIN, ROGER SHERMAN, and ROBERT R. LIVINGSTON.

It is usual, when committees are elected by ballot, that their names are arranged, in order, according to the number of votes which each has received. Mr. Jefferson, therefore, had received the highest, and Mr. Adams the next highest number of votes. The difference is said to have been but of a single vote. Mr. Jefferson and Mr. Adams, standing thus at the head of the committee, were requested, by the other members, to act as a sub-committee, to prepare the draught; and Mr. Jefferson drew up the paper. The original draught, as brought by him from his study, and submitted to the other members of the committee, with interlineations in the hand-writing of Dr. Franklin, and others in that of Mr. Adams, was in Mr. Jefferson's possession at the time of his death. The merit of this paper is Mr. Jefferson's. Some changes were made in it, on the suggestion of other members of the committee, and others by Congress while it was under discussion. But none of them altered the tone, the frame, the arrangement, or the general character of the instrument. As a composition, the declaration is Mr. Jefferson's. It is the production of his mind, and the high honor of it belongs to him, clearly and absolutely.

It has sometimes been said, as if it were a derogation from the merits of this paper, that it contains nothing new; that it only states grounds of proceeding, and presses topics of argument, which had often been stated and pressed before. But it was not the object of the Declaration to produce any thing new. It was not to invent reasons for independence, but to state those which governed the Congress. For great and sufficient causes, it was proposed to declare independence; and the proper business of the paper to be drawn was to set forth those causes, and justify the authors of the measure, in any event of fortune, to the country and to posterity. The cause of American independence, moreover, was now to be presented to the world in such manner, if it might so be, as to engage its sympathy, to command its respect, to attract its admiration; and in an assembly of most able and distinguished men, THOMAS JEFFERSON had the high honor of being the selected advocate of this cause. To say that he performed his great work well, would be doing him injustice. To say that he did excellently well, admirably well, would be inadequate and halting praise. Let us rather say, that he so discharged the duty assigned him, that all Americans may well rejoice that the work of drawing the title deed of their liberties devolved on his hands.

With all its merits, there are those who have thought that there was one thing in the declaration to be regretted; and that is, the asperity and apparent anger with which it speaks of the person of the king; the industrious ability with which it accumulates and charges upon him, all the injuries which the colonies had suffered from the mother country. Possibly some degree of injustice, now or hereafter, at home or abroad, may be done to the character of Mr. Jefferson, if this part of the declaration be not placed in its proper light. Anger or resentment, certainly, much less personal reproach and invective, could not properly find place, in a composition of such high dignity, and of such lofty and permanent character.

A single reflection on the original ground of dispute between England and the Colonies is sufficient to remove any unfavorable impression in this respect.

The inhabitants of all the Colonies, while Colonies, admitted themselves bound by their allegiance to the king; but they disclaimed altogether the authority of Parliament; holding themselves, in this respect, to resemble the condition of Scotland and Ireland before the respective unions of those kingdoms with England, when they acknowledged allegiance to the same king, but had each its separate legislature. The tie, therefore, which our Revolution was to break did not subsist between us and the British Parliament, or between us and the British Government in the aggregate, but directly between us and the king himself.

The Colonies had never admitted themselves subject to Parliament. That was precisely the point of the original controversy. They had uniformly denied that Parliament had authority to make laws for them. There was, therefore, no subjection to Parliament to be thrown off. But allegiance to the king did exist, and had been uniformly acknowledged; and down to 1775 the most solemn assurances had been given that it was not intended to break that allegiance or throw it off. Therefore, as the direct object and only effect of the Declaration, according to the principles on which the controversy had been maintained on our part, were to sever the tie of allegiance which bound us to the king, it was properly and necessarily founded on acts of the crown itself, as its justifying causes. Parliament is not so much as mentioned in the whole instrument. When odious and oppressive acts are referred to, it is done by charging the king with confederating with others "in pretended acts of legislation"; the object being constantly to hold the king himself directly responsible for those measures which were the grounds of separation. Even the precedent of the English Revolution was not overlooked, and in this case, as well as in that, occasion was found to say that the king had *abdicated* the government. Consistency with the principles upon which resistance began, and with all the previous state papers issued by Congress, required that the Declaration should be bottomed on the misgovernment of the king; and therefore it was properly framed with that aim and to that end. The king was known, indeed, to have acted, as in other cases, by his ministers, and with his Parliament; but as our ancestors had never admitted themselves subject either to ministers or to Parliament, there were no reasons to be given for now refusing obedience to their authority. This clear and obvious necessity of founding the Declaration on the misconduct of the king himself, gives to that instrument its personal application, and its character of direct and pointed accusation.

The Declaration having been reported to Congress by the committee, the resolution itself was taken up and debated on the first day of July, and again on the second, on which last day it was agreed to and adopted, in these words:—

"*Resolved,* That the United Colonies are, and of right ought to be, free and independent States; that they are absolved from all allegiance to the British crown, and that all political connection between them and the state of Great Britain is, and ought to be, totally dissolved."

Having thus passed the main resolution, Congress proceeded to consider the reported draught of the Declaration. It was discusssed on the second, and third, and FOURTH days of the month, in committee of the whole; and on the last of those days, being reported from that committee, it received the final approbation and sanction of Congress. It was ordered, at the same time, that copies be sent to the several States, and that it be proclaimed at the head of the army. The Declaration thus published did not bear the names of the members, for as yet it had not been signed by them. It was authenticated, like other papers of the Congress, by the signatures of the President and Secretary. On the 19th of July, as appears by the secret journal, Congress "*Resolved,* That the Declaration, passed on the fourth, be fairly engrossed on parchment, with the title and style of 'THE UNANIMOUS DECLARATION OF THE THIRTEEN UNITED STATES OF AMERICA'; and that the same, when engrossed, be signed by every member of Congress." And on the SECOND DAY OF AUGUST following, "the Declaration, being engrossed and compared at the table, was signed by the members." So that it happens, fellow-citizens, that we pay these honors to their memory on the anniversary of that day (2d of August) on which these great men actually signed their names to the Declaration. The Declaration was thus made, that is, it passed, and was adopted as an act of Congress, on the fourth of July; it was then signed, and certified by the President and Secretary, like other acts. The FOURTH OF JULY, therefore, is the ANNIVERSARY OF THE DECLARATION. But the signatures of the members present were made to it, being then engrossed on parchment, on the second day of August. Absent members afterwards signed, as they came in; and indeed it bears the names of some who were not chosen members of Congress until after the fourth of July. The interest belonging to the subject, will be sufficient, I hope, to justify these details.

The Congress of the Revolution, fellow-citizens, sat with closed doors, and no report of its debates was ever made. The discussion, therefore, which accompanied this great measure, has never been preserved, except in memory and by tradition. But it is, I believe, doing no injustice to others to say, that the general opinion was, and uniformly has been, that in debate, on the side of independence, JOHN ADAMS had no equal. The great author of the Declaration himself has expressed that opinion uniformly and strongly. "JOHN ADAMS," said he, in the hearing of him who has now the honor to address you, "JOHN ADAMS was our colossus on the floor. Not graceful, not elegant, not always fluent, in his public addresses, he yet came out with a power, both of thought and of expression, which moved us from our seats."

For the part which he was here to perform, Mr. Adams doubtless was eminently fitted. He possessed a bold spirit which disregarded danger, and a sanguine reliance on the goodness of the cause, and the virtues of the people, which led him to overlook all obstacles. His character, too, had been formed in troubled times. He had been rocked in the early storms of the controversy, and had acquired a decision and a hardihood proportioned to the severity of the discipline which he had undergone.

He not only loved the American cause devoutly, but had studied and understood it. It was all familiar to him. He had tried his powers on the questions which it involved, often and in various ways; and brought to their consideration whatever of argument or illustration the history of his own country, the history of England, or the stores of ancient or legal learning could furnish. Every grievance enumerated in the long catalogue of the Declaration had been the subject of his discussion, and the object of his remonstrance and reprobation. From 1760, the Colonies, the rights of the Colonies, the liberties of the Colonies, and the wrongs inflicted on the Colonies, had engaged his attention; and it has surprised those who have the opportunity of witnessing it, with what full remembrance, and with what prompt recollection he could refer, in his extreme old age to every act of Parliament affecting the Colonies, distinguishing and stating their respective titles, sections and provisions; and to all the Colonial memorials, remonstrances, and petitions, with whatever else belonged to the intimate and exact history of the times from that year to 1775. It was, in his own judgment, between these years that the American people came to a full understanding and thorough knowledge of their rights, and a fixed resolution of maintaining them; and bearing himself an active part in all important transactions, the controversy with England being then in effect the business of his life, facts, dates, and particulars made an impression which was never effaced. He was prepared, therefore, by education and discipline, as well as by natural talent and natural temperament, for the part which he was now to act.

The eloquence of Mr. Adams resembled his general character, and formed, indeed, a part of it. It was bold, manly, and energetic; and such the crisis required. When public bodies are to be addressed on momentous occasions, when great interests are at stake, and strong passions excited, nothing is valuable in speech farther than as it is connected with high intellectual and moral endowments. Clearness, force, and earnestness are the qualities which produce conviction. True eloquence, does not consist in speech. It cannot be brought from far. Labor and learning may toil for it, but they will toil in vain. Words and phrases may be marshalled in every way, but they cannot compass it. It must exist in the man, in the subject, and in the occasion. Affected passion, intense expression, the pomp of declamation, all may aspire to it; they cannot reach it. It comes, if it come at all, like the outbreaking of a fountain from the earth, or the bursting forth of volcanic fires, with spontaneous, original, native force. The graces taught in the schools, the costly ornaments and studied contrivances of speech, shock and disgust men, when their own lives, and the fate of their wives, their children, and their country, hang on the decision of the hour. Then words have lost their power, rhetoric is vain, and all elaborate oratory contemptible. Even genius itself then feels rebuked and subdued, as in the presence of higher qualities. Then patriotism is eloquent; then self devotion is eloquent. The clear conception, outrunning the deductions of logic, the high purpose, the firm resolve, the dauntless spirit, speaking on the tongue, beaming from the eye, informing every feature, and urging the whole man onward, right onward to his object—this, this is eloquence; or rather it is something greater and higher than all eloquence, it is action, noble, sublime, godlike action.

In July, 1776, the controversy had passed the stage of argument. An appeal had been made to force, and opposing armies were in the field. Congress, then, was to decide whether the tie which had so long bound us to the parent state was to be severed at once, and severed forever. All the Colonies had signified their resolution to abide by this decision, and the people looked for it with the most intense anxiety. And surely, fellow-citizens, never, never were men called to a more important political deliberation. If we contemplate it from the point where they then stood, no question could be more full of interest; if we look at it now, and judge of its importance by its effects, it appears of still greater magnitude.

Let us, then, bring before us the assembly, which was about to decide a question thus big with the fate of empire. Let us open their doors and look in upon their deliberations. Let us survey the anxious and care-worn countenances, let us hear the firm-toned voices, of this band of patriots.

HANCOCK presides over the solemn sitting; and one of those not yet prepared to pronounce for absolute independence is on the floor, and is urging his reasons for dissenting from the declaration.

"Let us pause! This step, once taken, can never be retraced. This resolution, once passed, will cut off all hope of a reconciliation. If success attend the arms of England, we shall then be no longer colonies, with charters and privileges; these will all be forfeited by this act; and we shall be in the condition of other conquered people, at the mercy of the conquerors. For ourselves, we may be ready to run the hazard; but are we ready to carry the country to that length? Is success so probable as to justify it? Where is the military, where the naval power, by which we are to resist the whole strength of the arm of England, for she will exert that strength to the utmost? Can we rely on the constancy and perseverance of the people? or will they not act as the people of other countries have acted, and wearied with a long war, submit, in the end, to a worse oppression? While we stand on our own ground, and insist on redress of grievances, we know we are right, and are not answerable for consequences. Nothing, then, can be imputed to us. But if we now change our object, carry our pretensions farther, and set up for absolute independence, we shall lose the sympathy of mankind. We shall no longer be defending what we possess, but struggling for something which we never did possess, and which we have solemnly and uniformly disclaimed all intention of pursuing, from the very outset of the troubles. Abandoning thus our old ground, of resistance only to arbitrary acts of oppression, the nations will believe the whole to have been mere pretence, and they will look on us, not as injured, but as ambitious subjects. I shudder before this responsibility. It will be on us, if, relinquishing the ground on which we have stood so safely, we now proclaim independence, and carry on the war for that object, while these cities burn, these pleasant fields whiten and bleach with the bones of their owners, and these streams run blood. It will be upon us, it will be upon us, if, failing to maintain this unseasonable and ill-judged declaration, a sterner despotism, maintained by military power, shall be established over our posterity, when we ourselves, given up by an exhausted, a harrassed, a misled people, shall have expiated our rashness and atoned for our presumption on the scaffold."

It was for Mr. Adams to reply to arguments like these. We know his opinions, and we know his character. He would commence with his accustomed directness and earnestness.

"Sink or swim, live or die, survive or perish, I give my hand and my heart to this vote. It is true, indeed that in the beginning that we aimed not at independence. But there's a Divinity which shapes our ends. The injustice of England has driven us to arms; and, blinded to her own interest for our good, she has obstinately persisted, till independence is now within our grasp. We have but to reach forth to it, and it is ours. Why, then should we defer the Declaration? Is any man so weak as now to hope for a reconciliation with England, which shall leave either safety to the country and its liberties, or safety to his own life and honor? Are not you, sir, who sit in that chair, is not he, our venerable colleague near you, are you not both already the proscribed and predestined objects of punishment and vengeance? Cut off from all hope of royal clemency, what are you, what can you be, while the power of England remains, but outlaws? If we postpone independence, do we mean to carry on, or give up, the war? Do we mean to submit to the measures of Parliament, Boston Port Bill and all? Do we mean to submit, and consent that we ourselves shall be ground to powder, and our country and its rights trodden down in the dust? I know we do not mean to submit. We never shall submit. Do we intend to violate that most solemn obligation ever entered into by men, that plighting, before God, of our sacred honor to Washington, when putting him forth to incur the dangers of War, as well as the political hazards of the times, we promised to adhere to him, in every extremity, with our fortunes and our lives! I know there is not a man here, who would not rather see a general conflagration sweep over the land, or an earthquake sink it, than one jot or tittle of that plighted faith fall to the ground. For myself, having, twelve months ago, in this place, moved you, that George Washington be appointed commander of the forces raised, or to be raised, for defence of American liberty, may my right hand forget her cunning, and my tongue cleave to the roof of my mouth, if I hesitate or waver in the support I give him.

"The war, then, must go on. We must fight it through. And if the war must go on, why put off longer the Declaration of Independence? That measure will strengthen us. It will give us character abroad. The nations will treat with us, which they can never do while we acknowledge ourselves subjects, in arms against our sovereign. Nay, I maintain that England herself will sooner treat for peace with us on the footing of independence, than consent, by repealing her acts, to acknowledge that her whole conduct towards us has been a course of injustice and oppression. Her pride will be less wounded by submitting to that course of things which now predestinates our independence, than by yielding the points in controversy to her rebellious subjects. The former she would regard as the result of fortune; the latter she would feel as her own deep disgrace. Why, then, why then, Sir, do we not as soon as possible change this from a civil to a national war? And since we must fight it through, why not put ourselves in a state to enjoy all the benefits of victory, if we gain the victory?

"If we fail, it can be no worse for us. But we shall not fail. The cause will raise up armies; the cause will create navies. The people, the people, if we are true to them, will carry us, and will carry themselves, gloriously through this struggle. I care not how fickle other people have been found. I know the people of these Colonies, and I know that resistance to British aggression is deep and settled in their hearts and cannot be eradicated. Every Colony, indeed, has expressed its willingness to follow, if we but take the lead. Sir, the Declaration will inspire the people with increased courage. Instead of a long and bloody war for the restoration of privileges, for redress of grievances, for chartered immunities, held under a British king, set before them the glorious object of entire independence, and it will breathe into them anew the breath of life. Read this Declaration at the head of the army; every sword will be drawn from its scabbard, and the solemn vow uttered, to maintain it, or to perish on the bed of honor. Publish it from the pulpit; religion will approve it, and the love of religious liberty will cling round it, resolved to stand with it or fall with it. Send it to the public halls; proclaim it there; let them hear it who heard the first roar of the enemy's cannon; let them see it who saw their brothers and their sons fall on the field of Bunker Hill, and in the street of Lexington and Concord, and the very walls will cry out in its support.

"Sir, I know the uncertainty of human affairs, but I see, I see clearly, through this day's business. You and I, indeed, may rue it. We may not live to the time when this Declaration shall be made good. We may die; die colonists; die slaves; die, it may be, ignominiously and on the scaffold. Be it so. Be it so. If it be the pleasure of Heaven that my country shall require the poor offering of my life, the victim shall be ready, at the appointed hour of sacrifice, come when that hour may. But while I do live, let me have a country, or at least the hope of a country, and that a free country.

"But whatever may be our fate, be assured, be assured that this Declaration will stand. It may cost treasure, and it may cost blood; but it will stand, and it will richly compensate for both. Through the thick gloom of the present, I see the brightness of the future, as the sun in heaven. We shall make this a glorious, an immortal day. When we are in our graves, our children will honor it. They will celebrate it with thanksgiving, with festivity, with bonfires, and illuminations.

On its annual return they will shed tears, copious, gushing tears, not of subjection and slavery, not of agony and distress, but of exultation, of gratitude, and of joy. Sir, before God, I believe the hour is come. My judgment approves this measure, and my whole heart is in it. All that I have, and all that I am, and all that I hope, in this life, I am now ready here to stake upon it; and I leave off as I begun, that live or die, survive or perish, I am for the Declaration. It is my living sentiment, and by the blessing of God it shall be my dying sentiment, Independence, *now,* and INDEPENDENCE FOR EVER."

And so that day shall be honored, illustrious prophet and patriot! so that day shall be honored, and as often as it returns, thy renown shall come along with it, and the glory of thy life, like the day of thy death, shall not fail from the remembrance of men.

It would be unjust, fellow-citizens, on this occasion, while we express our veneration for him who is the immediate subject of these remarks, were we to omit a most respectful, affectionate, and grateful mention of those other great men, his colleagues, who stood with him, and with the same spirit, the same devotion, took part in the interesting transaction. HANCOCK, the proscribed HANCOCK, exiled from his home by a military governor, cut off by proclamation from the mercy of the crown,—Heaven reserved for him the honor of putting this great question to the vote, and of writing his own name first, and most conspicuously, on that parchment which spoke defiance to the power of the crown of England. There, too, is the name of that other proscribed patriot, SAMUEL ADAMS, a man who hungered and thirsted for the independence of his country; who thought the Declaration halted and lingered, being himself not only ready, but eager for it, long before it was proposed; a man of the deepest sagacity, the clearest foresight, and the profoundest judgment in men. And there is GERRY, himself among the earliest and the foremost of the patriots, found when the battle of Lexington summoned them to common counsels, by the side of WARREN; a man who lived to serve his country at home and abroad, and to die in the second place in the government. There, too, is the inflexible, the upright, the Spartan character, ROBERT TREAT PAINE. He also lived to serve his country through the struggle, and then withdrew from her councils, only that he might give his labors and his life to his native State, in another relation. These names, fellow-citizens, are the treasures of the Commonwealth; and they are treasures which grow brighter by time.

It is now necessary to resume the narrative, and to finish with great brevity the notice of the lives of those whose virtues and services we have met to commemorate.

Mr. Adams remained in Congress from its first meeting till November, 1777, when he was appointed Minister to France. He proceeded on that service in the February following, embarking in the frigate Boston, from the shore of his native town, at the foot of Mount Wollaston. The year following, he was appointed commissioner to treat of peace with England. Returning to the United States, he was a delegate from Braintree in the Convention for framing the Constitution of this Commonwealth, in 1780. At the latter end of the same year, he again went abroad in the diplomatic service of the country, and was employed at various courts, and occupied with various negociations, until 1788. The particulars of these interesting and important services this occasion does not allow time to relate. In 1782 he concluded our first treaty with Holland. His negociations with that republic, his efforts to persuade the States-General to recognize our independence, his incessant and indefatigable exertions to represent the American cause favorably on the Continent, and to counteract the designs of its enemies, open and secret, and his successful undertaking to obtain loans, on the credit of a nation yet new and unknown, are among his most arduous, most useful, most honorable services. It was his fortune to bear a part in the negociation for peace with England, and in something more than six years from the Declaration which he had so strenuously supported, he had the satisfaction of seeing the minister plenipotentiary of the crown subscribe his name to the instrument which declared that his "Britannic Majesty acknowledged the United States to be free, sovereign, and independent." In these important transactions, Mr. Adams' conduct received the marked approbation of Congress and of the country.

While abroad, in 1787, he published his Defence of the American Constitutions; a work of merit and ability, though composed with haste, on the spur of a particular occasion, in the midst of other occupations, and under circumstances not admitting of careful revision. The immediate object of the work was to counteract the weight of opinions advanced by several popular European writers of that day, M. Turgot, the Abbe de Mably, and Dr. Price, at a time when the people of the United States were employed in forming and revising their systems of government.

Returning to the United States in 1788, he found the new government about going into operation, and was himself elected the first Vice President, a situation which he filled with reputation for eight years, at the expiration of which he was raised to the Presidential chair, as immediate successor to the immortal Washington. In this high station he was succeeded by Mr. Jefferson, after a memorable controversy between their respective friends, in 1801; and from that period his manner of life has been known to all who hear me. He has lived for five-and-twenty years, with every enjoyment that could render old age happy. Not inattentive to the occurrences of the times, political cares have yet not materially, or for any long time, disturbed his repose. In 1820 he acted as elector of President and Vice President, and in the same year we saw him, then at the age of eighty-five, a member of the Convention of this Commonwealth called to revise the Constitution. Forty years before, he had been one of those who formed that Constitution; and he had now the pleasure of witnessing that there was little which the people desired to change. Possessing all his faculties to the end of his long life, with an unabated love of reading and contemplation, in the centre of interesting circles of friendship and affection, he was blessed in his retirement with whatever of repose and felicity the condition of man allows. He had, also, other enjoyments. He saw around him that prosperity and general happiness which had been the object of his public cares and labors. No man ever beheld more clearly, and for a longer time, the great and beneficial effects of the services rendered by himself to his country. That liberty which he so early defended, that independence of which he was so able an advocate and supporter, he saw, we trust, firmly and securely established. The population of the country thickened around him faster, and extended wider, than his own sanguine predictions had anticipated; and the wealth, respectability, and power of the nation sprang up to a magnitude which it is quite impossible he could have expected to witness in his day. He lived also to behold those principles of civil freedom which had been developed, established, and practically applied in America, attract attention, command respect, and awaken imitation, in other regions of the globe; and well might, and well did he exclaim, "Where will the consequences of the American Revolution end?"

If any thing yet remains to fill this cup of happiness, let it be added, that he lived to see a great and intelligent people bestow the highest honor in their gift where he had bestowed his own kindest parental affections and lodged his fondest hopes. Thus honored in life, thus happy at death, he saw the JUBILEE, and he died; and with the last prayers which trembled on his lips was the fervent supplication for his country, "Independence for ever!"

Mr. Jefferson, having been occupied in the years 1778 and 1779 in the important service of revising the laws of Virginia, was elected Governor of that State, as successor to Patrick Henry, and held the situation when the State was invaded by the British arms. In 1781 he published his Notes on Virginia, a work which attracted attention in Europe as well as America, dispelled many misconceptions respecting this continent, and gave its author a place among men distinguished for science. In November, 1783, he again took his seat in the Continental Congress, but in May following was appointed Minister Plenipotentiary, to act abroad, in the negociation of commercial treaties, with Dr. Franklin and Mr. Adams. He proceeded to France in execution of this mission, embarking at Boston; and that was the only occasion on which he ever visited this place. In 1785 he was appointed Minister to France, the duties of which situation he continued to perform until October, 1789, when he obtained leave to retire, just on the eve of that tremendous revolution which has so much agitated the world in our times. Mr. Jefferson's discharge of his diplomatic duties was marked by great ability, diligence, and patriotism; and while he resided at Paris, in one of the most interesting periods, his character for intelligence, his love of knowledge, and of the society of learned men, distinguished him in the highest circles of the French capital. No court in Europe had at that time in Paris a representative commanding or enjoying higher regard, for political knowledge or for general attainments, than the minister of this then infant republic. Immediately on his return to his native country, at the organization of the government under the present Constitution, his talents and experience recommended him to President Washington for the first office in his gift. He was placed at the head of the Department of State. In this situation, also, he manifested conspicuous ability. His correspondence with the ministers of other powers residing here, and his instructions to our own diplomatic agents abroad, are among our ablest state papers. A thorough knowledge of the laws and usages of nations, perfect acquaintance with the immediate subject before him, great felicity, and still greater facility, in writing, show themselves in whatever his official situation called on him to make. It is believed by competent judges, that the diplomatic intercourse of the government of the United States, from the first meeting of the Continental Congress in 1774 to the present time, taken together, would not suffer in respect to the talent with which it has been conducted, by comparison with any thing which other and older governments can produce; and to the attainment of this respectability and distinction Mr. Jefferson has contributed his full part.

On the retirement of General Washington from the presidency, and the election of Mr. Adams to that office, in 1797, he was chosen

Vice-President. While presiding, in this capacity, over the deliberations of the senate, he compiled and published a Manual of
Parliamentary Practice, a work of more labor and more merit, than
is indicated by its size. It is now received, as the general standard, by
which proceedings are regulated, not only in both Houses of Congress,
but in most of the other legislative bodies in the country. In 1801,
he was elected President, in opposition to Mr. Adams, and re-elected
in 1805, by a vote approaching towards unanimity.

From the time of his final retirement from public life, in 1808,
Mr. Jefferson lived as became a wise man. Surrounded by affectionate friends, his ardor in the pursuit of knowledge undiminished, with
uncommon health, and unbroken spirits, he was able to enjoy largely
the rational pleasures of life, and to partake in that public prosperity,
which he had so much contributed to produce. His kindness and
hospitality, the charm of his conversation, the ease of his manners,
the extent of his acquirements, and especially the full store of revolutionary incidents, which he possessed, and which he knew when
and how to dispense, rendered his abode in a high degree attractive
to his admiring countrymen, while his high public and scientific
character drew towards him every intelligent and educated traveller
from abroad. Both Mr. Adams and Mr. Jefferson had the pleasure of
knowing that the respect, which they so largely received, was not
paid to their official stations. They were not men made great by
office; but great men, on whom the country for its own benefit had
conferred office. There was that in them, which office did not give,
and which the relinquishment of office, did not, and could not take
away. In their retirement, in the midst of their fellow citizens, themselves private citizens, they enjoyed as high regard and esteem, as
when filling the most important places of public trust.

There remained to Mr. Jefferson yet one other work of patriotism
and beneficence, the establishment of a University in his native state.
To this object he devoted years of incessant and anxious attention,
and by the enlightened liberality of the legislature of Virginia, and
the co-operation of other able and zealous friends, he lived to see it
accomplished. May all success attend this infant seminary; and may
those who enjoy its advantages, as often as their eyes shall rest on the
neighboring height, recollect what they owe to their disinterested
and indefatigable benefactor; and may letters honor him who thus
labored in the cause of letters.

Thus useful, and thus respected, passed the old age of Thomas
Jefferson. But time was on its ever ceaseless wing, and was now
bringing the last hour of this illustrious man. He saw its approach,

with undisturbed serenity. He counted the moments, as they passed, and beheld that his last sands were falling. That day, too, was at hand, which he had helped to make immortal. One wish, one hope—if it were not presumptuous—beat in his fainting breast. Could it be so—might it please God—he would desire—once more—to see the sun—once more to look abroad on the scene around him, on the great day of liberty. Heaven, in its mercy, fulfilled that prayer. He saw that sun—he enjoyed its sacred light—he thanked God, for this mercy, and bowed his aged head to the grave. *"Felix non vitæ tantum claritate, sed etiam opportunitate mortis."*

The last public labor of Mr. Jefferson naturally suggests the expression of the high praise which is due, both to him and to Mr. Adams, for their uniform and zealous attachment to learning, and to the cause of general knowledge. Of the advantages of learning, indeed, and of literary accomplishments, their own characters were striking recommendations, and illustrations. They were scholars, ripe and good scholars; widely acquainted with ancient, as well as modern literature, and not altogether uninstructed in the deeper sciences. Their acquirements, doubtless, were different, and so were the particular objects of their literary pursuits; as their tastes and characters, in these respects, differed like those of other men. Being, also, men of busy lives, with great objects, requiring action, constantly before them, their attainments in letters did not become showy, or obtrusive. Yet, I would hazard the opinion, that if we could now ascertain all the causes which gave them eminence and distinction, in the midst of the great men with whom they acted, we should find, not among the least, their early acquisition in literature, the resources which it furnished, the promptitude and facility which it communicated, and the wide field it opened, for analogy and illustration; giving them, thus, on every subject, a larger view, and a broader range, as well for discussion, as for the government of their own conduct.

Literature sometimes, and pretensions to it much oftener, disgusts, by appearing to hang loosely on the character, like something foreign or extraneous, not a part, but an ill-adjusted appendage; or by seeming to overload and weigh it down, by its unsightly bulk, like the productions of bad taste in architecture, where there is massy and cumbrous ornament, without strength or solidity of column. This has exposed learning, and especially classical learning, to reproach. Men have seen that it might exist, without mental superiority, without vigor, without good taste, and without utility. But in such cases classical learning has only not inspired natural talent; or, at most, it has but made original feebleness of intellect, and natural bluntness of perception, something more conspicuous. The question, after all, if it be a question, is whether literature, ancient as well as modem, does not assist a good understanding, improve natural good taste, add polished armor to native strength and render its possessor, not only more capable of deriving private happiness from contemplation and reflection, but more accomplished, also, for action in the affairs of life, and especially for public action. Those whose memories we now honor, were learned men; but their learning was kept in its proper place, and made subservient to the uses and objects of life. They were scholars not common, nor superficial; but their scholarship was so in keeping with their character, so blended and inwrought, that careless observers, or bad judges, not seeing an ostentatious display of it, might infer that it did not exist; forgetting, or not knowing, that classical learning, in men who act in conspicuous public stations, perform duties which exercise the faculty of writing, or address popular, deliberative, or judicial bodies, is often felt, where it is little seen, and sometimes felt more effectually, because it is not seen at all.

But the cause of knowledge, in a more enlarged sense, the cause of general knowledge and of popular education, had no warmer friends, nor more powerful advocates, than Mr. Adams and Mr. Jefferson. On this foundation, they knew the whole republican system rested; and this great and all-important truth they strove to impress, by all the means in their power. In the early publication already referred to, Mr. Adams expresses the strong and just sentiment, that the education of the poor is more important, even to the rich themselves, than all their own riches. On this great truth, indeed, is founded that unrivalled, that invaluable political and moral institution, our own blessing and the glory of our fathers, the New England system of free schools.

As the promotion of knowledge had been the object of their regard through life, so these great men made it the subject of their testamentary bounty. Mr. Jefferson is understood to have bequeathed his library to the University of Virginia, and that of Mr. Adams is bestowed on the inhabitants of Quincy.

Mr. Adams and Mr. Jefferson, fellow-citizens, were successively Presidents of the United States. The comparative merits of their respective administrations for a long time agitated and divided public opinion. They were rivals, each supported by numerous and powerful portions of the people, for the highest office. This contest, partly the cause and partly the consequence of the long existence of two great political parties in the country, is now part of the history of our government. We may naturally regret that any thing should have occurred to create difference and discord between those who had acted harmoniously and efficiently in the great concerns of the Revolution. But this is not the time, nor this the occasion, for entering into the grounds of that difference, or for attempting to discuss the merits of the question which it involves. As practical questions, they were canvassed when the measures which they regarded were acted on and adopted; and as belonging to history, the time had not come for their consideration.

It is, perhaps, not wonderful, that, when the Constitution of the United States first went into operation, different opinions should be entertained as to the extent of the powers conferred by it. Here was a natural source of diversity of sentiment. It is still less wonderful, that that event, nearly contemporary with our government under the present Constitution, which so entirely shocked all Europe, and disturbed our relations with her leading powers, should be thought, by different men, to have different bearings on our own prosperity; and that the early measures adopted by the government of the United States, in consequence of this new state of things, should be seen in opposite lights. It is for the future historian, when what now remains of prejudice and misconception shall have passed away, to state these different opinions, and pronounce impartial judgment. In the mean time, all good men rejoice, and well may rejoice, that the sharpest differences sprung out of measures which, whether right or wrong, have ceased with the exigencies that gave them birth, and have left no permanent effect, either on the Constitution or on the general prosperity of the country. This remark, I am aware, may be supposed to have its exception in one measure, the alteration of the Constitution as to the mode of choosing President; but it is true in its general application. Thus the course of policy pursued towards France in 1798, on the one hand, and the measures of commercial restriction commenced in 1807, on the other, both subjects of warm and severe opposition, have passed away and left nothing behind them. They were temporary, and whether wise or unwise, their consequences were limited to their respective occasions. It is equally clear, at the same time, and it is equally gratifying, that those measures of both administrations which were of durable importance, and which drew after them momentous and long remaining consequences, have received general approbation. Such was the organization, or rather the creation, of the navy, in the administration of Mr. Adams; such the acquisition of Louisiana in that of Mr. Jefferson. The country, it may safely be added, is not likely to be willing either to approve, or to reprobate, indiscriminately, and in the aggregate, all the measures of either or of any, administration. The dictate of reason and of justice is, that, holding each one his own sentiments on the points of difference, we imitate the great men themselves in the forbearance and moderation which they have cherished, and in the mutual respect and kindness which they have been so much inclined to feel and to reciprocate.

No men, fellow-citizens, ever served their country with more entire exemption from every imputation of selfish and mercenary motives, than those to whose memory we are paying these proofs of respect. A suspicion of any disposition to enrich themselves, or to profit by their public employments, never rested on either. No sordid motive approached them. The inheritance which they have left to their children is of their character and their fame.

Fellow-citizens, I will detain you no longer by this faint and feeble tribute to the memory of the illustrious dead. Even in other hands, adequate justice could not be done to them, within the limits of this occasion. Their highest, their best praise, is your deep conviction of their merits, your affectionate gratitude for their labors and their services. It is not my voice, it is this cessation of ordinary pursuits, this arresting of all attention, these solemn ceremonies, and this crowded house, which speak their eulogy. Their fame, indeed, is safe. That is now treasured up beyond the reach of accident. Although no sculptured marble should rise to their memory, nor engraved stone bear record of their deeds, yet will their remembrance be as lasting as the land they honored. Marble columns may, indeed, moulder into dust, time may erase all impress from the crumbling stone, but their fame remains; for with AMERICAN LIBERTY it rose, and with AMERICAN LIBERTY ONLY can it perish. It was the last swelling peal of yonder choir, "THEIR BODIES ARE BURIED IN PEACE, BUT THEIR NAME LIVETH EVERMORE." I catch that solemn song, I echo that lofty strain of funeral triumph, "THEIR NAME LIVETH EVERMORE."

Of the illustrious signers of the Declaration of Independence there now remains only CHARLES CARROLL. He seems an aged oak, standing alone on the plain, which time has spared a little longer after all its contemporaries have been levelled with the dust. Venerable object! we delight to gather round its trunk, while yet it stands, and to dwell beneath its shadow. Sole survivor of an assembly of as great men as the world has witnessed, in a transaction one of the most important that history records, what thoughts, what interesting reflections, must fill his elevated and devout soul! If he dwell on the past, how touching its recollections; if he survey the present, how happy, how joyous, how full of the fruition of that hope, which his ardent patriotism indulged; if he glance at the future, how does the prospect of his country's advancement almost bewilder his weakened conception! Fortunate, distinguished patriot! Interesting relic of the past! Let him know that, while we honor the dead, we do not forget the living; and that there is not a heart here which does not fervently pray, that Heaven may keep him yet back from the society of his companions.

And now, fellow-citizens, let us not retire from this occasion without a deep and solemn conviction of the duties which have devolved upon us. This lovely land, this glorious liberty, these benign institutions, the dear purchase of our fathers, are ours; ours to enjoy, ours to preserve, ours to transmit. Generations past and generations to come hold us responsible for this sacred trust. Our fathers, from behind, admonish us, with their anxious paternal voices; posterity calls out to us, from the bosom of the future; the world turns hither its solicitous eyes; all, all conjure us to act wisely, and faithfully, in the relation which we sustain. We can never, indeed, pay the debt which is upon us; but by virtue, by morality, by religion, by the cultivation of every good principle and every good habit, we may hope to enjoy the blessing, through our day, and to leave it unimpaired to our children. Let us feel deeply how much of what we are and of what we possess we owe to this liberty, and to these institutions of government. Nature has, indeed, given us a soil which yields bounteously to the hand of industry, the mighty and fruitful ocean is before us, and the skies over our heads shed health and vigor. But what are lands, and seas, and skies, to civilized man without society, without knowledge, without morals, religious culture; and how can these be enjoyed, in all their extent and all their excellence, but under the protection of wise institutions and a free government? Fellow-citizens, there is not one of us, there is not one of us here present, who does not, at this moment, and at every moment, experience, in his own condition, and in the condition of those most near and dear to him, the influence and the benefits of this liberty and these institutions. Let us then acknowledge the blessing, let us feel it deeply and powerfully, let us cherish a strong affection for it, and resolve to maintain and perpetuate it. The blood of our fathers, let it not have been shed in vain; the great hope of posterity, let it not be blasted.

The striking attitude, too, in which we stand to the world around us, a topic to which, I fear, I advert too often, and dwell on too long, cannot be altogether omitted here. Neither individuals nor nations can perform their part well, until they understand and feel its importance, and comprehend and justly appreciate all the duties belonging to it. It is not to inflate national vanity, nor to swell a light and empty feeling of self-importance, but it is that we may judge justly of our situation, and of our own duties, that I earnestly urge upon you this consideration of our position and our character among the nations of the earth. It cannot be denied, but by those who would dispute against the sun, that with America, and in America, a new era commences in human affairs. This era is distinguished by free representative governments, by entire religious liberty, by improved systems of national intercourse, by a newly awakened and an unconquerable spirit of free inquiry, and by a diffusion of knowledge through the community, such as has been before altogether unknown and unheard of. America, America, our country, fellow-citizens, our own dear and native land, is inseparably connected, fast bound up, in fortune and by fate, with these great interests. If they fall, we fall with them; if they stand, it will be because we have maintained them. Let us contemplate, then, this connection, which binds the prosperity of others to our own; and let us manfully discharge all the duties which it imposes. If we cherish the virtues and the principles of our fathers, Heaven will assist us to carry on the work of human liberty and human happiness. Auspicious omens cheer us. Great examples are before us. Our own firmament now shines brightly upon our path. Washington is in the clear, upper sky. These other stars have now joined the American constellation; they circle round their centre, and the heavens beam with new light. Beneath this illumination let us walk the course of life, and at its close devoutly commend our beloved country, the common parent of us all, to the Divine Benignity.

LUDWIG VAN BEETHOVEN (1770–1827)

by Franz Grillparzer (1827)

*Ludwig van Beethoven was a German composer, widely
remembered as the most important musical figure during the
transition from the Classical Era to the Romantic Era. The
following eulogy was composed by Franz Grillparzer and
delivered by the actor and orator Heinrich Anschutz at
Beethoven's funeral in Vienna. Grillparzer was Austria's
most notable playwright, and a longtime personal friend of
Beethoven.*

As WE STAND here at the grave of the deceased, we are, as it were,
the representatives of a whole nation, of the German people in its
entirety, grieving at the fall of the one, highly celebrated half of the
remaining vanished glory of indigenous art, of the nation's flourish-
ing spirit. To be sure, the hero of German poesy, Goethe, still lives—
and may he live long!—but the last master of sonorous song, of
music's sweet voice, the heir to Handel's immortal fame and Bach's,
the heir to Haydn and Mozart, has passed away, and we stand weep-
ing by the torn strings of faded harmony.

Of faded harmony! Let me call him so! For here was an artist, and
what he was, he was only through art. The thorns of life had wounded
him deeply; as a shipwrecked man clings to the shore, so he fled into
your arms, O Art, equally glorious sister of the good and the true,
comforter of suffering, begotten on high. He held fast to you, and
even when the gate was closed through which you had gained entrance
to him and spoke to him; when his deaf ear made him blind to your
features, still he carried your image in his heart, and when he died,
it still lay upon his breast.

He was an artist, and who has arisen beside him? As the behemoth storms through the seas, so he strained the boundaries of his art. From the cooing of the dove to the rolling of thunder, from the most intricately woven of idiosyncratic artistic devices to the terrifying point where achieved form becomes the lawless clashing forces of nature, he had reckoned everything, grasped everything. Those who come after him will not be able to continue, they will have to begin, for the predecessor halted only where art itself halts....

He was an artist, but also a human being. A human being in the word's fullest meaning. Because he shut himself off from the world, they called him hostile, and because he avoided emotion, unfeeling. Oh, he who knows himself to be hard does not flee! It is precisely the excess of emotion that shuns emotion. When he fled the world, it was because in the depths of his loving heart he found no weapon to resist it; when he withdrew from people, it occurred after he had given them his all and received nothing in return. He remained lonely because he found no other. But until his death he retained a humane heart toward all people, a fatherly one to his family, devoted his talent and life to the whole world!

So he was, so he died, so he shall live for all time.

You, however, who have followed our lead thus far, govern your pain! You have not lost him, you have gained him. Not until the gates of our life close behind us do the gates to the temple of immortality spring open. There he stands among the great of all times, untouchable, forever. Therefore depart from his place of rest, mourning but composed, and whenever in life the power of his creations overwhelms you like a gathering storm, whenever your tears flow in the midst of a still unborn generation, remember this hour and think: we were there when they buried him, and when he died, we wept.

DANIEL WEBSTER (1782–1852)

by Amasa McCoy (1852)

*Daniel Webster was an early American statesman, known
for his staunch support of Federalism and his great skill as
an orator. He served as both Congressman and Senator for
Massachusetts, and as the 14th and 19th Secretary of State.
The following funeral oration was delivered at the First
Presbyterian Church at Ballston Spa, New York, by Amasa
McCoy, a professor of logic and rhetoric at the National
Law School.*

THE TOLLING BELLS of twice ten thousand steeples proclaim that we
have met with no ordinary loss. Populous and opulent cities, thousands of miles from each other, celebrate these obsequies with all that
can engage the imagination, and impress the heart. Even in a retired
village, which makes no pretensions to parade, and where there is
nothing of magnificence, save the sombre pomp of nature herself,
the citizens of Ballston Spa, without distinction of party; the Board
of Supervisors, representing every town in the County of Saratoga;
the members of the Ballston Institute, coming from different sections
of the State; the students of the National Law School, representing
more than half the States of the Union; have assembled, under these
sable hangings, to join in the sublime lament which is now being
sung by the nation. These expressions of public sorrow, however
numerous and solemn, can be of no use, it is true, to the dead. But
they may justly administer to the consolation of the living. To echo
words once uttered by those lips, which because they are sealed in
death, we are now convened: the tears which flow, and the honors
that are paid, when the founders of the Republic die, give hope that
the Republic itself will be immortal.

DANIEL WEBSTER, Secretary of State in the United States, died at his farm at Marshfield, on the morning of the 24th of October. Just ten days ago, his mortal remains were laid away in his family vault. At the time of his death he had passed, some nine months, the limit assigned by the Psalmist to mortal man. Yet had we never come to associate with him the idea of decay. The whole of this long period was filled up with busy and laborious days in the service of his country. He was born, he lived, he died, in a century and a country of Freedom. He first saw the light amid her mountain home, and he died where she lifts her radiant form to enjoy the ocean breeze.

His death, since its occurrence, has engrossed the columns of the press; it has put the marts and the harbors of commerce in mourning; it has been solemnly noticed by the bar and the bench in the Courts of Justice; in the departments of State; and in the mansion of the Executive. And what bespeaks still more a public sense of calamity, it even stopped, and that within a week of the day of ballot, the whole machinery of a national election.

Meantime, while we have been witnessing this first spontaneous outburst of sorrow, and while more elaborate and sumptuous expressions are but just beginning, these unwelcome tidings have crossed the Atlantic, and deepened the grief of a nation already, like ourselves, clothed in the habiliments of mourning. The event by this time has been noticed with honor in hundreds of English journals; it has afflicted the members of the profession in the courts of Westminster; it has been mentioned on the floors of Parliament; it has penetrated the cloisters of Oxford and Cambridge. And before the action yet to be taken by the State Legislatures, the Supreme Federal Judiciary, and the Houses of Congress; the intelligence, in the order of its course, will have carried grief to the heart of every lover of freedom in the nations of Europe; and where less will be expressed than felt, because of the padlock on the lip of Liberty. So that, after all that has been done, and all that will be, that which will not be done, will redound most to the honor of the great American.

The public journals have certainly laid the country under many obligations, by their incredible industry in collecting facts respecting this extraordinary life. By so doing they have not only contributed vastly to our edification, but I submit that every fresh particular only increases our respect for the character of the deceased. The colossal proportions of his intellect had become a proverb; but the impression I think is now general, that great injustice has been done to the qualities of his heart. The tongue of scandal had been busy in bold affirmations respecting great frailties and infirmities. No reflecting man ever doubted that much of this was the invention of political rancor, and a curious proneness there is to seek for weakness in the great. Whatever of this is true, no one should now seek to extenuate, out of regard to the influence of example. The ancient maxim, that nothing should be said of the dead but what is favorable, the better ethics of our time justly repudiates. History, when true to its mission, is a dread tribunal; and while it will not allow the least injustice to the dead, it will not be unmindful of its duty to the living. In the mean time, it cannot be denied that many persons whose minds had been abused, are taken by surprise by the numerous and authentic evidences of the genial excellencies which gave warmth and coloring to his character. The nation had been so engrossed with the grandeur of his public career, that few were prepared for any such statement as that his greatness dilated when he entered the social circle. And it is fit in this temple of worship to invite those, if any such there be, who have assumed to use his name to give respectability to their own delinquencies, to ponder now upon some other things. Let them remember that vulgar infidelity never polluted his lips. That nothing ever escaped him in his public speeches, nothing in private conversation, disrespectful to the truths of Christianity. That he was a devout believer in divine Revelation. That he studied the scriptures more than many whose high vocation it is to expound them. That he was faithful in his attendance upon the services of the sanctuary. That the attributes of the Deity, as displayed in his works, overflowed his capacious nature with the enthusiasm of devotion.

And for my own part, I join with those who say that none of his great deeds in life give them such ideas of moral grandeur, as the manner of his death. I see him shake the Capitol in his wrath, when a violent hand is laid upon the Constitution; and yet it does not affect me with such an elevated sense of human greatness, as to mark the meek serenity with which he suffers the pangs of death, and abides the good pleasure of his God. His implicit faith in the blood of Christ, his parting blessings upon his family and domestics, his unmurmuring resignation in the last mortal agony,—tell me, ye who minister at the altar, was not here enough to have suggested to the Christian poet all his sublime conceptions of the chamber where the good man meets his fate?

When Mark Anthony appeared before the citizens of Rome, to pronounce his funeral oration over the dead body of Cæsar, his first endeavor was to refute the principal accusation of Cæsar's enemies.

A grave charge has been preferred against the deceased whom we deplore, in connection with one of his last acts in the Senate, and which it is not to be concealed, in the minds of many, and of some before me, rests at this moment as a cloud upon his memory. The charge is now of over two years' standing. What men have urged and insisted upon again and again, becomes rooted and grounded in their very nature. The matter in question has become a part of that feeling, hardly less inveterate than religious bigotry, the spirit of party. How idle it would be to think of removing it, I am well enough persuaded; but that the subject would be referred to on such an occasion might naturally be expected. I deem it expedient to touch upon it in very brief terms at this stage of my remarks.

Some persons go as far as this. The Compromise Measures adopted by Congress in 1850, tended to perpetuate a great evil. Evil should not be done even to sustain the arch of the Union. To such persons I would say, what I may not now reason out, that there are numerous evils which are the natural consequences of society. But to disband society would be a greater evil. Whoever remains in society, then, acts upon the principle of choosing the least of evils. Society is held together only by mutual compromise. The science of governing, to a great extent, is but the science of expedients. The philosopher deals only in abstract truth, and may always be consistent with himself. But between the theories and the practical action of legislators and rulers, there must sometimes be a variance.

Such extreme ground, however, is probably occupied by no one present. You frankly admit, if you could believe that the Compromise measures were essential to the integrity of the Union, you would no longer condemn those who voted for them. But you hold that there was no danger of any section seceding; and I understand your chief ground of confidence is this. That secession would have been contrary to their own interests. I ask, is it an unheard-of thing that men should act contrary to their own interests? especially men of pride and spirit, and most especially when they believe, or even imagine that any injustice is being done them? Were there not thousands of men, as intelligent and as honest as yourselves, who did believe some such compromise necessary? And have not multitudes who then condemned such legislation, since avowed their approval? Was not the measure acquiesced in by hundreds of ministers of religion, whose learning and piety make them the objects of reverence? Did a majority of both houses of Congress, did so many of their number, of patriotism hitherto above suspicion, walk in open day to the shambles of corruption, and traffic away the accumulated honor of life? Did Millard Fillmore do so; did Henry Clay; did Daniel Webster? When Nullification was coiling its fatal folds around this body politic, entire fruit of the revolution, and just about to send to its extremities the icy chill of death, you need not be told whose mighty arm it was that slew the monster as with a battle axe. If you have writ your annals true, alone he did it. This great champion of public liberty, whose whole fame was associated with its defence, and who saw that many would now brand him as an apostate and traitor, do you believe that he was condemned also by his own conscience? Have those who have been so unsparing of censure ever summed up the penalty he paid for taking this step? Reproach, reproach, from how many quarters; with what bitterness; and how long sustained! And this from oldest friends, upon whom the heart had learned to lean for support. The stab of Brutus, you know, that was the unkindest cut of all. If then, my friend and fellow-citizen, you cannot yet view this matter as I do, but must still insist in your heart, that he was guilty of a grievous fault,—at least, at least, you will not refuse to remember how grievously he hath answered it. And while no powers of persuasion can efface from your memory the single evil you have contended he did, that American heart within you, whose depths he has so often stirred as with the notes of battle and of victory, is surely too just and magnanimous to insist upon interring with his bones all that he ever did of good.

In common with the whole country, fellow-citizens, you have frequently reviewed, since its termination, Mr. Webster's great career. If it had not occurred to you before, you must now be impressed with the fact, that of the many distinguished citizens of his day, few owed less to fortuitous circumstances. Mr. Webster was not a man whose fame grew up over night. He owed his eminence to no accident, no compromise of factions, no chance of battle, no freak of fortune. None of his influence was acquired by flattering the people, but only by serving them. He more than once opposed a farther introduction into the government of the popular element; and in doing so, used the whole weight of his influence and talent. He not only repudiated the idea of a Democracy; for that is dreamed of by no one. But he evidently had faith in nothing less than the representative Republic, with all its checks and balances, as framed by the fathers. He acquired none of his distinction then, by introducing sweeping reforms in government. Indeed I undertake to say, that the most general characteristic of that whole career which the country is now contemplating with so much reverence is that of the great conservator. He borrowed no honor from office, for his mere entry into it covered it with lustre forever; and whoever might be elevated to the Presidency, Webster still continued the most eminent citizen of the Republic. The explanation of Mr. Webster's fame consists simply, in wonderful native endowments, disciplined by the last severity of culture, and displayed in professional and public service. To eloquence, to law, to civil polity, he devoted more study than most public men to all united. If Buffon, as he said, owed ten or twelve volumes of his writings to his servant, who forced him to rise at six,—it would be interesting, if it could be ascertained, to know what proportion of Mr. Webster's greatness is ascribable to his having risen at four.

The extinction of this great light afflicts no class more sorely than that scattered brotherhood who make up the republic of letters. In our part of that realm he was chief. No other man in this country ever exercised in so large a measure that sway over the human mind which belongs to literature. His supremacy over men was in proportion as they were educated. In Boston he reigned in all the sovereignty of reason. Had this whole country been made up of Bostons——

More than any other American of his day, more than any Englishman, Mr. Webster's style was chaste, lucid, and perspicuous. Every sentence was a crystal. He scattered among the people no ambiguous words. When Webster had spoken, you might differ from him indeed; but you knew his meaning. Whatever he touched, he not only adorned, but he shed over it a perpetual light. Such was the literary excellence of Mr. Webster's speech, that its influence did not cease with its delivery. There was always a charm over the printed report, that attracted and captivated innumerable readers. There were men of his day, and Mr. Clay was one of them, who exercised a more talismanic sway over their immediate hearers; but who spoke with such commanding eloquence to the nation? When it was known that Webster was to speak, is it any exaggeration to say that the Republic was one eager auditory? Give me a name if ye can, for glory like this: never to have risen, but millions hung upon his lips; never to have sat down, but millions were wiser men and better patriots. Webster's printed speeches were re-read, and put carefully away and committed. How many of his sentences, laden with noble truth and glowing patriotism, have become familiar as household words! Plutarch informs us that so thoroughly were the priests instructed in the writings of Numa, that the law–giver, assured that they would be preserved in spirit and in letter, ordered them to be burned with his body. Such is the impression made upon the minds of his countrymen by the productions of Mr. Webster, that had all written record of them been interred with his remains, every principle and precept could be collected from the memory of living men; and all his great orations, I doubt not, could be restored to print, word for word.

His sentiments are not only engraven on the minds of his countrymen, but they blend themselves with the surface of the country itself. Spots which the blood of our fathers have consecrated, this great master of eloquence has made classic. Even Bunker Hill, of hallowed memory, has borrowed additional interest and renown from his transcendent powers of speech. They have given birth indeed to the noblest monument of that eventful day. Any country, any people could have erected the granite obelisk. Of his contemporaries, who but the great New England orator could have delivered such discourses. It is not intimated that Bunker Hill Monument is not everything that could reasonably be asked. Lifting itself from that memorable summit, "rising over the land, and over the sea, and visible at their homes, to three hundred thousand citizens of Massachusetts," it is indeed a stupendous structure. And yet it is less imposing and majestic than the orations pronounced there by Mr. Webster. "Towering high above the column which our hands have builded, beheld, not by a single city, or a single state, ascends the colossal grandeur" of these sublimer remembrancers.

The influence of Mr. Webster's speeches was not limited to this country. In this connection permit one born under another government, and among a people at that time prejudiced beyond belief, to say that my own experience furnishes me with data, which from the good fortune of your birth, you would probably omit to take into the account. Happening to fall in with these great productions, I not only bowed in homage to the talents of the author, but immediately conceived respect, then admiration, and before I got through, enthusiasm and reverence, for the history, the great men, and the institutions of America. I said to myself that in the wonderful attributes of this great orator, and the heroic virtues of his countrymen whom he celebrates, is more than realized, what in Berkeley, a century and a quarter ago, seemed an extravagant flight, even for poetry, that here should rise up, and here should be sung,

> "The good and great inspiring epic rage,
> The wisest heads and noblest hearts."

Thus does it happen, that for the high privilege of American citizenship, for such a proud distinction, and crowning felicity, I am indebted to the sway of his living words, to whom in death, from the fullness of a swolen heart, I now make this poor acknowledgment Plato thanked heaven that he was born in the same age with Socrates. What a heart should I have, if it did not overflow with gratitude, that I have not only been thus far contemporary with the deceased, have experienced the divine luxury of his thought, and heard two orations from his lips, but that I am now entitled against the world to claim a share in his immense renown.

> "Praise enough
> To fill th' ambition of a private man,
> That WEBSTER's language was his mother tongue,
> And CLAY's great name compatriot with his own."

I have spoken of my native Province as at that time prejudiced beyond belief, against whatever pertained to the neighboring Republic. I rejoice to do it justice. Such was the respect they had come to entertain for the citizen now deceased, that when in one of its villages the announcement was made that he was dead, the people gave expression to their feelings in a salute of an hundred guns from English artillery.

Not only in the Hulseman letter, at the Plymouth dinner, and on the Greek question, but on numerous other occasions, Mr. Webster's resistless eloquence, defining the position, and speaking the sentiment of the American Republic, has fulmined over Europe,

> "To Macedon and Artaxerxes' throne,"

Those who make it out so clearly to their own satisfaction that he was guilty of such astonishing apostasy, let them not fail to notice this. That his death breaks a spell of dread to Absoluteism. Tyrants rejoice that Webster has fallen!

A full survey of the public life and services of Mr. Webster, can be taken only by his biographer. Let those who assume such an enumeration, not omit to include the following. That out of the treasury of his single intellect, he has paid another installment on the debt of civilization, we owe the mother Empire. It consists not alone in the light he has shed upon the sciences of international law, and civil polity. Virgil considered himself covered with glory, when he was called a pillar of the Latin tongue; and English scholars, in the fine enthusiasm, and high magnanimity of letters, will acknowledge with feelings of admiration and gratitude, that even to that gorgeous temple, whose base, and whose dome were the productions of a Shakspeare, the doric contributions of the great American orator have given additional strength, sublimity and grandeur.

Cicero thought Socrates used such language as Jupiter would, had he talked in the Greek. The English of Webster suggests the same notion of majesty. And if Cicero had given us his idea of the fabled deity in the act and attitude of speaking, it is by no means certain that he would have invested him with a more imposing presence. Conceptions of this kind are furnished in poetry, which have been things of joy to the scholars of many generations. But I question whether votaries of letters most familiar with the heathen Jove of Homer, the Trojan leader of Virgil, the royal Dane of Shakspeare, and the primitive great sire of Milton, ever had in their mind's eye, a figure which so impressed the heart, as when they gazed upon the solemn front, and eye sublime of our illustrious countryman. Not only have European masters in sculpture hung over his bust enamoured, as a model beyond even their finest ideal; but persons of no culture whatever, equally strangers to his fame, and to the enthusiasm of poetry and art, have given involuntary utterance to the sentiment of the admiring Queen of Carthage,

"Quem sese ore ferens!"

These outward indications of power, without example in his own age, added immensely, as might be supposed to the grandeur of his spoken eloquence. Of other orators, the audience made his present speech the guage of his intellect. And I suppose it often happened that Mr. Webster did his utmost; but with that massive amplitude of brow before you, and that vision and faculty divine, it was impossible to believe it. Bring forward what he might, you still said, the greatest is behind. Make ever so great a conquest, the spectators reported:

> "Yet half his strength, he put not forth, but check'd
> His thunder in mid-volley."

And when the historian, glorying in his theme, shall have recounted to the men of another age, the mighty feats of his genius, it needs must cap the climax of their wonder to be told; that such was his superb exterior, and so vast in promise, that he left his contemporaries in doubt, had he been called to meet a crisis so much greater, or grapple with an adversary so much more formidable, whether he had it not in him, to have achieved in one single triumph, what would have eclipsed the sum of his others.

It would be very proper in the presence of so much aspiration for professional honor, to dwell at some length upon the character of the deceased as a lawyer. And in adequate hands what more noble theme for discourse. But an attempt at such an analysis of his mind, or such summing up of his attainments by any one who has not devoted to the law his twenty years of vigils, would amount in my esteem, to irreverent presumption. Let us leave this part of the subject then, after expressing only what is in the mind of every educated man in the country. His published arguments at the bar, have never yet been spoken of as less than consummate models of forensic discussion. And the proportion of his admirers is not small, who insist that this is the theatre where the prowess of his mind achieved its greatest feats. As has been said by an old man eloquent, a patriarch of college presidents, respecting Hamilton: he strode through the cause with the club of Hercules, and left nothing living in his path. If you inquire who stands at the head of the profession in any given city or State, different persons will give you a different name; whereas not only now in the generosity of funeral eulogium, but any time during the last third of his life, and that by universal acclaim, the first place at the Bar of the American Union was accorded to Webster. And when of all this assembly there remains not on earth the slightest vestige of remembrance, posterity will marvel as we do now, at this amazing triumph of intellect; to have won the palm which cost Pinckney and Wirt the sustained struggle of a life; and yet at the same time, in the higher path of statesmanship, which they almost entirely avoided, to have clomb to equal pre-eminence; and in addition to all this, and perhaps for the first time in the history of America, to have given a classic to the language.

A glance still briefer at Mr. Webster's achievements in the field of diplomacy. They contributed very greatly to extend his European fame, and certainly rank among his highest claims to the gratitude of his own country. The announcement of his death will come home with great additional effect to Americans who are now travelling abroad; for they have felt, as they tell us, that his name ever surrounded them as with a guard of protection and of honor. His correspondence with the English Envoy in 1842, not only shed vast light upon the law of nations, and afford a sublime illustration of the compass and divinity of human reason; but they cleared up many difficulties between the United States and England, which at intervals for half a century, had threatened to involve these countries in all the horrors of war. They were settled by this great son of peace, satisfactorily, and forever; without war, and without dishonor. And it may be urged with justice, that the papers which at that time emanated from the Secretary of State, contributed greatly to inaugurate a new era in the intercourse of nations. They impressed upon the general heart of the world, what Richelieu utters in handing his weapon of war to his page:

> *"Take away the sword—*
> *States can be saved without it!"*

It has come to be a very frequent remark, what a pity our greatest men cannot be President; and surely there never has been more occasion for regret than in the case of Webster. What a superb piece of rhetoric would it have been, what a feast, what a banquet of reason, and with what a glow of patriotic pride would every American have perused his inaugural address. What annual messages would have illustrated the policy and enriched the literature of the country. What dignity, what strength, what splendor in his administration. The Presidential chair would have borrowed lustre from the talents and the fame of such an incumbent. For the first time since the line of Revolutionary Presidents, the highest office in the nation would have been adorned with its highest statesmanship. The Union, the Constitution, Peace, and every great interest of peace, would have smiled secure under a ruler at once so wise, so mild, so firm. There are many persons present, differing from him on questions of public interest, who would not have voted for him; but there is no one in this audience, there is no one in this Republic who would not have contemplated with proud emotion, institutions which could first produce such a citizen, and then give him his place according to the specifie gravity of nature.

Such would have been the general feeling at home. While abroad, and among foreign powers, as it was said of Washington, it is not probable that any prince or potentate of his day, would have commanded more respect and consideration. Throned emperors and kings would have read in this grand embodiment, all the elements that mould up our conception of a consummate magistrate:

"And by these claim their greatness, not by blood."

It is usual to say on such occasions that the Presidency could have added nothing to his fame. Such a reflection may possibly be of some solace to afflicted feeling, but it certainly will not stand the test of logical analysis. Mr. Webster, it is true, was a more eminent man than any President of his day; indeed the Secretaries of State for many years form a more distinguished line of Statesmen than the Presidents. Still the highest post in the government would have made even Mr. Webster's talents more conspicuous. "Pyramids are pyramids in vales." Doubtless; yet however great the structure, it is imposing in proportion to the elevation of its site. Mr. Webster, nevertheless, amassed a reputation on so huge a scale, that any such regrets on his account are almost unconscionable. Five million votes, nor fifty million votes, could have done for him what he did for himself. The truth is, that regrets of this kind, and indeed this whole aggregate of sorrow, spreading the Commonwealth as with a pall, is not for the dead, but for the living. And I, the humblest of all my fellow-citizens,—lifted into notice but for an hour by this sad occasion, and soon to return as is my wont, to the pursuits of retirement—with no title to consideration, save as I utter the words of truth—the least of all priests in this vast service of the grave; yet as such, possessing the ear of the congregation assembled—I assume to summon the American community into the forum of its own conscience. I arraign it before the bar of the world. I anticipate the verdict of posterity. Ye who have ears to hear, and hearts to understand, incline to what I say, for I speak no idle words. Hearken to the judgment of your children, and your children's children, to be affirmed by every succeeding age. And this it is: That in withholding from one who partook so largely of the spirit, and the wisdom, and the patriotism of Washington, the highest power for good which the Constitution entrusts to a single citizen,—*A duty has not been performed. A work of patriotism has not been completed.*

Friends and fellow-citizens: If such thoughts afflict us with compunctious visitings, and full well I know they do, let us remember that they are of use only as they breed resolutions for the future. For the past, for the past, they are unavailing. Daniel Webster is no longer among the living. The glory of the forum, the chief of the Senate, the mighty minister, great man of language,

> "Farewell, a long farewell, to all thy greatness!"

That drama of vigorous heroism is closed. On a stage, not darkened, but rather of heightened splendor, the curtain has fallen. Not as the ordinary great; nor yet as Socrates, like a philosopher; but with the sublimer exit of a Christian, he has gone from our sight forever. Oh, if this were not the solemn fact—if you had but just awakened from a sleep—if you were assured that these impressions of death at Marshfield, of the ensign of the Republic everywhere in crape, of ten thousand men at a private funeral; that these were not reality, but only the dismal fancies of a dream,—that instead of being in his grave, Daniel Webster was still at his post, as a faithful sentinel on the watch-towers of Liberty—if you could hear there in the darkness of the night his veteran footstep—especially if you should ask as was our wont in a moment of fear, *"Watchman, what of the night?"* and your ear should suddenly be greeted with those grand old tones, so full, resonant and joyous—*"All's well, all's well,"*—Oh! how this whole auditory would start to its feet; and what a burst of transport would shake this solid building to its base! But alas, these tears we are shedding, they are not the tears of joy, but of grief. And what event but the death of Webster, could have drawn from us so many. Had each of us lost his father, the stroke could hardly have fallen with more subduing effect. Why, here we touch the secret—*We have lost the second Father of his country.* God in heaven, be thou the father of an orphaned people!

When in July, two years ago, death removed an incumbent of the Executive, so strong in the confidence of his countrymen, you well remember how bitter and how universal was the sense of bereavement. It is no disparagement to say that his great office was worthily supplied by his immediate successor. What too often had been only an ingenious stroke of flattery, might have been quoted in this instance of accession, with honesty and truth:

> *"Sol occubuit; nox nulla secuta est."*

But now, ere yon moon had four times filled her horn, we are called upon to suffer the double eclipse of Clay and Webster. In lesser lights indeed the horizon is not wanting. And such is the tried prudence of the people themselves, and such, if they avail themselves of it, the reflected radiance of luminaries no longer seen, that I do not say they will stumble and fall. But alas, alas! how long may we have to await the appearance again of two orbs of such magnitude and splendor, to fill our hearts with joy, and our country with glory!

I know indeed the last accents of his lips—*"I still live;"* and I have marked with sensibility the eagerness of the nation to extract from them something to solace its smitten feelings. Already in the valley of the shadow of death, it was in his mind only, that the soul had not yet glided from the shore of its mortality. In that solemn instant it was farthest from him possible to indulge the thought of the ancient, *"vivit enim, vivet que semper."* Yet the bleeding heart of the nation, so lonesome and desolate, is surely warranted in cherishing such a sentiment. All that was mortal of Daniel Webster, is indeed dead. In the presence of a great cloud of witnesses, it was committed to the sacred soil of the Pilgrims. But his words, his works, his wisdom; the influence of his example, patriotism and deeds—these were not so interred. Heaven vouchsafes to a few superior natures a life to come, even in this world. There are those who rule us from their urns. Yes,

> "Thou art mighty yet!
> Thy spirit walks abroad."

Walk ever abroad, illustrious shade! Thy counsels and precepts are engraven on our memory; but oh, if in the economy of God, it is allowed to exert a directer influence—if patriots who die the death of the righteous are ever permitted to revisit their earthly seats—then, ever-venerated spirit, infuse into thy countrymen yet more of thy prudence, self-devotion, and wisdom!

All the editions I have seen of Mr. Webster's speeches have on the back of the volume a gold leaf figure of the Capitol at Washington. There is a fitness in this device. Consider how completely identified are his name and efforts with that great palace of the laws. With the House of Representatives, the Chamber of the Senate, the Supreme Federal Judiciary, and with the wing in course of erection, as orator at the laying of its corner-stone. Then what an expansive spirit of patriotism pervades those volumes: a school of rhetoric for the nation, instinct with nationality. In this respect, indeed, they are but the counterpart of his own feelings and character. Party and sectional foes might whisper suspicion with their lips; they might impugn his motives; they might wound his honor; and yet—who but one of his countrymen would credit it; and who that is a countryman disputes it?—it had come to be a piece of the American heart to believe that Webster would see that the Republic suffered no harm. That not only her interests, but her honor and her fame would come out of the fiery ordeal, as he himself would say, without the smell of smoke upon her garments. You have all doubtless met the verses which represent a captain's son on board of a ship in a terrific tempest. Veteran sailors are in tears of despair, and marvelling at his calmness, they ask the boy, "Are you not afraid?" The noble little fellow, a very picture of surprise, glancing at the stern, asks his interrogators, *"Is not my father at the helm?"* Such was the abiding faith of the nation in this more than Palinurus of the State. Whatever might be the peril, how dark soever the heavens,

"Though the strained mast should quiver as a reed,"

the people still asked, if you expressed alarm, *Is not Webster at the helm?*

Such was the universal sense of his fidelity and patriotism. Nor was it over estimated. Love of country, and of the whole country, was the ever present, and ever paramount passion of his being; it penetrated, and pervaded and engrossed it. Applying the entire energies of his robust, luminous, and comprehensive intellect, to the high ministries of its constitution, it was the great mission of his life to defend and expound it, to illustrate and hallow. His first entry into public life was in the service of the whole Union; and the summons of death found him still in its harness. No sooner had his eye fallen on her constitution, than he folded it to his heart as the first love of his boyhood; and the latest stroke of his pen ere it must be laid down forever, attests his loyalty and devotion. And having indentified himself conspicuously with every great interest at home, and more than any citizen of his time, enhanced her reputation abroad; in age, as in manhood, and in youth, still earlier than the sun in toiling for her glory; having thus exhausted his strength, his spirit, and his life, in the service of the country at large; he bequeathed at his death, to every American citizen, to every several man, in one massive and sumptuous assemblage, the rich inheritance of his name, his works, his example and renown.

I am afraid it is one of the solemn lessons of history that unto all states, as to men, it is appointed once to die. Certainly none now in existence gives more vigorous promise than that of England. And yet her eloquent historian has permitted himself to anticipate a time when some traveller from New Zealand shall, in the midst of a vast solitude, take his stand on a broken arch of London bridge, to sketch the ruins of St. Paul's. It is the most earnest prayer of every heart before me that the people may prove themselves so intelligent, virtuous and prudent, that the Capitol of the American Republic will stand forever. This, my friends, at least is sure; that while that great temple of Freedom does stand, it shall be as one vast Cenotaph to Webster. And as a sight of that hallowed dome, shall first recall to the beholder the memory of Webster; so shall come first to his lip, the epitaph now on the general heart of the nation: WELL DONE, GOOD AND FAITHFUL SERVANT.

CHARLOTTE BRONTË (1816–1855)

by William Makepeace Thackeray (1860)

Charlotte Brontë was an English novelist, best known as the author of Jane Eyre *and* The Professor. *William Makepeace Thackeray, author of* Vanity Fair, *was both a contemporary and a friend of Brontë, and wrote the following remembrance as an introduction to Brontë's posthumously published novel fragment,* Emma.

NOT MANY DAYS since I went to visit a house where in former years I had received many a friendly welcome. We went in to the owner's—an artist's—studio. Prints, pictures, and sketches hung on the walls as I had last seen and remembered them. The implements of the painter's art were there. The light which had shone upon so many, many hours of patient and cheerful toil, poured through the northern window upon print and bust, lay figure and sketch, and upon the easel before which the good, the gentle, the beloved Leslie laboured. In this room the busy brain had devised, and the skilful hand executed, I know not how many of the noble works which have delighted the world with their beauty and charming humour. Here the poet called up into pictorial presence, and informed with life, grace, beauty, infinite friendly mirth and wondrous naturalness of expression, the people of whom his dear books told him the stories,—his Shakspeare, his Cervantes, his Molière, his Le Sage. There was his last work on the easel—a beautiful fresh smiling shape of Titania, such as his sweet guileless fancy imagined the *Midsummer Night's* queen to be. Gracious, and pure, and bright, the sweet smiling image glimmers on the canvas. Fairy elves, no doubt, were to have been grouped around their mistress in laughing clusters. Honest Bottom's grotesque head and form are indicated as reposing by the side of the consummate beauty. The darkling forest would have grown around them, with the stars glittering from the midsummer sky: the flowers at the queen's feet, and the boughs and foliage about her, would have been peopled with gambolling sprites and fays. They were dwelling in the artist's mind no doubt, and would have been developed by that patient, faithful, admirable genius: but the busy brain stopped working, the skilful hand fell lifeless, the loving, honest heart ceased to beat. What was she to have been—that fair Titania—when perfected by the patient skill of the poet, who in imagination saw the sweet innocent figure, and with tender courtesy and caresses, as it were, posed and shaped and traced the fair form? Is there record kept anywhere of fancies conceived, beautiful, unborn? Some day will they assume form in some yet undeveloped light? If our bad unspoken thoughts are registered against us, and are written in the awful account, will not the good thoughts unspoken, the love and tenderness, the pity, beauty, charity, which pass through the breast, and cause the heart to throb with silent good, find a remembrance, too? A few weeks more, and this lovely offspring of the poet's conception would have been complete—to charm the world with its beautiful mirth. May there not be some sphere unknown to us where it may have an existence? They say our words, once out of our lips, go travelling in *omne ævum,* reverberating for ever and ever. If our words, why not our thoughts? If the Has Been, why not the Might Have Been?

Some day our spirits may be permitted to walk in galleries of fancies more wondrous and beautiful than any achieved works which at present we see, and our minds to behold and delight in masterpieces which poets' and artists' minds have fathered and conceived only.

With a feeling much akin to that with which I looked upon the friend's—the admirable artist's—unfinished work, I can fancy many readers turning to these—the last pages which were traced by Charlotte Brontë's hand. Of the multitude that has read her books, who has not known and deplored the tragedy of her family, her own most sad and untimely fate? Which of her readers has not become her friend? Who that has known her books has not admired the artist's noble English, the burning love of truth, the bravery, the simplicity, the indignation at wrong, the eager sympathy, the pious love and reverence, the passionate honour, so to speak, of the woman? What a story is that of that family of poets in their solitude yonder on the gloomy northern moors! At nine o'clock at night, Mrs. Gaskell tells, after evening prayers, when their guardian and relative had gone to bed, the three

poetesses—the three maidens, Charlotte, and Emily, and Anne—
Charlotte being the "motherly friend and guardian to the other two"—
"began, like restless wild animals, to pace up and down their parlour,
'making out' their wonderful stories, talking over plans and projects,
and thoughts of what was to be their future life."

One evening, at the close of 1854, as Charlotte Nicholls sat with
her husband by the fire, listening to the howling of the wind about
the house, she suddenly said to her husband, "If you had not been
with me, I must have been writing now." She then ran upstairs, and
brought down, and read aloud, the beginning of a new tale. When
she had finished, her husband remarked, "The critics will accuse you
of repetition." She replied, "Oh! I shall alter that. I always begin two
or three times before I can please myself." But it was not to be. The
trembling little hand was to write no more. The heart, newly awakened to love and happiness, and throbbing with maternal hope, was
soon to cease to beat; that intrepid outspeaker and champion of truth,
that eager, impetuous redresser of wrong, was to be called out of the
world's fight and struggle, to lay down the shining arms, and to be
removed to a sphere where even a noble indignation *cor ulterius
nequit lacerare,* and where truth complete, and right triumphant, no
longer need to wage war.

I can only say of this lady, *vidi tantum.* I saw her first just as I rose
out of an illness from which I had never thought to recover. I remember the trembling little frame, the little hand, the great honest eyes.
An impetuous honesty seemed to me to characterize the woman.
Twice I recollect she took me to task for what she held to be errors
in doctrine. Once about Fielding we had a disputation. She spoke
her mind out. She jumped too rapidly to conclusions. (I have smiled
at one or two passages in the *Biography,* in which my own disposition
or behaviour forms the subject of talk.) She formed conclusions that
might be wrong, and built up whole theories of character upon them.
New to the London world, she entered it with an independent,
indomitable spirit of her own; and judged of contemporaries, and
especially spied out arrogance or affectation, with extraordinary
keenness of vision. She was angry with her favourites if their conduct
or conversation fell below her ideal. Often she seemed to me to be
judging the London folk prematurely: but perhaps the city is rather
angry at being judged. I fancied an austere little Joan of Arc marching in upon us, and rebuking our easy lives, our easy morals. She
gave me the impression of being a very pure, and lofty, and high-
minded person. A great and holy reverence of right and truth seemed

to be with her always. Such, in our brief interview, she appeared to me. As one thinks of that life so noble, so lonely—of that passion for truth—of those nights and nights of eager study, swarming fancies, invention, depression, elation, prayer; as one reads the necessarily incomplete, though most touching and admirable history of the heart that throbbed in this one little frame—of this one amongst the myriads of souls that have lived and died on this great earth—this great earth?—this little speck in the infinite universe of God,—with what wonder do we think of to-day, with what awe await to-morrow, when that which is now but darkly seen shall be clear! As I read this little fragmentary sketch, I think of the rest. Is it? And where is it? Will not the leaf be turned some day, and the story be told? Shall the deviser of the tale somewhere perfect the history of little EMMA's griefs and troubles? Shall TITANIA come forth complete with her sportive court, with the flowers at her feet, the forest around her, and all the stars of summer glittering overhead?

How well I remember the delight, and wonder, and pleasure with which I read *Jane Eyre,* sent to me by an author whose name and sex were then alike unknown to me; the strange fascinations of the book; and how with my own work pressing upon me, I could not, having taken the volumes up, lay them down until they were read through! Hundreds of those who, like myself, recognized and admired that master-work of a great genius, will look with a mournful interest and regard and curiosity upon this, the last fragmentary sketch from the noble hand which wrote *Jane Eyre.*

HENRY DAVID THOREAU (1817–1862)

by Ralph Waldo Emerson (1862)

Henry David Thoreau was an American author, philosopher, poet, and Transcendentalist. His most lasting works are Walden, *a reflection on two years he spent living close to nature, and* Civil Disobedience, *an essay about the importance of putting one's conscience before one's allegiance to government. The following eulogy was delivered by Ralph Waldo Emerson, a fellow Transcendentalist, who for many years was Thoreau's mentor and closest friend.*

HENRY DAVID THOREAU was the last male descendant of a French ancestor who came to this country from the Isle of Guernsey. His character exhibited occasional traits drawn from this blood in singular combination with a very strong Saxon genius.

He was born in Concord, Massachusetts, on the 12th of July, 1817. He was graduated at Harvard College in 1837, but without any literary distinction. An iconoclast in literature, he seldom thanked colleges for their service to him, holding them in small esteem, whilst yet his debt to them was important. After leaving the University, he joined his brother in teaching a private school, which he soon renounced. His father was a manufacturer of lead-pencils, and Henry applied himself for a time to this craft, believing he could make a better pencil than was then in use. After completing his experiments, he exhibited his work to chemists and artists in Boston, and having obtained their certificates to its excellence and to its equality with the best London manufacture, he returned home contented. His friends congratulated him that he had now opened his way to fortune. But he replied that he should never make another pencil. "Why should I? I would not do again what I have done once." He resumed his endless walks and miscellaneous studies, making every day some new acquaintance with Nature, though as yet never speaking of zoology or botany, since, though very studious of natural facts, he was incurious of technical and textual science.

At this time, a strong, healthy youth, fresh from college, whilst all his companions were choosing their profession, or eager to begin some lucrative employment, it was inevitable that his thoughts should be exercised on the same question, and it required rare decision to refuse all the accustomed paths, and keep his solitary freedom at the cost of disappointing the natural expectations of his family and friends: all the more difficult that he had a perfect probity, was exact in securing his own independence, and in holding every man to the like duty. But Thoreau never faltered. He was a born protestant. He declined to give up his large ambition of knowledge and action for any narrow craft or profession, aiming at a much more comprehensive calling, the art of living well. If he slighted and defied the opinions of others, it was only that he was more intent to reconcile his practice with his own belief. Never idle or self-indulgent, he preferred, when he wanted money, earning it by some piece of manual labor agreeable to him, as building a boat or a fence, planting, grafting, surveying, or other short work, to any long engagements. With his hardy habits and few wants, his skill in wood-craft, and his powerful arithmetic, he was very competent to live in any part of the world. It would cost him less time to supply his wants than another. He was therefore secure of his leisure.

A natural skill for mensuration, growing out of his mathematical knowledge, and his habit of ascertaining the measures and distances of objects which interested him, the size of trees, the depth and extent of ponds and rivers, the height of mountains, and the air-line distance of his favorite summits—this, and his intimate knowledge of the territory about Concord, made him drift into the profession of land-surveyor. It had the advantage for him that it led him continually into new and secluded grounds, and helped his studies of Nature. His accuracy and skill in this work were readily appreciated, and he found all the employment he wanted.

He could easily solve the problems of the surveyor, but he was daily beset with graver questions, which he manfully confronted. He interrogated every custom, and wished to settle all his practice on an ideal foundation. He was a protestant *à l'outrance*, and few lives contain so many renunciations. He was bred to no profession; he never married; he lived alone; he never went to church; he never voted;

he refused to pay a tax to the State; he ate no flesh, he drank no wine, he never knew the use of tobacco; and, though a naturalist, he used neither trap nor gun. He chose, wisely, no doubt, for himself, to be the bachelor of thought and Nature. He had no talent for wealth, and knew how to be poor without the least hint of squalor or inelegance. Perhaps he fell into his way of living without forecasting it much, but approved it with later wisdom. "I am often reminded," he wrote in his journal, "that, if I had bestowed on me the wealth of Croesus, my aims must be still the same, and my means essentially the same." He had no temptations to fight against—no appetites, no passions, no taste for elegant trifles. A fine house, dress, the manners and talk of highly cultivated people were all thrown away on him. He much preferred a good Indian, and considered these refinements as impediments to conversation, wishing to meet his companion on the simplest terms. He declined invitations to dinner-parties, because there each was in every one's way, and he could not meet the individuals to any purpose. "They make their pride," he said, "in making their dinner cost much; I make my pride in making my dinner cost little." When asked at table what dish he preferred, he answered, "The nearest." He did not like the taste of wine, and never had a vice in his life. He said, "I have a faint recollection of pleasure derived from smoking dried lily-stems, before I was a man. I had commonly a supply of these. I have never smoked anything more noxious."

He chose to be rich by making his wants few, and supplying them himself. In his travels, he used the railroad only to get over so much country as was unimportant to the present purpose, walking hundreds of miles, avoiding taverns, buying a lodging in farmers' and fishermen's houses, as cheaper, and more agreeable to him, and because there he could better find the men and the information he wanted.

There was somewhat military in his nature not to be subdued, always manly and able, but rarely tender, as if he did not feel himself except in opposition. He wanted a fallacy to expose, a blunder to pillory, I may say required a little sense of victory, a roll of the drum, to call his powers into full exercise. It cost him nothing to say No; indeed, he found it much easier than to say Yes. It seemed as if his first instinct on hearing a proposition was to controvert it, so impatient was he of the limitations of our daily thought. This habit, of course, is a little chilling to the social affections; and though the companion would in the end acquit him of any malice or untruth, yet it mars conversation. Hence, no equal companion stood in affectionate relations with one so pure and guileless. "I love Henry," said one of his friends, "but I cannot like him; and as for taking his arm, I should as soon think of taking the arm of an elm-tree."

Yet, hermit and stoic as he was, he was really fond of sympathy, and threw himself heartily and childlike into the company of young people whom he loved, and whom he delighted to entertain, as he only could, with the varied and endless anecdotes of his experiences by field and river. And he was always ready to lead a huckleberry-party or a search for chestnuts or grapes. Talking, one day, of a public discourse, Henry remarked that whatever succeeded with the audience was bad. I said, "Who would not like to write something which all can read, like 'Robinson Crusoe'? And who does not see with regret that his page is not solid with a right materialistic treatment, which delights everybody?" Henry objected, of course, and vaunted the better lectures which reached only a few persons. But, at supper, a young girl, understanding that he was to lecture at the Lyceum, sharply asked him whether his lecture would be a nice, interesting story, such as she wished to hear, or whether it was one of those old philosophical things that she did not care about. Henry turned to her, and bethought himself, and, I saw, was trying to believe that he had matter that might fit her and her brother, who was to sit up and go to the lecture, if it was a good one for them.

He was a speaker and actor of the truth—born such—and was ever running into dramatic situations from this cause. In any circumstance, it interested all bystanders to know what part Henry would take, and what he would say; and he did not disappoint expectation, but used an original judgment on each emergency. In 1845 he built himself a small framed house on the shores of Walden Pond, and lived there two years alone, a life of labor and study. This action was quite native and fit for him. No one who knew him would tax him with affectation. He was more unlike his neighbors in his thought than in his action. As soon as he had exhausted the advantages of that solitude, he abandoned it. In 1847, not approving some uses to which the public expenditure was applied, he refused to pay his town tax and was put in jail. A friend paid the tax for him, and he was released. The like annoyance was threatened the next year. But, as his friends paid the tax, notwithstanding his protest, I believe he ceased to resist. No opposition or ridicule had any weight with him. He coldly and fully stated his opinion without affecting to believe that it was the opinion of the company. It was of no consequence if everyone present held the opposite opinion. On one occasion he went to the University Library to procure some books. The librarian refused to lend them. Mr. Thoreau repaired to the President, who stated to him the rules and usages, which permitted the loan of books to resident graduates, to clergymen who were alumni, and to some others resident within a circle of ten miles' radius from the College. Mr. Thoreau explained to the President that the railroad had destroyed the old scale of distances—that the library was useless, yes, and President and College useless, on the terms of his rules—that the one benefit he owed to the College was its library—that, at this moment, not only his want of books was imperative, but he wanted a large number of books, and assured him that he, Thoreau, and not the librarian, was the proper custodian of these. In short, the President found the petitioner so formidable, and the rules getting to look so ridiculous, that he ended by giving him a privilege which in his hands proved unlimited thereafter.

No truer American existed than Thoreau. His preference of his country and condition was genuine, and his aversion from English and European manners and tastes almost reached contempt. He listened impatiently to news or *bon mots* gleaned from London circles; and though he tried to be civil, these anecdotes fatigued him. The men were all imitating each other, and on a small mould. Why can they not live as far apart as possible, and each be a man by himself? What he sought was the most energetic nature; and he wished to go to Oregon, not to London. "In every part of Great Britain," he wrote in his diary, "are discovered traces of the Romans, their funereal urns, their camps, their roads, their dwellings. But New England, at least, is not based on any Roman ruins. We have not to lay the foundations of our houses on the ashes of a former civilization."

But, idealist as he was, standing for abolition of slavery, abolition of tariffs, almost for abolition of government, it is needless to say he found himself not only unrepresented in actual politics, but almost equally opposed to every class of reformers. Yet he paid the tribute of his uniform respect to the Anti-Slavery party. One man, whose personal acquaintance he had formed, he honored with exceptional regard. Before the first friendly word had been spoken for Captain John Brown, he sent notices to most houses in Concord that he would speak in a public hall on the condition and character of John Brown, on Sunday evening, and invited all people to come. The Republican Committee, the Abolitionist Committee, sent him word that it was premature and not advisable. He replied, "I did not send to you for advice, but to announce that I am to speak." The hall was filled at an early hour by people of all parties, and his earnest eulogy of the hero was heard by all respectfully, by many with a sympathy that surprised themselves.

It was said of Plotinus that he was ashamed of his body, and 't is very likely he had good reason for it—that his body was a bad servant, and he had not skill in dealing with the material world, as happens often to men of abstract intellect. But Mr. Thoreau was equipped with a most adapted and serviceable body. He was of short stature, firmly built, of light complexion, with strong, serious blue eyes, and a grave aspect—his face covered in the late years with a becoming beard. His senses were acute, his frame well-knit and hardy, his hands strong and skillful in the use of tools. And there was a wonderful fitness of body and mind. He could pace sixteen rods more accurately than another man could measure them with rod and chain. He could find his path in the woods at night, he said, better by his feet than his eyes. He could estimate the measure of a tree very well by his eye; he could estimate the weight of a calf or a pig, like a dealer. From a box containing a bushel or more of loose pencils, he could take up with his hands fast enough just a dozen pencils at every grasp. He was a good swimmer, runner, skater, boatman, and would probably out-walk most countrymen in a day's journey. And the relation of body to mind was still finer than we have indicated. He said he wanted every stride his legs made. The length of his walk uniformly made the length of his writing. If shut up in the house, he did not write at all.

He had a strong common sense, like that which Rose Flammock, the weaver's daughter, in Scott's romance, commends in her father, as resembling a yardstick, which, whilst it measures dowlas and diaper, can equally well measure tapestry and cloth of gold. He had always a new resource. When I was planting forest-trees, and had procured half a peck of acorns, he said that only a small portion of them would be sound, and proceeded to examine them, and select the sound ones. But finding this took time, he said, "I think, if you put them all into water, the good ones will sink," which experiment we tried with success. He could plan a garden, or a house, or a barn; would have been competent to lead a "Pacific Exploring Expedition"; could give judicious counsel in the gravest private or public affairs.

He lived for the day, not cumbered and mortified by his memory. If he brought you yesterday a new proposition, he would bring you today another not less revolutionary. A very industrious man, and setting, like all highly organized men, a high value on his time, he seemed the only man of leisure in town, always ready for any excursion that promised well, or for conversation prolonged into late hours. His trenchant sense was never stopped by his rules of daily prudence, but was always up to the new occasion. He liked and used the simplest food, yet, when someone urged a vegetable diet, Thoreau thought all diets a very small matter, saying that "the man who shoots the buffalo lives better than the man who hoards at the Graham House." He said, "You can sleep near the railroad, and never be disturbed: Nature knows very well what sounds are worth attending to, and has made up her mind not to hear the railroad-whistle. But things respect the devout mind, and a mental ecstasy was never interrupted." He noted, what repeatedly befell him, that, after receiving from a distance a rare plant, he would presently find the same in his own haunts. And those pieces of luck which happen only to good players happened to him. One day, walking with a stranger, who inquired where Indian arrow-heads could be found, he replied, "Everywhere," and, stooping forward, picked one on the instant from the ground. At Mount Washington, in Tuckerman's Ravine, Thoreau had a bad fall and sprained his foot. As he was in the act of getting up from his fall, he saw for the first time the leaves of the *Arnica mollis*.

His robust common sense, armed with stout hands, keen perceptions, and strong will, cannot yet account for the superiority which shone in his simple and hidden life. I must add the cardinal fact, that there was an excellent wisdom in him, proper to a rare class of men, which showed him the material world as a means and symbol. This discovery, which sometimes yields to poets a certain casual and interrupted light, serving for the ornament of their writing, was in him an unsleeping insight; and whatever faults or obstructions of temperament might cloud it, he was not disobedient to the heavenly vision. In his youth, he said, one day, "The other world is all my art: my pencils will draw no other; my jack-knife will cut nothing else; I do not use it as a means." This was the muse and genius that ruled his opinions, conversation, studies, work, and course of life. This made him a searching judge of men. At first glance he measured his companion, and, though insensible to some fine traits of culture, could very well report his weight and calibere. And this made the impression of genius which his conversation sometimes gave.

He understood the matter in hand at a glance, and saw the limitations and poverty of those he talked with, so that nothing seemed concealed from such terrible eyes. I have repeatedly known young men of sensibility converted in a moment to the belief that this was the man they were in search of, the man of men, who could tell them all they should do. His own dealing with them was never affectionate, but superior, didactic—scorning their petty ways—very slowly conceding, or not conceding at all, the promise of his society at their houses, or even at his own. "Would he not walk with them?" He did not know. There was nothing so important to him as his walk; he had no walks to throw away on company. Visits were offered him from respectful parties, but he declined them. Admiring friends offered to carry him at their own cost to the Yellow-Stone River— to the West Indies—to South America. But though nothing could be more grave or considered than his refusals, they remind one in quite new relations of that fop Brummel's reply to the gentleman who offered him his carriage in a shower, "But where will you ride, then?"—and what accusing silences, and what searching and irresistible speeches, battering down all defences, his companions can remember!

Mr. Thoreau dedicated his genius with such entire love to the fields, hills, and waters of his native town, that he made them known and interesting to all reading Americans, and to people over the sea. The river on whose banks he was born and died he knew from its springs to its confluence with the Merrimack. He had made summer and winter observations on it for many years, and at every hour of the day and the night. The result of the recent survey of the Water Commissioners appointed by the State of Massachusetts he had reached by his private experiments, several years earlier. Every fact which occurs in the bed, on the banks, or in the air over it; the fishes, and their spawning and nests, their manners, their food; the shad-flies which fill the air on a certain evening once a year, and which are snapped at by the fishes so ravenously that many of these die of repletion; the conical heaps of small stones on the river-shallows, one of which heaps will sometimes overfill a cart—these heaps the huge nests of small fishes; the birds which frequent the stream, heron, duck, sheldrake, loon, osprey; the snake, muskrat, otter, woodchuck, and fox, on the banks; the turtle, frog, hyla, and cricket, which make the banks vocal—were all known to him, and, as it were, townsmen and fellow-creatures; so that he felt an absurdity or violence in any narrative of one of these by itself apart, and still more of its dimensions on an inch-rule, or in the exhibition of its skeleton, or the specimen of a squirrel or a bird in brandy. He liked to speak of the manners of the river, as itself a lawful creature, yet with exactness, and always to an observed fact. As he knew the river, so the ponds in this region.

One of the weapons he used, more important than microscope or alcohol-receiver to other investigators, was a whim which grew on him by indulgence, yet appeared in gravest statement, namely, of extolling his own town and neighborhood as the most favored centre for natural observation. He remarked that the Flora of Massachusetts embraced almost all the important plants of America—most of the oaks, most of the willows, the best pines, the ash, the maple, the beech, the nuts. He returned Kane's "Arctic Voyage" to a friend of whom he had borrowed it, with the remark, that "most of the phenomena noted might be observed in Concord." He seemed a little envious of the Pole, for the coincident sunrise and sunset, or five minutes' day after six months: a splendid fact, which Annursnuc had never afforded him. He found red snow in one of his walks, and told me that he expected to find yet the *Victoria regia* in Concord. He was the attorney of the indigenous plants, and owned to a preference of the weeds to the imported plants, as of the Indian to the civilized man—and noticed, with pleasure, that the willow bean-poles of his neighbor had grown more than his beans. "See these weeds," he said, "which have been hoed at by a million farmers all spring and summer, and yet have prevailed, and just now come out triumphant over all lanes, pastures, fields, and gardens, such is their vigor. We have insulted them with low names, too,—as Pigweed, Wormwood, Chickweed, Shad-Blossom." He says, "They have brave names, too—Ambrosia, Stellaria, Amelanchia, Amaranth, etc."

I think his fancy for referring everything to the meridian of Concord did not grow out of any ignorance or depreciation of other longitudes or latitudes, but was rather a playful expression of his conviction of the indifferency of all places, and that the best place for each is where he stands. He expressed it once in this wise: "I think nothing is to be hoped from you, if this bit of mould under your feet is not sweeter to you to eat than any other in this world, or in any world."

The other weapon with which he conquered all obstacles in science was patience. He knew how to sit immovable, a part of the rock he rested on, until the bird, the reptile, the fish, which had retired from him, should come back, and resume its habits, nay, moved by curiosity, should come to him and watch him.

It was a pleasure and a privilege to walk with him. He knew the country like a fox or a bird, and passed through it as freely by paths of his own. He knew every track in the snow or on the ground, and what creature had taken this path before him. One must submit abjectly to such a guide, and the reward was great. Under his arm he carried an old music-book to press plants; in his pocket, his diary and pencil, a spy-glass for birds, microscope, jack-knife, and twine. He wore straw hat, stout shoes, strong gray trousers, to brave shrub-oaks and smilax, and to climb a tree for a hawk's or a squirrel's nest. He waded into the pool for the water-plants, and his strong legs were no insignificant part of his armor. On the day I speak of he looked for the Menyanthes, detected it across the wide pool, and, on examination of the florets, decided that it had been in flower five days. He drew out of his breast-pocket his diary, and read the names of all the plants that should bloom on this day, whereof he kept account as a banker when his notes fall due. The Cypripedium not due till to-morrow. He thought, that, if waked up from a trance, in this swamp, he could tell by the plants what time of the year it was within two days. The redstart was flying about, and presently the fine grosbeaks, whose brilliant scarlet makes the rash gazer wipe his eye, and whose fine clear note Thoreau compared to that of a tanager which has got rid of its hoarseness. Presently he heard a note which he called that of the night-warbler, a bird he had never identified, had been in search of twelve years, which always, when he saw it, was in the act of diving down into a tree or bush, and which it was vain to seek; the only bird that sings indifferently by night and by day. I told him he must beware of finding and booking it, lest life should have nothing more to show him. He said, "What you seek in vain for, half your life, one day you come full upon all the family at dinner. You seek it like a dream, and as soon as you find it you become its prey."

His interest in the flower or the bird lay very deep in his mind, was connected with Nature—and the meaning of Nature was never attempted to be defined by him. He would not offer a memoir of his observations to the Natural History Society. "Why should I? To detach the description from its connections in my mind would make it no longer true or valuable to me: and they do not wish what belongs to it." His power of observation seemed to indicate additional senses. He saw as with microscope, heard as with ear-trumpet, and his memory was a photographic register of all he saw and heard. And yet none knew better than he that it is not the fact that imports, but the impression or effect of the fact on your mind. Every fact lay in glory in his mind, a type of the order and beauty of the whole.

His determination on Natural History was organic. He confessed that he sometimes felt like a hound or a panther, and, if born among Indians, would have been a fell hunter. But, restrained by his Massachusetts culture, he played out the game in this mild form of botany and ichthyology. His intimacy with animals suggested what Thomas Fuller records of Butler the apiologist, that "either he had told the bees things or the bees had told him." Snakes coiled round his leg; the fishes swam into his hand, and he took them out of the water; he pulled the woodchuck out of its hole by the tail, and took the foxes under his protection from the hunters. Our naturalist had perfect magnanimity; he had no secrets: he would carry you to the heron's haunt, or even to his most prized botanical swamp—possibly knowing that you could never find it again, yet willing to take his risks.

No college ever offered him a diploma, or a professor's chair; no academy made him its corresponding secretary, its discoverer, or even its member. Whether these learned bodies feared the satire of his presence. Yet so much knowledge of Nature's secret and genius few others possessed, none in a more large and religious synthesis. For not a particle of respect had he to the opinions of any man or body of men, but homage solely to the truth itself; and as he discovered everywhere among doctors some leaning of courtesy, it discredited them. He grew to be revered and admired by his townsmen, who had at first known him only as an oddity. The farmers who employed him as a surveyor soon discovered his rare accuracy and skill, his knowledge of their lands, of trees, of birds, of Indian remains, and the like, which enabled him to tell every farmer more than he knew before of his own farm; so that he began to feel a little as if Mr. Thoreau had better rights in his land than he. They felt, too, the superiority of character which addressed all men with a native authority.

Indian relics abound in Concord—arrow-heads, stone chisels, pestles, and fragments of pottery; and on the river-bank, large heaps of clam-shells and ashes mark spots which the savages frequented. These, and every circumstance touching the Indian, were important in his eyes. His visits to Maine were chiefly for love of the Indian. He had the satisfaction of seeing the manufacture of the bark-canoe, as well as of trying his hand in its management on the rapids. He was inquisitive about the making of the stone arrow-head, and in his last days charged a youth setting out for the Rocky Mountains to find an Indian who could tell him that: "It was well worth a visit to California to learn it." Occasionally, a small party of Penobscot Indians would visit Concord and pitch their tents for a few weeks in summer on the river-bank. He failed not to make acquaintance with the best of them; though he well knew that asking questions of Indians is like catechizing beavers and rabbits. In his last visit to Maine he had great satisfaction from Joseph Polis, an intelligent Indian of Oldtown, who was his guide for some weeks.

He was equally interested in every natural fact. The depth of his perception found likeness of law throughout Nature, and I know not any genius who so swiftly inferred universal law from the single fact. He was no pedant of a department. His eye was open to beauty, and his ear to music. He found these, not in rare conditions, but wheresoever he went. He thought the best of music was in single strains; and he found poetic suggestion in the humming of the telegraph-wire.

His poetry might be bad or good; he no doubt wanted a lyric facility and technical skill; but he had the source of poetry in his spiritual perception. He was a good reader and critic, and his judgment on poetry was to the ground of it. He could not be deceived as to the presence or absence of the poetic element in any composition, and his thirst for this made him negligent and perhaps scornful of superficial graces. He would pass by many delicate rhythms, but he would have detected every live stanza or line in a volume, and knew very well where to find an equal poetic charm in prose. He was so enamored of the spiritual beauty that he held all actual written poems in very light esteem in the comparison. He admired Æschylus and Pindar; but, when someone was commending them, he said that "Æschylus and the Greeks, in describing Apollo and Orpheus, had given no song, or no good one. They ought not to have moved trees, but to have chanted to the gods such a hymn as would have sung all their old ideas out of their heads, and new ones in." His own verses are often rude and defective. The gold does not yet run pure, is drossy and crude. The thyme and marjoram are not yet honey. But if he want lyric fineness and technical merits, if he have not the poetic temperament, he never lacks the causal thought, showing that his genius was better than his talent. He knew the worth of the Imagination for the uplifting and consolation of human life, and liked to throw every thought into a symbol. The fact you tell is of no value, but only the impression. For this reason his presence was poetic, always piqued the curiosity to know more deeply the secrets of his mind. He had many reserves, an unwillingness to exhibit to profane eyes what was still sacred in his own, and knew well how to throw a poetic veil over his experience. All readers of "Walden" will remember his mythical record of his disappointments:

"I long ago lost a hound, a bay horse, and a turtle-dove, and am still on their trail. Many are the travellers I have spoken concerning them, describing their tracks, and what calls they answered to. I have met one or two who had heard the hound, and the tramp of the horse, and even seen the dove disappear behind a cloud; and they seemed as anxious to recover them as if they had lost them themselves."

His riddles were worth the reading, and I confide, that, if at any time I do not understand the expression, it is yet just. Such was the wealth of his truth that it was not worth his while to use words in vain. His poem entitled "Sympathy" reveals the tenderness under that triple steel of stoicism, and the intellectual subtilty it could animate. His classic poem on "Smoke" suggests Simonides, but is better than any poem of Simonides. His biography is in his verses. His habitual thought makes all his poetry a hymn to the Cause of causes, the Spirit which vivifies and controls his own.

"I hearing get, who had but ears, And sight, who had but eyes before; I moments live, who lived but years, And truth discern, who knew but learning's lore."

And still more in these religious lines:

"Now chiefly is my natal hour, And only now my prime of life; I will not doubt the love untold, Which not my worth or want hath bought, Which wooed me young, and wooes me old, And to this evening hath me brought."

Whilst he used in his writings a certain petulance of remark in reference to churches or churchmen, he was a person of a rare, tender, and absolute religion, a person incapable of any profanation, by act or by thought. Of course, the same isolation which belonged to his original thinking and living detached him from the social religious forms. This is neither to be censured nor regretted. Aristotle long ago explained it, when he said, "One who surpasses his fellow-citizens in virtue is no longer a part of the city. Their law is not for him, since he is a law to himself."

Thoreau was sincerity itself, and might fortify the convictions of prophets in the ethical laws by his holy living. It was an affirmative experience which refused to be set aside. A truth-speaker he, capable of the most deep and strict conversation; a physician to the wounds of any soul; a friend, knowing not only the secret of friendship, but almost worshipped by those few persons who resorted to him as their confessor and prophet, and knew the deep value of his mind and great heart. He thought that without religion or devotion of some kind nothing great was ever accomplished: and he thought that the bigoted sectarian had better bear this in mind.

His virtues, of course, sometimes ran into extremes. It was easy to trace to the inexorable demand on all for exact truth that austerity which made this willing hermit more solitary even than he wished. Himself of a perfect probity, he required not less of others. He had a disgust at crime, and no worldly success would cover it. He detected paltering as readily in dignified and prosperous persons as in beggars, and with equal scorn. Such dangerous frankness was in his dealing that his admirers called him "that terrible Thoreau," as if he spoke when silent, and was still present when he had departed. I think the severity of his ideal interfered to deprive him of a healthy sufficiency of human society.

The habit of a realist to find things the reverse of their appearance inclined him to put every statement in a paradox. A certain habit of antagonism defaced his earlier writings—a trick of rhetoric not quite outgrown in his later, of substituting for the obvious word and thought its diametrical opposite. He praised wild mountains and winter forests for their domestic air, in snow and ice he would find sultriness, and commended the wilderness for resembling Rome and Paris. "It was so dry, that you might call it wet."

The tendency to magnify the moment, to read all the laws of Nature in the one object or one combination under your eye, is of course comic to those who do not share the philosopher's perception of identity. To him there was no such thing as size. The pond was a small ocean; the Atlantic, a large Walden Pond. He referred every minute fact to cosmical laws. Though he meant to be just, he seemed haunted by a certain chronic assumption that the science of the day pretended completeness, and he had just found out that the sevens had neglected to discriminate a particular botanical variety, had failed to describe the seeds or count the sepals. "That is to say," we replied, "the blockheads were not born in Concord; but who said they were? It was their unspeakable misfortune to be born in London, or Paris, or Rome; but, poor fellows, they did what they could, considering that they never saw Bateman's Pond, or Nine-Acre Corner, or

Becky-Stow's Swamp. Besides, what were you sent into the world for, but to add this observation?"

Had his genius been only contemplative, he had been fitted to his life, but with his energy and practical ability he seemed born for great enterprise and for command; and I so much regret the loss of his rare powers of action, that I cannot help counting it a fault in him that he had no ambition. Wanting this, instead of engineering for all America, he was the captain of a huckleberry-party. Pounding beans is good to the end of pounding empires one of these days; but if, at the end of years, it is still only beans!

But these foibles, real or apparent, were fast vanishing in the incessant growth of a spirit so robust and wise, and which effaced its defeats with new triumphs. His study of Nature was a perpetual ornament to him, and inspired his friends with curiosity to see the world through his eyes, and to hear his adventures. They possessed every kind of interest.

He had many elegances of his own, whilst he scoffed at conventional elegance. Thus, he could not bear to hear the sound of his own steps, the grit of gravel; and therefore never willingly walked in the road, but in the grass, on mountains and in woods. His senses were acute, and he remarked that by night every dwelling-house gives out bad air, like a slaughterhouse. He liked the pure fragrance of melilot. He honored certain plants with special regard, and, over all, the pond-lily—then, the gentian, and the Milcania scandens, and "life-everlasting," and a bass-tree which he visited every year when it bloomed, in the middle of July. He thought the scent a more oracular inquisition than the sight—more oracular and trustworthy. The scent, of course, reveals what is concealed from the other senses. By it he detected earthiness. He delighted in echoes, and said they were almost the only kind of kindred voices that he heard. He loved Nature so well, was so happy in her solitude, that be became very jealous of cities, and the sad work which their refinements and artifices made with man and his dwelling. The axe was always destroying his forest. "Thank God," he said, "they cannot cut down the clouds!" "All kinds of figures are drawn on the blue ground with this fibrous white paint."

I subjoin a few sentences taken from his unpublished manuscripts, not only as records of his thought and feeling, but for their power of description and literary excellence.

> "Some circumstantial evidence is very strong, as when you find a trout in the milk."

"The chub is a soft fish, and tastes like boiled brown paper salted."

"The youth gets together his materials to build a bridge to the moon, or, perchance, a palace or temple on the earth, and at length the middle-aged man concludes to build a wood-shed with them."

"The locust z-ing."

"Devil's-needles zigzagging along the Nut-Meadow brook."

"Sugar is not so sweet to the palate as sound to the healthy ear."

"I put on some hemlock-boughs, and the rich salt crackling of their leaves was like mustard to the ear, the crackling of uncountable regiments. Dead trees love the fire."

"The bluebird carries the sky on his back."

"The tanager flies through the green foliage as if it would ignite the leaves."

"If I wish for a horse-hair for my compass-sight, I must go to the stable; but the hair-bird, with her sharp eyes, goes to the road."

"Immortal water, alive even to the superficies."

"Fire is the most tolerable third party."

"Nature made ferns for pure leaves, to show what she could do in that line."

"No tree has so fair a hole and so handsome an instep as the beech."

"How did these beautiful rainbow-tints get into the shell of the fresh-water clam, buried in the mud at the bottom of our dark river?"

"Hard are the times when the infant's shoes are second-foot."

"We are strictly confined to our men to whom we give liberty."

"Nothing is so much to be feared as fear. Atheism may comparatively be popular with God himself."

"Of what significance the things you can forget? A little thought is sexton to all the world."

"How can we expect a harvest of thought who have not had a seed-time of character?"

"Only he can be trusted with gifts who can present a face of bronze to expectations."

"I ask to be melted. You can only ask of the metals that they be tender to the fire that melts them. To nought else can they be tender."

There is a flower known to botanists, one of the same genus with our summer plant called "Life-Everlasting," a *Gnaphalium* like that, which grows on the most inaccessible cliffs of the Tyrolese mountains, where the chamois dare hardly venture, and which the hunter, tempted by its beauty, and by his love (for it is immensely valued by the Swiss maidens) climbs the cliffs to gather, and is sometimes found dead at the foot, with the flower in his hand. It is called by botanists the *Gnaphalium leontopodium*, but by the Swiss *Edelweisse*, which signifies Noble Purity. Thoreau seemed to me living in the hope to gather this plant, which belonged to him of right. The scale on which his studies proceeded was so large as to require longevity, and we were the less prepared for his sudden disappearance. The country knows not yet, or in the least part, how great a son it has lost. It seems an injury that he should leave in the midst his broken task, which none else can finish—a kind of indignity to so noble a soul, that it should depart out of Nature before yet he has been really shown to his peers for what he is. But he, at least, is content. His soul was made for the noblest society; he had in a short life exhausted the capabilities of this world; wherever there is knowledge, wherever there is virtue, wherever there is beauty, he will find a home.

ABRAHAM LINCOLN (1809–1865)

by Frederick Douglass (1876)

Abraham Lincoln was the 16th President of the United States, best known for putting an end to slavery and stewarding the nation through the Civil War. The following oration was delivered by Frederick Douglass, a former slave, who went on to become one of the nation's leading abolitionists and statesmen, at the unveiling of the Freedmen's Monument in Lincoln Park, Washington, D.C.

FRIENDS AND FELLOW-CITIZENS:

I warmly congratulate you upon the highly interesting object which has caused you to assemble in such numbers and spirit as you have today. This occasion is in some respects remarkable. Wise and thoughtful men of our race, who shall come after us, and study the lesson of our history in the United States; who shall survey the long and dreary spaces over which we have traveled; who shall count the links in the great chain of events by which we have reached our present position, will make a note of this occasion; they will think of it and speak of it with a sense of manly pride and complacency.

I congratulate you, also, upon the very favorable circumstances in which we meet today. They are high, inspiring, and uncommon. They lend grace, glory, and significance to the object for which we have met. Nowhere else in this great country, with its uncounted towns and cities, unlimited wealth, and immeasurable territory extending from sea to sea, could conditions be found more favorable to the success of this occasion than here.

We stand today at the national center to perform something like a national act—an act which is to go into history; and we are here where every pulsation of the national heart can be heard, felt, and reciprocated. A thousand wires, fed with thought and winged with lightning, put us in instantaneous communication with the loyal and true men all over the country.

Few facts could better illustrate the vast and wonderful change which has taken place in our condition as a people than the fact of our assembling here for the purpose we have today. Harmless, beautiful, proper, and praiseworthy as this demonstration is, I cannot forget that no such demonstration would have been tolerated here twenty years ago. The spirit of slavery and barbarism, which still lingers to blight and destroy in some dark and distant parts of our country, would have made our assembling here the signal and excuse for opening upon us all the flood-gates of wrath and violence. That we are here in peace today is a compliment and a credit to American civilization, and a prophecy of still greater national enlightenment and progress in the future. I refer to the past not in malice, for this is no day for malice; but simply to place more distinctly in front the gratifying and glorious change which has come both to our white fellow-citizens and ourselves, and to congratulate all upon the contrast between now and then; the new dispensation of freedom with its thousand blessings to both races, and the old dispensation of slavery with its ten thousand evils to both races—white and black. In view, then, of the past, the present, and the future, with the long and dark history of our bondage behind us, and with liberty, progress, and enlightenment before us, I again congratulate you upon this auspicious day and hour.

Friends and fellow-citizens, the story of our presence here is soon and easily told. We are here in the District of Columbia, here in the city of Washington, the most luminous point of American territory; a city recently transformed and made beautiful in its body and in its spirit; we are here in the place where the ablest and best men of the country are sent to devise the policy, enact the laws, and shape the destiny of the Republic; we are here, with the stately pillars and majestic dome of the Capitol of the nation looking down upon us; we are here, with the broad earth freshly adorned with the foliage and flowers of spring for our church, and all races, colors, and conditions of men for our congregation—in a word, we are here to express, as best we may, by appropriate forms and ceremonies, our grateful sense of the vast, high, and preeminent services rendered to ourselves, to our race, to our country, and to the whole world by Abraham Lincoln.

The sentiment that brings us here to-day is one of the noblest that can stir and thrill the human heart. It has crowned and made glorious the high places of all civilized nations with the grandest and most enduring works of art, designed to illustrate the characters and perpetuate the memories of great public men. It is the sentiment which from year to year adorns with fragrant and beautiful flowers the graves of our loyal, brave, and patriotic soldiers who fell in defense of the Union and liberty. It is the sentiment of gratitude and appreciation, which often, in the presence of many who hear me, has filled yonder heights of Arlington with the eloquence of eulogy and the sublime enthusiasm of poetry and song; a sentiment which can never die while the Republic lives.

For the first time in the history of our people, and in the history of the whole American people, we join in this high worship, and march conspicuously in the line of this time-honored custom. First things are always interesting, and this is one of our first things. It is the first time that, in this form and manner, we have sought to do honor to an American great man, however deserving and illustrious. I commend the fact to notice; let it be told in every part of the Republic; let men of all parties and opinions hear it; let those who despise us, not less than those who respect us, know that now and here, in the spirit of liberty, loyalty, and gratitude, let it be known everywhere, and by everybody who takes an interest in human progress and in the amelioration of the condition of mankind, that, in the presence and with the approval of the members of the American House of Representatives, reflecting the general sentiment of the country; that in the presence of that august body, the American Senate, representing the highest intelligence and the calmest judgment of the country; in the presence of the Supreme Court and Chief-Justice of the United States, to whose decisions we all patriotically bow; in the presence and under the steady eye of the honored and trusted President of the United States, with the members of his wise and patriotic Cabinet, we, the colored people, newly emancipated and rejoicing in our blood-bought freedom, near the close of the first century in the life of this Republic, have now and here unveiled, set apart, and dedicated a monument of enduring granite and bronze, in every line, feature, and figure of which the men of this generation may read, and those of aftercoming generations may read, something of the exalted character and great works of Abraham Lincoln, the first martyr President of the United States.

Fellow-citizens, in what we have said and done today, and in what we may say and do hereafter, we disclaim everything like arrogance and assumption. We claim for ourselves no superior devotion to the character, history, and memory of the illustrious name whose monument we have here dedicated today. We fully comprehend the relation of Abraham Lincoln both to ourselves and to the white people of the United States. Truth is proper and beautiful at all times and in all places, and it is never more proper and beautiful in any case than when speaking of a great public man whose example is likely to be commended for honor and imitation long after his departure to the solemn shades, the silent continents of eternity. It must be admitted, truth compels me to admit, even here in the presence of the monument we have erected to his memory, Abraham Lincoln was not, in the fullest sense of the word, either our man or our model. In his interests, in his associations, in his habits of thought, and in his prejudices, he was a white man.

He was preeminently the white man's President, entirely devoted to the welfare of white men. He was ready and willing at any time during the first years of his administration to deny, postpone, and sacrifice the rights of humanity in the colored people to promote the welfare of the white people of this country. In all his education and feeling he was an American of the Americans. He came into the Presidential chair upon one principle alone, namely, opposition to the extension of slavery. His arguments in furtherance of this policy had their motive and mainspring in his patriotic devotion to the interests of his own race. To protect, defend, and perpetuate slavery in the states where it existed Abraham Lincoln was not less ready than any other President to draw the sword of the nation. He was ready to execute all the supposed guarantees of the United States Constitution in favor of the slave system anywhere inside the slave states. He was willing to pursue, recapture, and send back the fugitive slave to his master, and to suppress a slave rising for liberty, though his guilty master were already in arms against the Government. The race to which we belong were not the special objects of his consideration. Knowing this, I concede to you, my white fellow-citizens, a pre-eminence in this worship at once full and supreme. First, midst, and last, you and yours were the objects of his deepest affection and his most earnest solicitude. You are the children of Abraham Lincoln. We are at best only his step-children; children by adoption, children by forces of circumstances and necessity. To you it especially belongs to sound his praises, to preserve and perpetuate his memory, to multiply his statues, to hang his pictures high upon your walls, and commend his example, for to you he was a great and glorious friend and benefactor. Instead of supplanting you at his altar, we would exhort you to build high his monuments; let them be of the most costly material, of the most cunning workmanship; let their forms be symmetrical, beautiful, and perfect, let their bases be upon solid rocks, and their summits lean against the unchanging blue, overhanging sky, and let them endure forever! But while in the abundance of your wealth, and in the fullness of your just and patriotic devotion, you do all this, we entreat you to despise not the humble offering we this day unveil to view; for while Abraham Lincoln saved for you a country, he delivered us from a bondage, according to Jefferson, one hour of which was worse than ages of the oppression your fathers rose in rebellion to oppose.

Fellow-citizens, ours is no new-born zeal and devotion—merely a thing of this moment. The name of Abraham Lincoln was near and dear to our hearts in the darkest and most perilous hours of the Republic. We were no more ashamed of him when shrouded in clouds of darkness, of doubt, and defeat than when we saw him crowned with victory, honor, and glory. Our faith in him was often taxed and strained to the uttermost, but it never failed. When he tarried long in the mountain; when he strangely told us that we were the cause of the war; when he still more strangely told us that we were to leave the land in which we were born; when he refused to employ our arms in defense of the Union; when, after accepting our services as colored soldiers, he refused to retaliate our murder and torture as colored prisoners; when he told us he would save the Union if he could with slavery; when he revoked the Proclamation of Emancipation of General Fremont; when he refused to remove the popular commander of the Army of the Potomac, in the days of its inaction and defeat, who was more zealous in his efforts to protect slavery than to suppress rebellion; when we saw all this, and more, we were at times grieved, stunned, and greatly bewildered; but our hearts believed while they ached and bled. Nor was this, even at that time, a blind and unreasoning superstition. Despite the mist and haze that surrounded him; despite the tumult, the hurry, and confusion of the hour, we were able to take a comprehensive view of Abraham Lincoln, and to make reasonable allowance for the circumstances of his position. We saw him, measured him, and estimated him; not by stray utterances to injudicious and tedious delegations, who often tried his patience; not by isolated facts torn from their connection; not by any partial and imperfect glimpses, caught at inopportune moments; but by a broad survey, in the light of the stern logic of great events, and in view of that divinity which shapes our ends, rough hew them how we will, we came to the conclusion that the hour and the man of our redemption had somehow met in the person of Abraham Lincoln. It mattered little to us what language he might employ on special occasions; it mattered little to us, when we fully knew him, whether he was swift or slow in his movements; it was enough for us that Abraham Lincoln was at the head of a great movement, and was in living and earnest sympathy with that movement, which, in the nature of things, must go on until slavery should be utterly and forever abolished in the United States.

When, therefore, it shall be asked what we have to do with the memory of Abraham Lincoln, or what Abraham Lincoln had to do with us, the answer is ready, full, and complete. Though he loved Caesar less than Rome, though the Union was more to him than our freedom or our future, under his wise and beneficent rule we saw ourselves gradually lifted from the depths of slavery to the heights of liberty and manhood; under his wise and beneficent rule, and by measures approved and vigorously pressed by him, we saw that the handwriting of ages, in the form of prejudice and proscription, was rapidly fading away from the face of our whole country; under his rule, and in due time, about as soon after all as the country could tolerate the strange spectacle, we saw our brave sons and brothers laying off the rags of bondage, and being clothed all over in the blue uniforms of the soldiers of the United States; under his rule we saw two hundred thousand of our dark and dusky people responding to the call of Abraham Lincoln, and with muskets on their shoulders, and eagles on their buttons, timing their high footsteps to liberty and union under the national flag; under his rule we saw the independence of the black republic of Haiti, the special object of slave-holding aversion and horror, fully recognized, and her minister, a colored gentleman, duly received here in the city of Washington; under his rule we saw the internal slave-trade, which so long disgraced the nation, abolished, and slavery abolished in the District of Columbia; under his rule we saw for the first time the law enforced against the foreign slave trade, and the first slave-trader hanged like any other pirate or murderer; under his rule, assisted by the greatest captain of our age, and his inspiration, we saw the Confederate States, based upon the idea that our race must be slaves, and slaves forever, battered to pieces and scattered to the four winds; under his rule, and in the fullness of time, we saw Abraham Lincoln, after giving the slave-holders three months' grace in which to save their hateful slave system, penning the immortal paper, which, though special in its language, was general in its principles and effect, making slavery forever impossible in the United States. Though we waited long, we saw all this and more.

Can any colored man, or any white man friendly to the freedom of all men, ever forget the night which followed the first day of January, 1863, when the world was to see if Abraham Lincoln would prove to be as good as his word? I shall never forget that memorable night, when in a distant city I waited and watched at a public meeting, with three thousand others not less anxious than myself, for the word of deliverance which we have heard read today. Nor shall I ever forget the outburst of joy and thanksgiving that rent the air when the lightning brought to us the emancipation proclamation. In that happy hour we forgot all delay, and forgot all tardiness, forgot that the President had bribed the rebels to lay down their arms by a promise to withhold the bolt which would smite the slave-system with destruction; and we were thenceforward willing to allow the President all the latitude of time, phraseology, and every honorable device that statesmanship might require for the achievement of a great and beneficent measure of liberty and progress.

Fellow-citizens, there is little necessity on this occasion to speak at length and critically of this great and good man, and of his high mission in the world. That ground has been fully occupied and completely covered both here and elsewhere. The whole field of fact and fancy has been gleaned and garnered. Any man can say things that are true of Abraham Lincoln, but no man can say anything that is new of Abraham Lincoln. His personal traits and public acts are better known to the American people than are those of any other man of his age. He was a mystery to no man who saw him and heard him. Though high in position, the humblest could approach him and feel at home in his presence. Though deep, he was transparent; though strong, he was gentle; though decided and pronounced in his convictions, he was tolerant towards those who differed from him, and patient under reproaches. Even those who only knew him through his public utterance obtained a tolerably clear idea of his character and personality. The image of the man went out with his words, and those who read them knew him.

I have said that President Lincoln was a white man, and shared the prejudices common to his countrymen towards the colored race. Looking back to his times and to the condition of his country, we are compelled to admit that this unfriendly feeling on his part may be safely set down as one element of his wonderful success in organizing the loyal American people for the tremendous conflict before them, and bringing them safely through that conflict. His great mission was to accomplish two things: first, to save his country from dismemberment and ruin; and, second, to free his country from the great crime of slavery. To do one or the other, or both, he must have the earnest sympathy and the powerful cooperation of his loyal fellow-countrymen. Without this primary and essential condition to success his efforts must have been vain and utterly fruitless. Had he put the abolition of slavery before the salvation of the Union, he would have inevitably driven from him a powerful class of the American people and rendered resistance to rebellion impossible. Viewed from the genuine abolition ground, Mr. Lincoln seemed tardy, cold, dull, and indifferent; but measuring him by the sentiment of his country, a sentiment he was bound as a statesman to consult, he was swift, zealous, radical, and determined.

Though Mr. Lincoln shared the prejudices of his white fellow-countrymen against the Negro, it is hardly necessary to say that in his heart of hearts he loathed and hated slavery. The man who could say, "Fondly do we hope, fervently do we pray, that this mighty scourge of war shall soon pass away, yet if God wills it continue till all the wealth piled by two hundred years of bondage shall have been wasted, and each drop of blood drawn by the lash shall have been paid for by one drawn by the sword, the judgments of the Lord are true and righteous altogether," gives all needed proof of his feeling on the subject of slavery. He was willing, while the South was loyal, that it should have its pound of flesh, because he thought that it was so nominated in the bond; but farther than this no earthly power could make him go.

Fellow-citizens, whatever else in this world may be partial, unjust, and uncertain, time, time! is impartial, just, and certain in its action. In the realm of mind, as well as in the realm of matter, it is a great worker, and often works wonders. The honest and comprehensive statesman, clearly discerning the needs of his country, and earnestly endeavoring to do his whole duty, though covered and blistered with reproaches, may safely leave his course to the silent judgment of time. Few great public men have ever been the victims of fiercer denunciation than Abraham Lincoln was during his administration. He was often wounded in the house of his friends. Reproaches came thick and fast upon him from within and from without, and from opposite quarters. He was assailed by Abolitionists; he was assailed by slave-holders; he was assailed by the men who were for peace at any price; he was assailed by those who were for a more vigorous prosecution of the war; he was assailed for not making the war an abolition war; and he was bitterly assailed for making the war an abolition war.

But now behold the change: the judgment of the present hour is, that taking him for all in all, measuring the tremendous magnitude of the work before him, considering the necessary means to ends, and surveying the end from the beginning, infinite wisdom has seldom sent any man into the world better fitted for his mission than Abraham Lincoln. His birth, his training, and his natural endowments, both mental and physical, were strongly in his favor. Born and reared among the lowly, a stranger to wealth and luxury, compelled to grapple single-handed with the flintiest hardships of life, from tender youth to sturdy manhood, he grew strong in the manly and heroic qualities demanded by the great mission to which he was called by the votes of his countrymen. The hard condition of his early life, which would have depressed and broken down weaker men, only gave greater life, vigor, and buoyancy to the heroic spirit of Abraham Lincoln. He was ready for any kind and any quality of work. What other young men dreaded in the shape of toil, he took hold of with the utmost cheerfulness.

> "A spade, a rake, a hoe,
>   A pick-axe, or a bill;
> A hook to reap, a scythe to mow,
>   A flail, or what you will."

All day long he could split heavy rails in the woods, and half the night long he could study his English Grammar by the uncertain flare and glare of the light made by a pine-knot. He was at home in the land with his axe, with his maul, with gluts, and his wedges; and he was equally at home on water, with his oars, with his poles, with his planks, and with his boat-hooks. And whether in his flat-boat on the Mississippi River, or at the fireside of his frontier cabin, he was a man of work. A son of toil himself, he was linked in brotherly sympathy with the sons of toil in every loyal part of the Republic. This very fact gave him tremendous power with the American people, and materially contributed not only to selecting him to the Presidency, but in sustaining his administration of the Government.

Upon his inauguration as President of the United States, an office, even when assumed under the most favorable condition, fitted to tax and strain the largest abilities, Abraham Lincoln was met by a tremendous crisis. He was called upon not merely to administer the Government, but to decide, in the face of terrible odds, the fate of the Republic.

A formidable rebellion rose in his path before him; the Union was already practically dissolved; his country was torn and rent asunder at the center. Hostile armies were already organized against the Republic, armed with the munitions of war which the Republic had provided for its own defense. The tremendous question for him to decide was whether his country should survive the crisis and flourish, or be dismembered and perish. His predecessor in office had already decided the question in favor of national dismemberment, by denying to it the right of self-defense and self-preservation—a right which belongs to the meanest insect.

Happily for the country, happily for you and for me, the judgment of James Buchanan, the patrician, was not the judgment of Abraham Lincoln, the plebeian. He brought his strong common sense, sharpened in the school of adversity, to bear upon the question. He did not hesitate, he did not doubt, he did not falter; but at once resolved that at whatever peril, at whatever cost, the union of the States should be preserved. A patriot himself, his faith was strong and unwavering in the patriotism of his countrymen. Timid men said before Mr. Lincoln's inauguration, that we have seen the last President of the United States. A voice in influential quarters said, "Let the Union slide." Some said that a Union maintained by the sword was worthless. Others said a rebellion of 8,000,000 cannot be suppressed; but in the midst of all this tumult and timidity, and against all this, Abraham Lincoln was clear in his duty, and had an oath in heaven. He calmly and bravely heard the voice of doubt and fear all around him; but he had an oath in heaven, and there was not power enough on earth to make this honest boatman, backwoodsman, and broad-handed splitter of rails evade or violate that sacred oath. He had not been schooled in the ethics of slavery; his plain life had favored his love of truth. He had not been taught that treason and perjury were the proof of honor and honesty. His moral training was against his saying one thing when he meant another. The trust that Abraham Lincoln had in himself and in the people was surprising and grand, but it was also enlightened and well founded. He knew the American people better than they knew themselves, and his truth was based upon this knowledge.

Fellow-citizens, the fourteenth day of April, 1865, of which this is the eleventh anniversary, is now and will ever remain a memorable day in the annals of this Republic. It was on the evening of this day, while a fierce and sanguinary rebellion was in the last stages of its desolating power; while its armies were broken and scattered before the invincible armies of Grant and Sherman; while a great nation, torn and rent by war, was already beginning to raise to the skies loud anthems of joy at the dawn of peace, it was startled, amazed, and overwhelmed by the crowning crime of slavery—the assassination of Abraham Lincoln. It was a new crime, a pure act of malice. No purpose of the rebellion was to be served by it. It was the simple gratification of a hell-black spirit of revenge. But it has done good after all. It has filled the country with a deeper abhorrence of slavery and a deeper love for the great liberator.

Had Abraham Lincoln died from any of the numerous ills to which flesh is heir; had he reached that good old age of which his vigorous constitution and his temperate habits gave promise; had he been permitted to see the end of his great work; had the solemn curtain of death come down but gradually—we should still have been smitten with a heavy grief, and treasured his name lovingly. But dying as he did die, by the red hand of violence, killed, assassinated, taken off without warning, not because of personal hate—for no man who knew Abraham Lincoln could hate him—but because of his fidelity to union and liberty, he is doubly dear to us, and his memory will be precious forever.

Fellow-citizens, I end, as I began, with congratulations. We have done a good work for our race today. In doing honor to the memory of our friend and liberator, we have been doing highest honors to ourselves and those who come after us; we have been fastening ourselves to a name and fame imperishable and immortal; we have also been defending ourselves from a blighting scandal. When now it shall be said that the colored man is soulless, that he has no appreciation of benefits or benefactors; when the foul reproach of ingratitude is hurled at us, and it is attempted to scourge us beyond the range of human brotherhood, we may calmly point to the monument we have this day erected to the memory of Abraham Lincoln.

VOLTAIRE (1694–1778)

by Victor Hugo (1878)

Voltaire, born François-Marie Arouet, was widely consid-
ered to be the greatest French writer during the Enlightenment.
While he is mostly remembered for his satirical novel,
Candide, *he was also the author of more than a dozen*
plays, and countless works of philosophy and poetry. The
following oration was delivered by French author Victor
Hugo on the 100th anniversary of Voltaire's death.

A HUNDRED YEARS to-day a man died. He died immortal. He departed laden with years, laden with works, laden with the most illustrious and the most fearful of responsibilities, the responsibility of the human conscience informed and rectified. He went cursed and blessed, cursed by the past, blessed by the future; and these are the two superb forms of glory. On his death-bed he had, on the one hand, the acclaim of contemporaries and of posterity; on the other, that triumph of hooting and of hate which the implacable past bestows upon those who have combatted it. He was more than a man; he was an age. He had exercised a function and fulfilled a mission. He had been evidently chosen for the work which he had done by the Supreme Will, which manifests itself as visibly in the laws of destiny as in the laws of nature.

The eighty-four years which this man lived span the interval between the Monarchy at its apogee and the Revolution at its dawn. When he was born, Louis XIV still reigned; when he died, Louis XVI already wore the crown; so that his cradle saw the last rays of the great throne, and his coffin the first gleams from the great abyss.

Before going further, let us come to an understanding upon the word abyss. There are good abysses: such are the abysses in which evil is engulfed.

Since I have interrupted myself, allow me to complete my thought. No word imprudent or unsound will be pronounced here. We are here to perform an act of civilization. We are here to make affirmation of progress, to pay respect to philosophers for the benefits of philosophy, to bring to the Eighteenth century the testimony of the Nineteenth, to honor magnanimous combatants and good servants, to felicitate the noble effort of people, industry, science, the valiant march in advance, the toil to cement human concord; in one word, to glorify peace, that sublime, universal desire. Peace is the virtue of civilization; war is its crime. We are here, at this grand moment, in this solemn hour, to bow religiously before the moral law, and to say to the world, which hears France, this: There is only one power, conscience in the service of justice; and there is only one glory, genius in the service of truth. That said, I continue.

Before the Revolution the social structure was this—

At the base, the people;

Above the people, religion represented by the clergy;

By the side of religion, justice represented by the magistracy.

And, at that period of human society, what was the people? It was ignorance. What was religion? It was intolerance. And what was justice? It was injustice. Am I going too far in my words? Judge.

I will confine myself to the citation of two facts, but decisive.

At Toulouse, October 13, 1761, there was found in the lower story of a house a young man hanged. The crowd gathered, the clergy fulminated, the magistracy investigated. It was a suicide; they made of it an assassination. In what interest? In the interest of religion. And who was accused? The father. He was a Huguenot, and he wished to hinder his son from becoming a Catholic. There was here a moral monstrosity and a material impossibility; no matter! This father had killed his son; this old man had hanged this young man. Justice travailed, and this was the result. In the month of March, 1762, a man with white hair, Jean Calas, was conducted to a public place, stripped naked, stretched upon a wheel, the members bound upon it, the head hanging. Three men are there upon a scaffold, a magistrate, named David, charged to superintend the punishment, a priest to hold the crucifix, and the executioner with a bar of iron in his hand. The patient, stupefied and terrible, regards not the priest, and looks at the executioner. The executioner lifts the bar of iron, and breaks one of his arms. The victim groans and swoons. The magistrate comes forward; they make the condemned inhale salts; he returns to life. Then another stroke of the bar; another groan. Calas loses consciousness; they revive him and the executioner begins again; and, as each limb before being broken in two places receives two blows, that makes eight punishments. After the eighth swooning the priest offers him the crucifix to kiss; Calas turns away his head, and the executioner gives him the *coup de grâce;* that is to say, crushes in his chest with the thick end of the bar of iron. So died Jean Calas.

That lasted two hours. After his death the evidence of the suicide came to light. But an assassination had been committed. By whom? By the judges.

Another fact. After the old man, the young man. Three years later, in 1765, at Abbeville, the day after a night of storm and high wind, there was found upon the pavement of a bridge an old crucifix of worm-eaten wood, which for three centuries had been fastened to the parapet. Who had thrown down this crucifix? Who committed this sacrilege? It is not known. Perhaps a passer-by. Perhaps the wind. Who is the guilty one? The Bishop of Amiens launches a *monitoire*. Note what a *monitoire* was: it was an order to all the faithful, on pain of hell, to declare what they knew or believed they knew of such or such a fact; a murderous injunction, when addressed by fanaticism to ignorance. The *monitoire* of the Bishop of Amiens does its work; the town gossip assumes the character of the crime charged. Justice discovers, or believes it discovers, that on the night when the crucifix was thrown down, two men, two officers, one named La Barre, the other D'Etallonde, passed over the bridge of Abbeville, that they were drunk, and that they sang a guardroom song.

The tribunal was the Seneschalcy of Abbeville. The Seneschalcy of Abbeville was equivalent to the court of the Capitouls of Toulouse. It was not less just. Two orders for arrest were issued. D'Etallonde escaped, La Barre was taken. Him they delivered to judicial examination. He denied having crossed the bridge; he confessed to having sung the song. The Seneschalcy of Abbeville condemned him; he appealed to the Parliament of Paris. He was conducted to Paris; the sentence was found good and confirmed. He was conducted back to Abbeville in chains. I abridge. The monstrous hour arrives. They begin by subjecting the Chevalier de La Barre to the torture, ordinary and extraordinary, to make him reveal his accomplices. Accomplices in what? In having crossed a bridge and sung a song. During the torture one of his knees was broken; his confessor, on hearing the bones crack, fainted away. The next day, June 5, 1766, La Barre was drawn to the great square of Abbeville, where flamed a penitential fire; the sentence was read to La Barre; then they cut off one of his hands; then they tore out his tongue with iron pincers; then, in mercy, his head was cut off and thrown into the fire. So died the Chevalier de La Barre. He was nineteen years of age.

Then, O Voltaire! thou didst utter a cry of horror, and it will be thine eternal glory!

Then didst thou enter upon the appalling trial of the past; thou didst plead, against tyrants and monsters, the cause of the human race, and thou didst gain it. Great man, blessed be thou forever!

The frightful things which I have recalled were accomplished in the midst of a polite society; its life was gay and light; people went and came; they looked neither above nor below themselves; their indifference had become carelessness; graceful poets, Saint Aulaire, Boufflers, Gentil-Bernard, composed pretty verses; the court was all festival; Versailles was brilliant; Paris ignored what was passing; and then it was that, through religious ferocity, the judges made an old man die upon the wheel, and the priests tore out a child's tongue for a song.

In the presence of this society, frivolous and dismal, Voltaire alone, having before his eyes those united forces, the court, the nobility, capital; that unconscious power, the blind multitude; that terrible magistracy, so severe to subjects, so docile to the master, crushing and flattering, kneeling upon the people before the king; that clergy, vile *mélange* of hypocrisy and fanaticism; Voltaire alone, I repeat, declared war against that coalition of all the social iniquities, against that enormous and terrible world, and he accepted battle with it. And what was his weapon? That which has the lightness of the wind and the power of the thunderbolt—a pen.

With that weapon he fought; with that weapon he conquered.

Let us salute that memory.

Voltaire conquered; Voltaire waged the splendid kind of warfare, the war of one alone against all; that is to say, the grand warfare. The war of thought against matter, the war of reason against prejudice, the war of the just against the unjust, the war for the oppressed against the oppressor, the war of goodness, the war of kindness. He had the tenderness of a woman and the wrath of a hero. He was a great mind and an immense heart.

He conquered the old code and the old dogma. He conquered the feudal lord, the Gothic judge, the Roman priest. He raised the populace to the dignity of people. He taught, pacificated, and civilized. He fought for Sirven and Montbailly, as for Calas and La Barre; he accepted all the menaces, all the outrages, all the persecutions, calumny, and exile. He was indefatigable and immovable. He conquered violence by a smile, despotism by sarcasm, infallibility by irony, obstinacy by perseverance, ignorance by truth.

I have just pronounced the word *smile*. I pause at it. Smile! It is Voltaire.

Let us say it, pacification is the great side of the philosopher: in Voltaire the equilibrium always re-establishes itself at last. Whatever may be his just wrath, it passes, and the irritated Voltaire always gives place to the Voltaire calmed. Then in that profound eye the smile appears.

That smile is wisdom. That smile, I repeat, is Voltaire. That smile sometimes becomes laughter, but the philosophic sadness tempers it. Toward the strong it is mockery; toward the weak it is a caress. It disquiets the oppressor, and reassures the oppressed. Against the great it is raillery; for the little it is pity. Ah, let us be moved by that smile! It had in it the rays of the dawn. It illuminated the true, the just, the good, and what there is of worthy in the useful. It lighted up the interior of superstitions. Those ugly things it is salutary to see, he has shown. Luminous, that smile was fruitful also. The new society, the desire for equality and concession and that beginning of fraternity which called itself tolerance, reciprocal good-will, the just accord of men and right, reason recognized as the supreme law, the annihilation of prejudices and prescribed opinions, the serenity of souls, the spirit of indulgence and of pardon, harmony, peace—behold what has come from that great smile!

On the day—very near, without any doubt—when the identity of wisdom and clemency will be recognized, when the amnesty will be proclaimed, I affirm it! up there in the stars Voltaire will smile.

Between two servants of humanity, who appeared eighteen hundred years apart, there is a mysterious relation.

To combat Pharisaism; to unmask imposture; to overthrow tyrannies, usurpations, prejudices, falsehoods, superstitions; to demolish the temple in order to rebuild it, that is to say, to replace the false by the true; to attack a ferocious magistracy, a sanguinary priesthood; to take a whip and drive the money-changers from the sanctuary; to reclaim the heritage of the disinherited; to protect the weak, the poor, the suffering, the overwhelmed, to struggle for the persecuted and oppressed—that was the war of Jesus Christ! And who waged that war? It was Voltaire.

The completion of the evangelical work is the philosophical work; the spirit of mercy began, the spirit of tolerance continued. Let us say it with a sentiment of profound respect: Jesus wept; Voltaire smiled. Of that divine tear and that human smile is composed the sweetness of the present civilization.

Did Voltaire always smile? No. He was often indignant. You remarked it in my first words.

Certainly measure, reserve, proportion are reason's supreme law. We can say that moderation is the very respiration of the philosopher. The effort of the wise man ought to be to condense into a sort of serene certainty all the approximations of which philosophy is composed. But at certain moments the passion for the true rises powerful and violent, and it is within its right in so doing, like the stormy winds which purify. Never, I insist upon it, will any wise man shake those two august supports of social labor, justice and hope; and all will respect the judge if he is embodied justice, and all will venerate the priest if he represents hope. But if the magistracy calls itself torture, if the Church calls itself Inquisition, then Humanity looks them in the face, and says to the judge: I will none of thy law! and says to the priest: I will none of thy dogma! I will none of thy fire upon the earth and thy hell in the future! Then philosophy rises in wrath, and arraigns the judge before justice, and the priest before God!

That is what Voltaire did. It was grand.

What Voltaire was, I have said; what his age was, I am about to say.

Great men rarely come alone; large trees seem larger when they dominate a forest; there they are at home. There was a forest of minds around Voltaire; that forest was the Eighteenth century. Among those minds there were summits, Montesquieu, Buffon, Beaumarchais, and among others, two, the highest after Voltaire—Rousseau and Diderot. Those thinkers taught men to reason; reasoning well leads to acting well; justness in the mind becomes justice in the heart. Those toilers for progress labored usefully. Buffon founded naturalism; Beaumarchais discovered, outside of Molière, a kind of comedy till then almost unknown, the social comedy; Montesquieu made in law some excavations so profound that he succeeded in exhuming the right. As to Rousseau, as to Diderot, let us pronounce those two names apart; Diderot, a vast intelligence, inquisitive, a tender heart, a thirst for justice, wished to give certain notions as the foundation of true ideas, and created the encyclopædia. Rousseau rendered to woman an admirable service, completing the mother by the nurse, placing near one another those two majesties of the cradle. Rousseau, a writer, eloquent and pathetic, a profound oratorical dreamer, often divined and proclaimed political truth; his ideal borders upon the real; he had the glory of being the first man in France who called himself citizen. The civic fibre vibrates in Rousseau; that which vibrates in Voltaire is the universal fibre. One can say that in the fruitful Eighteenth century, Rousseau represented the people; Voltaire, still more vast, represented Man. Those powerful writers disappeared, but they left us their soul, the Revolution.

Yes, the French Revolution was their soul. It was their radiant manifestation. It came from them; we find them everywhere in that blest and superb catastrophe, which formed the conclusion of the past and the opening of the future. In that clear light, which is peculiar to revolutions, and which beyond causes permits us to perceive effects, and beyond the first plan the second, we see behind Danton Diderot, behind Robespierre Rousseau, and behind Mirabeau Voltaire. These formed those.

To sum up epochs, by giving them the names of men, to name ages, to make of them in some sort human personages, has only been done by three peoples, Greece, Italy, France. We say, the Age of Pericles, the Age of Augustus, the Age of Leo X, the Age of Louis XIV, the Age of Voltaire. These appellations have a great significance. This privilege of giving names to periods belonging exclusively to Greece, to Italy, and to France, is the highest mark of civilization. Until Voltaire, they were the names of the chiefs of states; Voltaire is more than the chief of a state; he is a chief of ideas; with Voltaire a new cycle begins. We feel that henceforth the supreme governmental power is to be thought. Civilization obeyed force; it will obey the ideal. It was the sceptre and the sword broken, to be replaced by the ray of light; that is to say, authority transfigured into liberty. Henceforth, no other sovereignty than the law for the people, and the conscience for the individual. For each of us, the two aspects of progress separate themselves clearly, and they are these: to exercise one's right; that is to say, to be a man; to perform one's duty; that is to say, to be a citizen.

Such is the signification of that word, the Age of Voltaire; such is the meaning of that august event, the French Revolution.

The two memorable centuries which preceded the Eighteenth, prepared for it; Rabelais warned royalty in "Gargantua," and Molière warned the Church in "Tartuffe." Hatred of force and respect for right are visible in those two illustrious spirits.

Whoever says to-day might makes right performs an act of the Middle Ages, and speaks to men three hundred years behind their time.

The Nineteenth century glorifies the Eighteenth century. The Eighteenth proposed, the Nineteenth concludes. And my last word will be the declaration, tranquil, but inflexible, of progress.

The time has come. The right has found its formula: human federation.

To-day, force is called violence, and begins to be judged; war is arraigned. Civilization, upon the complaint of the human race, orders the trial, and draws up the great criminal indictment of conquerors and captains. This witness, History, is summoned. The reality appears. The factitious brilliancy is dissipated. In many cases, the hero is a species of assassin. The peoples begin to comprehend that increasing the magnitude of a crime cannot be its diminution; that, if to kill is a crime, to kill much cannot be an extenuating circumstance; that, if to steal is a shame, to invade cannot be a glory; that *Te Deums* do not count for much in this matter; that homicide is homicide; that bloodshed is bloodshed; that it serves nothing to call one's self Cæsar or Napoleon; and that in the eyes of the eternal God, the figure of a murderer is not changed because, instead of a gallows-cap, there is placed upon his head an emperor's crown.

Ah! let us proclaim absolute truths. Let us dishonor war. No; glorious war does not exist. No; it is not good, and it is not useful, to make corpses. No; it cannot be that life travails for death. No; O mothers who surround me, it cannot be that war, the robber, should continue to take from you your children. No; it cannot be that women should bear children in pain, that men should be born, that people should plow and sow, that the farmer should fertilize the fields, and the workmen enrich the city, that industry should produce marvels, that genius should produce prodigies, that the vast human activity should, in presence of the starry sky, multiply efforts and creations, all to result in that frightful international exposition which is called a field of battle!

The true field of battle, behold it here! It is this rendezvous [at the Exposition, then open] of the masterpieces of human labor which Paris offers the world at this moment. The true victory is the victory of Paris.

Alas! we cannot hide it from ourselves that the present hour, worthy as it is of admiration and respect, has still some mournful aspects; there are still clouds upon the horizon; the tragedy of the peoples is not finished; war, wicked war, is still there, and it has the audacity to lift its head in the midst of this august festival of peace. Princes, for two years past, obstinately adhere to a fatal misunderstanding; their discord forms an obstacle to our concord, and they are ill-inspired to condemn us to the statement of such a contrast.

Let this contrast lead us back to Voltaire. In the presence of menacing possibilities, let us be more pacific than ever. Let us turn toward that great death, toward that great life, toward that great spirit. Let us bend before the venerated sepulcher. Let us take counsel of him whose life, useful to men, was extinguished a hundred years ago, but whose work is immortal. Let us take counsel of the other powerful thinkers, the auxiliaries of this glorious Voltaire—of Jean Jacques, of Diderot, of Montesquieu. Let us give the word to those great voices. Let us stop the shedding of human blood. Enough! enough! despots. Ah! barbarism persists; very well, let civilization be indignant. Let the Eighteenth century come to the help of the Nineteenth. The philosophers, our predecessors, are the apostles of the true; let us invoke those illustrious shades; let them, before monarchies meditating war, proclaim the right of man to life, the right of conscience to liberty, the sovereignty of reason, the holiness of labor, the blessedness of peace; and since night issues from the thrones, let light come from the tombs.

ULYSSES S. GRANT (1822–1885)

by Rev. Henry Ward Beecher (1885)

Ulysses S. Grant was a statesman and military leader who served as general and commander of the Union armies during the American Civil War, before going on to become the nation's 18th President. The following eulogy was delivered by noted abolitionist and Congregational Clergyman Henry Ward Beecher at Boston's Tremont Temple on October 22, 1885.

ANOTHER NAME IS added to the roll of those whom the world will not willingly let die. A few years since storm-clouds filled his heaven, and obloquy, slander and bitter lies rained down upon him.

The clouds are all blown away, under a serene sky he laid down his life, and the Nation wept. The path to his tomb is worn by the feet of innumerable pilgrims. The mildewed lips of Slander are silent, and even *Criticism* hesitates lest some incautious word should mar the history of the modest, gentle magnanimous Warrior.

The whole Nation watched his passage through humiliating misfortunes with unfeigned sympathy; the whole world sighed when his life ended! At his burial the unsworded hands of those whom he had fought lifted his bier and bore him to his tomb with love and reverence.

Grant made no claim to saintship. He was a man of like passions, and with as marked limitations as other men. Nothing could be more distasteful to his honest, modest soul while living, and nothing more unbecoming to his memory, than lying exaggerations and fulsome flatteries.

Men without faults are apt to be men without force. A round diamond has no brilliancy. Lights and shadows, hills and valleys, give beauty to the landscape. The faults of great and generous natures are often over-ripe goodness, or the shadows which their virtues cast.

Three elements enter into the career of a great citizen:

That which his ancestry gives;

That which opportunity gives;

That which his will develops.

Grant came from a sturdy New England stock; New England derived it from Scotland, Scotland bred it, at a time when Covenanters and Puritans were made—men of iron consciences hammered out upon the anvil of adversity. From N. E. the stream flowed to the Ohio, where it enriched the soil till it brought forth abundant harvests of great men. When it was Grant's time to be born, he came forth without celestial portents and his youth had in it no prophecy of his manhood. His boyhood was wholesome, robust, with a vigorous frame. With a heart susceptible of tender love, he yet was not social. He was patient and persistent. He loved horses, and could master them. That is a good sign.

Grant had no art of creating circumstances; opportunity must seek him, or else he would plod through life without disclosing the gifts which God hid in him. The gold in the hills cannot disclose itself. It must be sought and dug.

A sharp and wiry politician, for some reason of Providence, performed a generous deed, in sending young Grant to *West Point*. He finished his course there, distinguished as a skillfull and bold rider, with an inclination to mathematics, but with little taste for the theory and literature of war, but with sympathy for its external and material developments. In boyhood and youth he was marked by simplicity, candor, veracity and silence.

After leaving the Academy he saw service in Mexico, and afterward in California, but without conspicuous results.

Then came a clouded period, a sad life of irresolute vibration between self-indulgence and aspiration through intemperance. He resigned from the army, and at that time one would have feared that his life would end in eclipse. Hercules crushed two serpents sent to destroy him in his cradle. It was later in his life that Grant destroyed the enemy that "biteth like a serpent and stingeth like an adder."

At length he struck at the root of the matter. Others agree not to drink, which is good, Grant overcame the *wish* to drink—which is better. But the cloud hung over his reputation for many years, and threatened his ascendency when better days came. Of all his victories, many and great, this was the greatest that he conquered himself. His will was stronger than his passions.

Poor, much shattered, he essayed farming. Carrying wood for sale to St. Louis did not seem to be that for which he was created; neither did planting crops, or raising cattle.

Tanning is an honorable calling, and, to many, a road to wealth. Grant found no gold in the tan vat.

Then he became a listless merchant—a silent, unsocial and rather moody waiter upon petty traffic.

He was a good subaltern, a poor farmer, a worse tanner, a worthless trafficer. Without civil experience, without literary gifts, too diffident to be ambitious, too modest to put himself forward, too honest to be a politician, he was of all men the least likely to attain eminence, and absolutely unfitted, apparently, for pre-eminence; yet God's Providence selected him.

When the prophet Samuel went forth to annoint a successor to the impetuous and imperious King Saul, he caused all the children of Jesse to pass before him. He rejected one by one the whole band. At length the youngest called from among the flock came in, and the Lord said to Samuel, "Arise, this is *he*," and Samuel took the horn of oil and anointed him in the midst of his brethren, and the spirit of the Lord came upon him from that day forward. (1 Sam. 16.)

Ordained was Grant with the ointment of war—black and sulphurous.

Had Grant died at the tan-yard, or from behind the counter, the world would never have suspected that it had lost a hero. He would have fallen as an undistinguishable leaf among the millions cast down every year. His time had not come. It was plain that he had no capacity to create his opportunity. IT must find him out, or he would die ignoble and unknown!

It was coming! Already the clouds afar off were gathering. He saw them not. No figures were seen upon the dim horizon of the already near future.

The insulted flag; the garments rolled in blood; a million men in arms; the sulphurous smoke of battle; gorey heaps upon desperate battle fields; an army of slowly moving crippled heroes; graveyards populous as cities; they were all in the clouded horizon, though he saw them not!

Let us look upon the scene on which he was soon to exert a mighty energy.

This continent lay waiting for ages for the seed of civilization. At length a sower came forth to sow. While he sowed the good seed of liberty and Christian civilization, an enemy, darkling, sowed tares. They sprang up and grew together. The Constitution cradled both Slavery and Liberty. While yet ungrown they dwelt together in peace. They snarled in youth, quarreled when half grown, and fought when of full age. The final catastrophe was inevitable. No finesse, no device or compromise could withstand the inevitable. The conflict began in Congress; it drifted into commerce; it rose into the very air, and public sentiment grew hot, and raged in the pulpit, the forum, and in politics.

The South, like a queenly beauty, grew imperious and exacting; the North, like an obsequious suitor, knelt at her feet, only to receive contempt and mockery.

Both parties, Whig and Democrat, drank of the cup of her sorcery. It killed the Whig party. The Democrat was tougher, and was only besotted. A few, like John the Baptist, were preaching repentance, but, like him, they were in the wilderness, and seemed rude and shaggy fanatics.

If a wise moderation had possessed the South, if they had conciliated the North, if they had met the just scruples of honest men, who, hating slavery, dreaded the dishonor of breaking the compacts of the Constitution, the South might have held control for another hundred years. It was not to be. God sent a strong delusion upon them.

Nothing can be plainer than that all parties in the State were drifting in the dark, without any comprehension of the elemental causes at work. Without prescience or sagacity, like ignorant physicians, they prescribed at random; they sewed on patches, new compromise upon old garments, sought to conceal the real depth and danger of the gathering torrent by crying peace, peace, to each other. In short, they were seeking to medicate volcanoes and stop earthquakes by administering political quinine. The wise statesmen were bewildred and politicians were juggling fools.

The South had laid the foundation of her industry, her commerce, and her commonwealth upon slavery. It was slavery that inspired her councils, that engorged her philanthropy, that corrupted her political economy and theology, that disturbed all the ways of active politics; broke up sympathy between North and South. As Ahab met Elijah with, "Art thou he that troubleth Israel?" so Slavery charged the sentiments of Freedom with vexatious meddling and unwarrantable interference.

The South had builded herself upon the rock of Slavery. It lay in the very channels of Civilization, like some Flood Rock lying sullen off Hell Gate. The tides of controversy rushed upon it and split into eddies and swirling pools, bringing incessant disaster. The rock would not move. It must be removed. It was the South itself that furnished the engineers. Arrogance in Council sunk the shaft, Violence chambered the subterranean passages, and Infatuation loaded them with infernal dynamite. All was secure. Their rock was their fortress. The hand that fired upon Sumter exploded the mine, and tore the fortress to atoms. For one moment it rose into the air like spectral hills—for one moment the waters rocked with wild confusion, then settled back to quiet, and the way of civilization was opened!

The spark that was kindled at Fort Sumter fell upon the North, like fire upon autumnal prairies. Men came together in the presence of this universal calamity with sudden fusion. They forgot all separations of politics, parties, or even of religion itself. It was a conflagration of patriotism. The bugle and the drum rang out in every neighborhood, the plow stood still in the furrow, the hammer dropped from the anvil, book and pen were forgotten, pulpit and forum, court and shop, felt the electric shock. Parties dissolved and reformed. The Democratic party sent forth a host of noble men, and swelled the Republican ranks, and gave many noble leaders and irresistible energy to the Hosts of War. The whole land became a military school, and officers and men began to learn the art and practice of war.

When once the North had organized its armies, there was soon disclosed an amiable folly of conciliation. It hoped for some peaceable way out of the war; generals seemed to fight so that no one should be hurt; they saw the mirage of future parties above the battlefield, and anxiously considered the political effect of their military conduct. They were fighting not to break down rebellion, but to secure a future presidency—or governorship. The South had smelted into a glowing mass. It believed in its course with an infatuation that would have been glorious if the cause had been better! It put its whole soul into it and struck hard!

The South fought for slavery and independence. The North fought for Union, but for political success after the War. Thus for two years, not unmarked by great deeds, the war lingered. Lincoln, sad and sorrowful, felt the moderation of his generals, and longed for a man of iron mould, who had but two words in his military vocabulary, VICTORY or ANNIHILATION.

He was coming! He was heard from at Henry and Donelson.

Three great names were rising to sight—Sherman, Thomas, Sheridan; and larger than either, Grant! With his advent the armies, with some repulses, went steadily forward, from conquering to conquer. Aside from all military qualities, he had one absorbing spirit—the Union must be saved, the rebellion must be beaten, the Confederate armies must be threshed to chaff as on a summer threshing floor. He had no political ambition, no imaginary reputation to preserve or gain. A great genius for grand strategy, a comprehension of complex and vast armies, caution, prudence and silence while preparing, an endless patience, an indomitable will, and a real, downright fighting quality.

Thus at length Grant was really born! He had lain in the nest for long as an infertile egg. The brooding of war hatched the egg, and an eagle came forth!

★ ★ ★

It is impossible to reach the full measure of Grant's military genius until we survey the greatness of this most extraordinary war of modern days, or it may be said of any age.

For more than four years there were more than a million men on each side, stretched out upon a line of between one and two thousand miles, and a blockade rigorously enforced along a coast of an equal extent. During that time, counting no battle in which there were not five hundred Union men engaged, there was fought more than two thousand engagements—two thousand two hundred and sixty-one of record.

Amid this sea of blood, there shot up great battles, that for numbers, fighting and losses, will rank with the great battles of the world.

In 1862 the losses by death, wounds and missing on each side, as extracted from Government Records, were:

	Union.	Confed.	Total.
1. Shiloh	13,500	10,699	24,199
2. Seven Pines and Fair Oaks	5,739	7,997	13,736
3. 7 Day Retreat and Malvern Hill	15,249	17,583	32,832
4. 2d Bull Run	7,800	3,700	11,100
5. Antietam	12,469	25,899	38,367

6. Fredericksburg..............................	12,353	4,576	16,929
7. Stone River.................................	11,578	25,560	37,138

1863.

8. Chancellorsville	16,030	12,281	28,311
9. Gettysburg....................................	23,186	31,621	54,807
10. Chicamauga	15,851	17,804	33,655
11. Chattanooga.................................	5,616	8,684	

1864.

12. Wilderness..................................	37,737	11,400	49,137
13. Spotsylvania................................	26,421	9,000	35,421
14. Cold Harbor................................	14,931	1,700	16,700
15. Petersburg	10,586	28,000	38,586
16. Chattanooga to Atlanta................	37,199		

Over 26,000 Northern soldiers died in prison, in captivity. If we reckon all who perished by violence and by sickness on both sides, nearly a million died in the War of Emancipation.

The number must be largely swelled if we add all who died at home, of sickness and wounds received in the campaign.

The Secretary of War, in his report, dated November 22, 1865, makes the following remarks, which show more than anything else the spirit animating the people of the loyal States: "On several occasions, when troops were promptly needed to avert impending disaster, vigorous exertion brought them into the field from remote States with incredible speed. Official reports show that after the disasters on the Peninsula, in 1862, over 80,000 troops were enlisted, organized, armed, equipped, and sent into the field in less than a month. 60,000 troops have repeatedly gone to the field within four weeks. 90,000 infantry were sent to the armies from the five States of Ohio, Indiana, Illinois, Iowa, and Wisconsin, within twenty days. When Lee's army surrendered, thousands of recruits were pouring in, and men were discharged from recruiting stations and rendezvous in every State."

Into this sulphurous storm of war Grant entered almost unknown. It was with difficulty that he could obtain a command. Once set forward, *Donelson, Shiloh, Vicksburg, Chicamauga, The Wilderness, Spotsylvania, Petersburg, Appomattox,* these were his footsteps. In four years he had risen, without political favor, from the bottom to the very highest command—not second to any living commander in all the world!

His plans were large, his undiscouraged will was patient to obduracy. He was not fighting for reputation, nor for the display of generalship, nor for a future Presidency. He had but one motive, and that as intense as life itself—the subjugation of the rebellion and the restoration of the broken Union. He embodied the feelings of the common people. He was their perfect representative. The war was waged for the maintenance of the Union, the suppression of armed resistance, and, at length, for the eradication of Slavery. Every step, from Donelson to Appomattox, evinced with increasing intensity this his one terrible purpose. He never wavered, turned aside, or dallied. He waded through blood to the horses' bridles.

In all this career he never lost courage or equanimity. With a million men, for whose movements he was responsible, he yet carried a tranquil mind, neither depressed by disasters, nor elated by success. Gentle of heart, familiar with all, never boasting, always modest— *Grant* came of the old self-contained stock, men of a simple force of being, which allied his genius to the great elemental forces of Nature, silent, invisible, irresistible. When his work was done, and the defeat of Confederate armies was final, this dreadful man of blood was tender toward his late adversaries as a woman toward her son. He imposed no humiliating conditions, spared the feelings of his antagonists, sent home the disbanded Southern men with food and with horses for working their crops, and when a revengeful spirit in the Executive Chair showed itself, and threatened the chief Southern Generals, Grant, with a holy indignation, interposed himself, and compelled his superior to relinquish his rash purpose.

There have been men—there are yet—for stupidity is long-lived— who regard Grant as only a man of luck. Surely he was! Is it not luck through such an ancestry to have had conferred upon him such a body, such a disposition, such greatness of soul, such patriotism unalloyed by ambition, such military genius, such an indomitable will, and such a capacity for handling the largest armies of any age?

For four years and more this man of continuous Luck, across a rugged continent, in the face of armies of men as brave as his own, commanded by Generals of extraordinary ability, performed every function of strategy in grand War, which Jomini attributes to Napoleon and his greatest marshals, and Napier to Wellington. Whether Grant could have conducted a successful retreat will never be known. He was never defeated.

Grant has been severely criticised for the waste of life. War is not created for the purpose of saving life, but by a noble spending of blood to save the Commonwealth. The great end which he achieved would have been cheaply gained, at double the expense.

After the Battle of the Wilderness he was styled the *Butcher*.

But we are not to forget the circumstances under which the conduct of the last great campaign was committed to him. For four years the heroic and patient Army of the Potomac had squandered blood and treasure without measure, and had gained not a step. With Generals many, excellently skilled in logistics, skillful in everything but success, they fought and retreated; they dug, they waded, they advanced and retreated. They went down to Richmond and looked upon it, and came back to defend Washington.

Their victories were fruitless. *Antietam* was ably fought, but weakly followed up. Gettysburg, with hideous slaughter, sent Lee back unpursued, undestroyed, though he waited three or four days, helpless, cooped-up and surely doomed had Sheridan or Grant been in Meade's place.

The Army of the Potomac needed a General who knew how to employ their splendid bravery, their all-enduring pluck. They had danced long enough; they had led off—changed partners—chasséd—they had gone into campaigns with slow and solemn music, but returned with quick-steps. They seemed desirous of making war so as not to exasperate the South.

Do not men know that nothing spends life faster than unfighting war? Disease is more deadly than the bullet. In all the war, but one out of every 42 that died were slain by the bullet, and one out of every 13 by disease. 6,000,000 men passed through the Hospitals during the war; over three million with malarial diseases.

It seemed doubtful whether the Government was putting down rebellion, or whether Lee was putting down the Government. An eminent critic says: "The fire and passion, downright earnestness and self-abandon that the South threw into the struggle at the outset and maintained for two full years, had, it must be admitted, so far impaired the morale of the Union forces, that while courage was nowhere wanting, self-confidence had been seriously diminished. This was especially true of the devoted and decimated Army of the Potomac, whose commanders, after the first battle of Bull Run, always appeared to be afraid of exasperating the enemy. Driving Lee to extremities was the one thing that they were all loth to do. They would fight to the last drop of blood to defend Washington, to hold their own, to preserve the Union, but to corner the enemy, to drive him to desperation, to make him shed the last drop of his own blood, was the one thing they would not do, and no amount of urging could make them do it. It was this *arrière pensée* that held the hand of McClellan and of Meade after Antietam and Gettysburg. Both of these engagements were victories for the Army of the Potomac, and both were robbed of their fruits by a lurking fear of the lion at bay. "They are 'shooing' the enemy out of Maryland," said Lincoln, with his peculiar aptness and homeliness."

When Grant came to the Army of the Potomac, he reversed the methods of all who preceded him. Braver soldiers never were, and Valiant Commanders; but the Generals had not learned the art of fighting with deadly intent. Peace is very good for peace, but war is organized Rage. It means destruction or it means nothing.

At the Battle of the Wilderness, Grant stripped his commissary train of its guards to fill a gap in the line of battle. When expostulated with for exposing his Army to the loss of all its provisions, his reply was:

"When this army is whipped, it will not want any provisions."

All Summer, all the Autumn, all the Winter, all the Spring, and early Summer again, he hammered Lee, with blow on blow, until, at Appomattox, the great, but not greatest, Southern General went to the ground.

Grant was a great fighter, but not a fighter only.

His mind took in the whole field of war—as wide and complex as any that ever Napoleon knew. He combined in his plans the operations of three Armies, and for the first time in the War, the whole of Union forces were acting in concert.

He had the patience of Fate, and the force of Thor. If he neglected the rules of war, as at Vicksburg, it was to make better rules, to those who were strong enough to employ them.

Counselors gave him materials. He formed his own plans. Abhorring *Show,* simple in manner, gentle in his intercourse, modest and even diffident in regard to his own personality, he seems to have been the only man in Camp who was ignorant of his own greatness. Never was a Commander better served, never were subordinates more magnanimously treated. The fame of his Generals was as dear to him as his own. Those who might have been expected to be his rivals, were his bosom friends. While there were envies and jealousies among minor officers, the great names, *Thomas, Sherman, Sheridan,* give to history a new instance of a great friendship between great Warriors.

Some future day a Napier will picture the final drama: the breaking up of Lee's right wing at Five Forks; Lee's retreat; Grant's grim, relentless pursuit; Sheridan, like a raging lion, heading off the fleeing armies, that were wearied, worn, decimated, conquered; and, at the end, the modesty of their Victorious General; the delicacy with which he treated his beaten foe; the humanity of the terms given to the men: sent away with food, and horses for their farms; all this will form a picture of *War and of Peace.*

He never forgot that the South was part of his country. The moment that the South lay panting and helpless upon the ground, Grant carried himself with magnanimous and sympathetic consideration. After the fall of Richmond he turned aside and returned to Washington without entering the conquered Capital.

When Johnston surrendered upon terms not agreeable to Lincoln, Stanton, like a roaring lion fearing to lose its prey, sent Grant to overrule him. He loved Sherman, and was unwilling to enter his camp lest he should seem to snatch from him the glory of his illustrious campaign. From a near town he enabled Sherman to reconstruct his terms, and accept Gen'l Johnston's surrender.

When Lincoln was dead, Vice-President Johnson became President; a man well fitted for carrying on a fight, but not skilled in Peace, with a morbid sense of Justice, he determined that the leaders of rebellion should be made to suffer as examples; as if the death of all the first-born, the desolation of every Southern home, the impoverished condition and bankruptcy of every citizen were not example enough! He ordered Lee to be arrested. Grant refused. When Johnson would have employed the Army to effect his purposes, Grant, with quick but noble rebellion, refused obedience to his superior, and, arranging to take from his hands all military control, repressed the President's wild temper and savage purpose of a dishonoring Justice.

Having brought the long and disastrous war to a close, in his own heart Grant would have chosen to have rested upon his laurels, and lived a retired military life. It was not to be permitted. He was called to the Presidency by universal acclaim, and it fell to him to conduct a campaign of Reconstruction even more burdensome than the war.

It would seem impossible to combine in one, eminent civil and military genius. To a certain extent they have elements in common. But the predominant element in war is organized *Force;* of civil government, *Influence.* Statesmanship is less brilliant than Generalship, but requires a different and a higher moral and intellectual genius.

God is frugal in creating great men—men great enough to hold in eminence, the elements of a great General and of a great Ruler. Washington was eminent in Statesmanship—but then he was not a great General. At any rate, he had no opportunity to develop the fact.

Alexander was a mere brutal fighter.

Cesar as Emperor differed from Cesar as General only as a sword sheathed differs from a sword unsheathed.

Frederick the Great was simply a Military Ruler.

Napoleon came near to combine the two elements in the earlier period of his career, but the genius of Force gradually weakened that sense of right and justice on which Statesmanship must rest.

Grant had in him the element of great Statesmanship; but neither his education, nor his training, nor the desperate necessities of war, gave it a fair chance of development in a condition of things which bewildered the wisest statesmen.

The tangled skein of affairs would have tasked a Cavour or a Bismarck. The Period of Reconstruction is yet too near our war-inflamed eyes to be philosophically judged.

1. Came the disbanding of the army. That was so easily done that the world has never done justice to the marvel. The soldiers of three great armies dropped their arms at the word of command, dissolved their organizations, and disappeared. To-day the mightiest force on earth, to-morrow they were not! As a summer storm darkens the whole heavens, shakes the ground with its thunder, and empties its quiver of lightning, and is gone in an hour, as if it had never been, so was it with both armies. Neither in the South nor in the North was there a cabal of officers, nor any affray of soldiers—for every soldier was yet more a citizen.

In this resumption of citizen life, Grant, accompanied by his most brilliant Generals, led the way. He hated war, its very insignia, and in foreign lands refused to witness military pageants. He had had enough of war. He loved peace.

When advanced to the Presidency, three vital questions were to be solved.

1. The status of the four million Emancipated Slaves.

2. The adjustment of the political relations of the dislocated States.

3. The restraint and control of that gulf-stream of Finance which threatened to wash out the foundations of honest industry, and which brought to the Nation more moral mischief than had the whole war itself. We are in peril from golden quicksands yet.

Grant was eminently wise upon this question. His veto saved the country from a vitiated and corrupting circulation.

The exaltation of the domestic African to immediate Citizenship was the most audacious act of faith and fidelity that ever was witnessed.

Their fidelity to the duties of bondage was most Christian. In all the war, knowing that their emancipation was to be gained or lost, there was never an insurrection, nor a recorded instance of cruelty or insubordination. This came not from cowardice; for, when, in the later periods of the war, they were enlisted and drilled, they made soldiers so brave as to extort admiration and praise from prejudice itself. They deserved their liberty for their good conduct.

But, were they prepared for Citizenship? The safety of our civil economy rests upon the intelligence of the citizen. But the slaves in mass were greatly ignorant.

It was a political necessity to arm them with the ballot as a means of self-defense.

In many of the Southern States a probationary state would have been wiser, but in others it would have remanded them to substantial bondage.

In this grand department of Statesmanship General Grant accepted the views of the most eminent Republicans, Stanton, Chase, Sumner, Thad. Stevens, Fessenden, Sherman, Garfield, Conkling, Evarts, and of all the great leaders.

In the readjustment of the political relations of the South he was wise, generous, and magnanimous in his career. Not a line in letter, speech or message can be found that would wound the self-respect of Southern citizens.

When the dangerous heresy of a Greenback currency had gained political power, and Congress was disposed to open the flood-gates of a rotten currency, his veto, an act of courage, turned back the deluge and saved the land from a whole generation of mischief. Had he done but this one thing, he would have deserved well of History.

The respects in which he fell below the line of sound Statesmanship—and these are not a few—are to be attributed to the influence of advisers whom he had taken into his confidence. Such was his loyalty to friendship that it must be set down as a fault—a fault rarely found among public men.

Many springs of mischief were opened which still flow. When it was proposed to nominate Grant for a third term, the real objections to the movement among wise and dispassionate men was not so much against Grant as against the staff which would come in with him.

On the whole, if one considers the intrinsic difficulty of the question belonging to his administration, the stormy days of politics and parties during his eight years, it must be admitted that the country owes to his unselfish disposition, to his general wisdom, to his unsullied integrity, if not the meed of wisest yet the reputation of one who, pre-eminent in war, was eminent in administration, more perhaps by the wisdom of a noble nature than by that intelligence which is bred only by experience. Imperious counselors and corrupt parasites dimmed the light of his political administration.

We turn from Grant's public life to his unrestful private life. After a return from a tour of the world, during which he met on all hands a distinguished reception, he ventured upon the dangerous road of speculation. The desire of large wealth was deep-seated in Grant's soul. His early experience of poverty had probably taken away from it all romance. Had wealth been sought by a legitimate production of real property, he would have added one more laurel to his career. But, with childlike simplicity of ignorance, he committed all he had to the wild chances of legalized gambling. But a few days before the humiliating crash came, he believed himself to be worth three millions of dollars! What service had been rendered for it? What equivalent of industry, skill, productiveness, distribution or convenience? None. Did he never think that this golden robe, with which he designed to clothe his declining years, was woven of air, was in its nature unsubstantial, and not reputable? His success was a gorgeous bubble, reflecting on its brilliant surface all the hues of heaven, but which grew thinner as it swelled larger. A touch dispelled the illusion, and left him poor.

It is a significant proof of the impression produced upon the public mind of the essential honesty of his mind, and of the simplicity of his ignorance of practical business, that the whole nation condoned his folly, and believed in his intentional honesty. But the iron had entered his soul. That which all the hardships of war, and the wearing anxieties of public administration could not do, the shame and bitterness of this great Bankruptcy achieved.

The resisting forces of his body gave way. A disease in ambush sprang forth and carried him captive. Patiently he sat in the region and shadow of death. A mild heroism of gentleness and patience hovered about him. The iron will that had upheld him in all the vicissitudes of war, still in a gracious guise sustained his lingering hours.

His household love, never tarnished, never abated, now roused him to one last heroic achievement—to provide for the future of his family. No longer were there golden hopes for himself. The vision of wealth had vanished. But love took its place, and under weakness, pain and anguish, he wrought out a history of his remarkable career. A kindly hand administered the trust. It has amply secured his loved household from want.

When the last lines were written, he laid back upon his couch and breathed back his great Soul to God, whom he had worshiped unostentatiously after the manner of his fathers.

A man he was without vices, with an absolute hatred of lies, and an ineradicable love of truth, of a perfect loyalty to friendship, neither envious of others nor selfish for himself. With a zeal for the public good, unfeigned, he has left to memory only such weaknesses as connect him with humanity, and such virtues as will rank him among heroes.

The tidings of his death, long expected, gave a shock to the whole world. Governments, Rulers, Eminent Statesmen and Scholars from all civilized nations gave sincere tokens of sympathy. For the hour, sympathy rolled as a wave over all our own land. It closed the last furrow of war, it extinguished the last prejudice, it effaced the last vestige of hatred, and cursed be the hand that shall bring them back!

Johnston and Buckner on one side, Sherman and Sheridan upon the other of his bier, he has come to his tomb a silent symbol that Liberty had conquered Slavery, Patriotism Rebellion, and Peace War.

He rests in peace. No drum or cannon shall disturb his rest.

Sleep, Hero, until another trumpet shall shake the heavens and the earth. Then come forth to glory in immortality.

EMILY DICKINSON (1830–1886)

by Susan Gilbert Dickinson (1886)

Emily Dickinson was an American poet from Amherst, Massachusetts. Although she was never recognized for her work during her lifetime, she is now widely considered one of the most important American poets of the nineteenth century. The following obituary was written by Emily Dickinson's sister-in-law, Susan Gilbert Dickinson, and published in the Springfield Republican *on May 18, 1886.*

THE DEATH OF Miss Emily Dickinson, daughter of the late Edward Dickinson, at Amherst on Saturday, makes another sad inroad on the small circle so long occupying the old family mansion. It was for a long generation overlooked by death, and one passing in and out there thought of old-fashioned times, when parents and children grew up and passed maturity together, in lives of singular uneventfulness unmarked by sad or joyous crises. Very few in the village, except among the older inhabitants, knew Miss Emily personally, although the facts of her seclusion and intellectual brilliancy were familiar Amherst traditions. There are many houses among all classes into which treasures of fruit and flowers and ambrosial dishes for the sick and well were constantly sent, that will forever miss those evidences of her unselfish consideration, and mourn afresh that she screened herself from close acquaintance. As she passed on in life, her sensitive nature shrank from much personal contact with the world, and more and more turned to her own large wealth of individual resources for companionship, sitting thenceforth, as some one said of her, "in the light of her own fire." Not disappointed with the world, not an invalid until within the past two years, not from any lack of sympathy, not because she was insufficient for any mental work or social career—her endowments being so exceptional—but the "mesh of her soul," as Browning calls the body, was too rare, and the sacred quiet of her own home proved the fit atmosphere for her worth and work. All that must be inviolate. One can only speak of "duties beautifully done"; of her gentle tillage of the rare flowers filling her conservatory, into which, as into the heavenly Paradise, entered nothing that could defile, and which was ever abloom in frost or sunshine, so well she knew her chemistries; of her tenderness to all in the home circle; her gentlewoman's grace and courtesy to all who served in house and grounds; her quick and rich response to all who rejoiced or suffered at home, or among her wide circle of friends the world over. This side of her nature was to her the real entity in which she rested, so simple and strong was her instinct that a woman's hearthstone is her shrine. Her talk and her writings were like no one's else, and although she never published a line, now and then some enthusiastic literary friend would turn love to larceny, and cause a few verses surreptitiously obtained to be printed. Thus, and through other natural ways, many saw and admired her verses, and in consequence frequently notable persons paid her visits, hoping to overcome the protest of her own nature and gain a promise of occasional contributions, at least, to various magazines. She withstood even the fascinations of Mrs. Helen Jackson, who earnestly sought her co-operation in a novel of the No Name series, although one little poem somehow strayed into the volume of verse which appeared in that series. Her pages would ill have fitted even so attractive a story as "Mercy Philbrick's Choice," unwilling though a large part of the literary public were to believe that she had no part in it. "Her wagon was hitched to a star,"—and who could ride or write with such a voyager? A Damascus blade gleaming and glancing in the sun was her wit. Her swift poetic rapture was like the long glistening note of a bird one hears in the June woods at high noon, but can never see. Like a magician she caught the shadowy apparitions of her brain and tossed them in startling picturesqueness to her friends, who, charmed with their simplicity and homeliness as well as profundity, fretted that she had so easily made palpable the tantalizing fancies forever eluding their bungling, fettered grasp. So intimate and passionate was her love of Nature, she seemed herself a part of the high March sky, the summer day and bird-call. Keen and eclectic in her literary tastes, she sifted libraries to Shakespeare and Browning; quick as the lightning in her intuitions and analyses, she seized the kernel instantly, almost impatient of the fewest words, by which she must make her revelation. To her, life was rich and all aglow with God and immortality. With no creed, no formulated faith, hardly knowing the names of dogmas, she walked this life with the gentleness and reverence of old saints, with the firm step of martyrs who sing while they suffer. How better note the flight of this "soul of fire in a shell of pearl" than by her own words? —

> Morns like these, we parted;
> Noons like these, she rose;
> Fluttering first, then firmer,
> To her fair repose.

WALT WHITMAN (1819–1892)

by Robert Ingersoll (1892)

Walt Whitman was an American poet and essayist, best remembered for his landmark collection of poetry, Leaves of Grass. *Robert Ingersoll was a lawyer, politician, and noted agnostic, who was widely considered one of the greatest orators of his time. After sharing a lifelong friendship, Ingersoll delivered the following eulogy at Walt Whitman's funeral on March 30, 1892.*

MY FRIENDS: AGAIN we, in the mystery of Life, are brought face to face with the mystery of Death. A great man, a great American, the most eminent citizen of this Republic, lies dead before us, and we have met to pay a tribute to his greatness and his worth.

I know he needs no words of mine. His fame is secure. He laid the foundations of it deep in the human heart and brain. He was, above all I have known, the poet of humanity, of sympathy. He was so great that he rose above the greatest that he met without arrogance, and so great that he stooped to the lowest without conscious condescension. He never claimed to be lower or greater than any of the sons of men.

He came into our generation a free, untrammeled spirit, with sympathy for all. His arm was beneath the form of the sick. He sympathized with the imprisoned and despised, and even on the brow of crime he was great enough to place the kiss of human sympathy.

One of the greatest lines in our literature is his, and the line is great enough to do honor to the greatest genius that has ever lived. He said, speaking of an outcast: "Not till the sun excludes you do I exclude you."

His charity was wide as the sky, and wherever there was human suffering, human misfortune, the sympathy of Whitman bent above it as the firmament bends above the earth.

He was built on a broad and splendid plan—ample, without appearing to have limitations—passing easily for a brother of mountains and seas and constellations; caring nothing for the little maps and charts with which timid pilots hug the shore, but giving himself freely with recklessness of genius to winds and waves and tides; caring for nothing as long as the stars were above him. He walked among men, among writers, among verbal varnishers and veneerers, among literary milliners and tailors, with the unconscious majesty of an antique god.

He was the poet of that divine democracy which gives equal rights to all the sons and daughters of men. He uttered the great American voice; uttered a song worthy of the great Republic. No man ever said more for the rights of humanity, more in favor of real democracy, of real justice. He neither scorned nor cringed, was neither tyrant nor slave. He asked only to stand the equal of his fellows beneath the great flag of nature, the blue and stars.

He was the poet of Life. It was a joy simply to breathe. He loved the clouds; he enjoyed the breath of morning, the twilight, the wind, the winding streams. He loved to look at the sea when the waves burst into the whitecaps of joy. He loved the fields, the hills; he was acquainted with the trees, with birds, with all the beautiful objects of the earth. He not only saw these objects, but understood their meaning, and he used them that he might exhibit his heart to his fellow-men.

He was the poet of Love. He was not ashamed of that divine passion that has built every home in the world; that divine passion that has painted every picture and given us every real work of art; that divine passion that has made the world worth living in and has given some value to human life.

He was the poet of the natural, and taught men not to be ashamed of what is natural. He was not only the poet of democracy, not only the poet of the great Republic, but he was the poet of the human race. He was not confined to the limits of this country, but his sympathy went out over the seas to all the nations of the earth.

He stretched out his hand, and felt himself the equal of all kings and all princes, and the brother of all men, no matter how high, no matter how low.

He has uttered more supreme words than any writer of our century, possibly of almost any other. He was, above all things, a man, and above genius, above all the snow-capped peaks of intelligence, above all art, rises the true man. Greater than all is the true man, and he walked among his fellow-men as such.

He was the poet of Death. He accepted all life and all death, and he justified all. He had the courage to meet all, and was great enough and splendid enough to harmonize all and to accept all there is of life as a divine melody.

You know better than I what his life has been, but let me say one thing. Knowing, as he did, what others can know and what they cannot, he accepted and absorbed all theories, all creeds, all religions, and believed in none. His philosophy was a sky that embraced all clouds and accounted for all clouds. He had a philosophy and a religion of his own, broader, as he believed—as I believe—than others. He accepted all, he understood all, and he was above all.

He was absolutely true to himself. He had frankness and courage, and he was as candid as light. He was willing that all the sons of men should be absolutely acquainted with his heart and brain. He had nothing to conceal. Frank, candid, pure, serene, noble, and yet for years he was maligned and slandered, simply because he had the candor of nature. He will be understood yet, and that for which he was condemned—his frankness, his candor—will add to the glory and greatness of his fame.

He wrote a liturgy for mankind; he wrote a great and splendid psalm of life, and he gave to us the gospel of humanity—the greatest gospel that can be preached.

He was not afraid to live, not afraid to die. For many years he and death were near neighbors. He was always willing and ready to meet and greet this king called death, and for many months he sat in the deepening twilight waiting for the night, waiting for the light.

He never lost his hope. When the mists filled the valleys, he looked upon the mountain tops, and when the mountains in darkness disappeared, he fixed his gaze upon the stars.

In his brain were blessed memories of the day, and in his heart were mingled the dawn and dusk of life.

He was not afraid; he was cheerful every moment. The laughing nymphs of day did not desert him. They remained that they might clasp the hands and greet with smiles the veiled and silent sisters of the night. And when they did come, Walt Whitman stretched his hand to them. On one side were the nymphs of the day, and on the other the silent sisters of the night, and so, hand in hand, between smiles and tears, he reached his journey's end.

From the frontier of life, from the western wave-kissed shore, he sent us messages of content and hope, and these messages seem now like strains of music blown by the "Mystic Trumpeter" from Death's pale realm.

To-day we give back to Mother Nature, to her clasp and kiss, one of the bravest, sweetest souls that ever lived in human clay.

Charitable as the air and generous as Nature, he was negligent of all except to do and say what he believed he should do and say.

And I to-day thank him, not only for you but for myself, for all the brave words he has uttered. I thank him for all the great and splendid words he has said in favor of liberty, in favor of man and woman, in favor of motherhood, in favor of fathers, in favor of children, and I thank him for the brave words he has said of death.

He has lived, he has died, and death is less terrible than it was before. Thousands and millions will walk down into the "dark valley of the shadow" holding Walt Whitman by the hand. Long after we are dead the brave words he has spoken will sound like trumpets to the dying.

And so I lay this little wreath upon this great man's tomb. I loved him living, and I love him still.

CHARLES TIFFANY (1812–1902)

by Annabel Goan (1902)

Charles Tiffany was an American businessman, most noted for starting the iconic Tiffany & Co.® brand, and for creating the first retail catalog. The following eulogy was delivered by Annabel Goan, a longtime friend of Tiffany, at his memorial service at New York's Madison Square Presbyterian Church on February 20, 1902.

WHEN THE COMMUNITY loses a prominent man like Mr. Charles L. Tiffany, who died February 18, the world is interested in learning the causes of his success and what his influence has been upon his fellows. Few men have a strenuous business life of seventy years. Half that time is the usual length of a man's active connection with the business community, but Mr. Tiffany, from the time of the administration of President Jackson, was a potent factor in the commercial life of New York.

His great business was unique in its command of public confidence and in the harmony of its internal organization. The principle upon which he worked from the beginning to the end of his long career was "to give the public the best quality of goods and the finest service that could be secured." This was his unceasing endeavor. He established a standard in silverware that raised the quality of silver sold not only throughout the United States but in Europe also. He had an ideal for his business and he lived up to it. Absolute undeviating honesty, even in the smallest detail of the business, was the key note.

A lady traveling in Japan was questioning the Japanese Commissioner of Education about the integrity of a certain prominent Japanese merchant. "You can rely on his word," he answered, "as you can on that of the famous Mr. Tiffany of New York. You know his word is unquestioned the world over." That sort of a reputation is not made in a day or by simply having honest intentions and impulses, but by living up to one's conscientious standard every day and by having sufficient force to require others to do likewise.

Mr. Tiffany was a strict disciplinarian and, like other successful men, had a discriminating insight into human character and was an excellent judge of men and their capacity. His men were selected with care and retained for many years; they were as devoted and faithful a body of men as could be found anywhere. Their term of service ranged from fifty years down, over a hundred having been with him over a quarter of a century. This long term of service was also true of the domestics in his home.

There was a personal tie between Mr. Tiffany and his employees more binding than a merely business connection that sweetened life on both sides. They really cared for each other.

During those past months of his confinement, the tender attentions of these many men, more freely expressed than in the days of his robust health, were received by him with a lively appreciative gratitude. Among the numerous gifts sent to the sickroom was a basket of choice fruit marked "From the boys to our beloved chief." Long after the fruit was gone, he kept the basket and card where he could see them. That he had the love and esteem of the men who worked for him and with him every day and knew him better than any others could was a great comfort to him as he approached the closing days of his life.

None knew better than he how to show a delicate attention, and every little kindness extended to him received his personal acknowledgment. In these days of careless manners, Mr. Tiffany was conspicuous for the dignity of his bearing and his courtesy of the olden time, a happy reminder of that stately generation of fastidious men and women of which he was one of the few eminent examples left to us. He impressed a stranger as a man of cool reserve, but to those who were admitted to his friendship, he was a man of intense enthusiasm. To those who had his friendship, it will be a most cherished memory.

His influence over younger men was not toward luxurious living, as might be supposed, but toward a marked simplicity. He admired economy.

He had no scheme for the salvation of the human race, but his unconscious personal influence upon those who came within its range was tremendously helpful, stimulating one to do one's best.

It is a privilege to have known a man who was absolutely sincere; who failed not in fidelity to his largest and smallest duties; who had an unswerving sense of justice of man to man; who had lifted a business out of the usual sordidness until, by its successful organization, it was more like a social work of art with which men were proud to have their names identified and to which they were glad to give loving service.

Perhaps never again will this personal element so permeate a business house—the times have changed.

SUSAN B. ANTHONY (1820–1906)

by Rev. Anna Howard Shaw (1906)

Susan B. Anthony was an American social reformer, abo-
litionist, and political activist who served as president of the
National American Woman Suffrage Association. Although
she died almost 15 years before the 19th amendment gave
women the right to vote, she is widely credited for laying
the foundation of the movement for women's suffrage in
America. The following eulogy was delivered by Reverend
Anna Howard Shaw, a fellow leader of the women's suffrage
movement, and one of the first women to be ordained as a
Methodist minister in the United States.

YOUR FLAGS AT half-mast tell of a nation's loss, but there are no symbols and no words which can tell the love and sorrow which fill our hearts. And yet out of the depths of our grief arise feelings of truest gratitude for the beauty, the tenderness, the nobility of example, of our peerless leader's life. There is no death for such as she. There are no last words of love. The ages to come will revere her name. Unnumbered generations of the children of men shall rise up to call her blessed. Her words, her work, and her character will go on to brighten the pathway and bless the lives of all peoples. That which seems death to our unseeing eyes is to her translation. Her work will not be finished, nor will her last word be spoken while there remains a wrong to be righted, or a fettered life to be freed in all the earth.

You do well to strew her bier with palms of victory, and crown her with unfading laurel, for never did more victorious hero enter into rest.

Her character was well poised; she did not emphasize one characteristic to the exclusion of others; she taught us that the real beauty of a true life is found in the harmonious blending of diverse elements, and her life was the epitome of her teaching. She merged a keen sense of justice with the deepest love; her masterful intellect never for one moment checked the tenderness of her emotions; her splendid self-assertion found its highest realization in perfect self-surrender; she demonstrated the divine principle that the truest self-development must go hand in hand with the greatest and most arduous service for others.

Here was the most harmoniously developed character I have ever known—a living soul whose individuality was blended into oneness with all humanity. She lived, yet not she; humanity lived in her. Fighting the battle for individual freedom, she was so lost to the consciousness of her own personality that she was unconscious of existence apart from all mankind.

Her quenchless passion for her cause was that it was yours and mine, the cause of the whole world. She knew that where freedom is there is the center of power. In it she saw potentially all that humanity might attain when possessed by its spirit. Hence her cause, perfect equality of rights, of opportunity, of privilege for all, civil and political, was to her the bed-rock upon which all true progress must rest. Therefore she was nothing, her cause was everything; she knew no existence apart from it; in it she lived and moved and had her being. It was the first and last thought of each day; it was the last word upon her faultering lips; to it her flitting soul responded when the silenced voice could no longer obey the will, and she could only answer our heart-broken questions with the clasp of her trembling hand.

She was in the truest sense a reformer, unhindered in her service by the narrowness and negative destructiveness which often so sadly hampers the work of true reform. Possessed by an unfaltering conviction of the primary importance of her own cause, she nevertheless recognized that every effort by either one or many earnest souls toward what they believed to be a better or saner life should be met in a spirit of encouragement and helpfulness. She recognized that it was immeasurably more desirable to be honestly and earnestly seeking that which in its attainment might not prove good than to be hypocritically subservient to the truth through a spirit of selfish fear or fawning at the beck of power. She instinctively grasped the truth underlying all great movements which have helped the progress of the ages, and did not wait for an individual nor a cause to win popularity before freely extending to its struggling life a hand of helpful comradeship. She was never found in the cheering crowd that follows an already victorious standard. She left that to the time-servers who divide the spoil after they have crucified their Savior. She was truly great; great in her humility and utter lack of pretension.

On her eightieth birthday this noble soul could truthfully say in response to the words of loving appreciation from those who showered garlands all about her: "I am not accustomed to demonstrations of gratitude or of praise. I have ever been a hewer of wood and a drawer of water to this movement. I know nothing, I have known nothing of oratory or rhetoric. Whatever I have has been done because I wanted to see better conditions, better surroundings, better circumstances for women."

Speaking of her Lady Henry Somerset said: "She has the true sign of greatness in that she is absolutely without pretension. No woman of fame has ever so thoroughly made this impression of modesty and unselfishness upon my mind." This was the impression which she made upon all who knew her, and leaving her presence one would say, "How humble she is!" Viewing her life achievements, one exclaims, "How transcendently great she is!" No wonder she has won a name and fame worldwide and that she has turned the entire current of human conviction. One indeed wrote truly who said of her: "She has lived a thousand years if achievements can measure the length of life."

She whose name we honor, whose friendship we reverence, whose love we prize as a deathless treasure, would say this is not an hour for grief or despair—"If my life has achieved anything, if I have lived to any purpose, carry on the work I have to lay down."

In our last conversation, when her prophetic soul saw what we dare not even think, she said: "I leave my work to you and to the others who have been so faithful—promise that you will never let it go down or lessen our demands. There is so much to be done. Think of it! I have struggled for sixty years for a little bit of justice and die without securing it."

Oh, the unutterable cruelty of it! The time will come when at these words every American heart will feel the unspeakable shame and wrong of such a martyrdom.

She did not gain the little bit of freedom for herself, but there is scarcely a civilized land, not even our own, in which she has not been instrumental in securing for some woman that to which our leader did not attain. She did not reach the goal, but all along the weary years what marvellous achievements, what countless victories! The whole progress has been a triumphal march, marked by sorrow and hardship, but never by despair. The heart sometimes longed for sympathy and the way was long, and oh! so lonely; but every step was marked by some evidence of progress, some wrong righted, some right established.

We have followed her leadership until we stand upon the mount of vision where she to-day leaves us. The promised land lies just before us. It is for us to go forward and take possession. Without faltering, without a desertion from our ranks, without delaying even to mourn the loss of our departed leader, the faithful host is marching on. Already the call to advance is heard along the line, and one devoted young follower writes: "There are hundreds of us now, her followers, who will try to keep up the work she so nobly began and brought so nearly to completion. We will work the harder to try to compensate the world for her loss." Another writes: "I believe as you go forth to your labors you will find less opposition and far more encouragement than heretofore. The world is profoundly stirred by the loss of our great leader, and in consequence the lukewarm are becoming zealous, the prejudiced are disarming, the suffragists are renewing their vows of fidelity to the cause for which Miss Anthony lived and died. Her talismanic words, the last she ever uttered before a public audience, 'Failure is impossible,' should be inscribed on our banners and engraved on our hearts."

She has not only blessed us in the legacy of her life and work, but she has left us the dearest legacy of her love. The world knew Miss Anthony as the courageous, earnest, unfaltering champion of a great principle, and the friend of all reforms. Those of us who knew her best knew that she was all this and more; that she was one of the most home-making and home-loving of women. To her home her heart always turned with tenderest longing, and for the one who made home possible she felt the most devoted love and gratitude. She inscribed upon the first volume of her life history, "To my youngest sister, Mary, without whose faithful and constant home-making there could have been no freedom for the out-going of her grateful and affectionate sister."

To this home-making sister the affection of every loyal heart will turn, and we, her coworkers, will love and honor her, not alone for this devotion to her sister, but for her loyal comradeship and faithful service in our great cause. She is our legacy of love, and it will be the joy of every younger sister to bestow upon her the homage of our affection.

On the heights alone such souls meet God. In silent communion they learn life's sublimest lessons. They are the world's real heroes. Hers was an heroic life. By it she teaches us that the philosophy of the ancients is wrong; that it is not true that men are made heroic by indifference to life and death, but by learning to love something more than life. Her heroism was the heroism of an all-absorbing love, a love which neither indifference, nor persecution, nor misrepresentation, nor betrayal, nor hatred, nor flattery could quench; a heroism which would suffer her to see and to know nothing but the power of injustice and hatred to destroy, and the power of justice and love to develop, all that is best and noblest in human character. To such ends the causes which such souls espouse "Failure is impossible." Truly did Dean Thomas say in her address at our National Convention: "Of such as you were the lines of the poet Keats written—

> They shall be remembered forever,
> They shall be alive forever,
> They shall be speaking forever,
> The people shall hear them forever."

ANDREW CARNEGIE (1835–1919)

by John H. Finley (1920)

Andrew Carnegie was a Scottish-born American business-man and industrialist who is credited with leading the late-nineteenth-century expansion of the steel industry, in addition to being one of the nation's most prolific philan-thropists. The following address was delivered by New York State Education Commissioner John Huston Finley at a memorial service in Carnegie's honor on April 25, 1920.

HE WAS A weaver's lad—this boy bearing the name of the practical disciple, Andrew, who became the patron saint of Scotland. I say "practical," for it was Andrew who said when asked how the thousands on the shores of Galilee were to be fed: "There is a lad here which hath five barley loaves and two small fishes, but what are they among so many?" And had this disciple beheld, in the year of his Lord 1847, in the land to which he had become patron saint, the want and misery due to the stopping of the hand looms by the coming of steam machines, and had then seen this wee Dunfermline lad, he might have made much the same remark: "There's a lad here wi' his five senses and twa' sma' han's, but what are they amang sae mony?"

We say that it was a miracle that was performed on the shores of Galilee, when the boy's meagre store was suddenly multiplied to feed the thousands. Was it not as great a miracle that the seemingly petty store of the weaver's lad was transferred (in what is but a moment of time in His sight, to whom a thousand years are but as yester-day)—transformed not only into food, but books and music and pictures and other human blessings: and not for a few thousands only, but for millions?

In this miracle the Scotch lad had, to be sure, an active, aggressive, shrewd part, but it was no less a miracle, and it was one (and I say it in all reverence) that could not have been wrought even by the Almighty with the aid of this eager lad anywhere else than in the free air of America.

I suspect that my knowledge of chemistry is no greater than that of Lord Morley, whose observations about phosphorus in iron ore have just been read, but I am informed that there are mysterious substances known to chemists as "catalysts" which have such potency that they bring into solution elements before seemingly insoluble and yet are themselves apparently unchanged—substances often so infinitesimal in relation to the effects they produce that it is (according to one who was a teacher in a Carnegie laboratory) as if you were "to dissolve a whole island by throwing a few crystals upon it." So the catalytic, robust, sunny spirit of this youth, who never grew old, did incomparable, incommensurate things in the earth.

It was not merely nor chiefly that he touched the ore that was lying in the far hills beyond Superior, and transferred it from there into a girder, a bridge, a steel rail, a bit of armour plate, a beam for a sky-scraper, and in utter silence, as I have witnessed the process in the flaming sheds of Pittsburgh, with the calm pushing and pulling of a few levers, the accurate shovelling by a few hands and the deliberate testing by a few eyes—wonderful as that all was and is.

And it was not even that in every luminous, white-hot ingot swung in the steel mills in the smoky valley of the Youghiogheny there was something for the pension of a university professor, something for an artist in New York or Paris, something for an astronomer on a California mountain, something for the mathematician over his computations, something for the historian over his archives, something for the teacher in the school upon the hill above, something for every worshiper in hundreds of kirks and churches, something for every one of hundreds of thousands of readers in libraries from Scotland to California, as a result of the multiplication of the childish store in his hands as he stood an immigrant lad on the shores of America, with a "fair and free field" before him. For besides those there were gifts to millions more than were reached directly and indirectly by the steel ingots. These were gifts of the alchemy of his personality that touched the spirits and imaginations of men. The material gifts were like those of Prometheus who bestowed upon mortal man the

"bright glory
Of fire that all arts spring from."

His supreme gifts to mankind were, however, not those of a demigod, a Titan, working with the elements of the earth and looking down upon them as inferior creatures for whom he had made sacrifices. They were those of a very human, mortal man who loved his fellow-men, who suffered and fought and wept and rejoiced with them as one of them.

He, no doubt, would not wish me to trace the name Andrew, which his Scotch mother gave him, back to the Greek, but it was in its origin Greek nevertheless, the Greek name for "man," and he might have belonged to any age of men beginning with that of Moses or Pericles. He could have stood unembarrassed before any ruler from Pharaoh to Napoleon, and did so stand before the emperors, kings and presidents of his own day. Long before he became famous for his wealth, I have read, he was a personal friend of Gladstone, Matthew Arnold, Herbert Spencer, John Morley, and James Bryce. And, after he had become a world figure, he was still the friend of the lowliest and the poorest.

He was a triumphant democrat with a genius for friendships, as great as the genius in the field in which the word "genius" has been transmuted into the "engine" and the "engineer" with a passionate love for America, with an international mind having an orbit of concern for the cosmos (but with Dunfermline and Pittsburgh as its two foci) and with a love for all things beautiful, but with a preordained taste for that which had a Caledonian form or fragrance or melody in it; the "auld gray toon"; the abbey bell sounding the curfew; the scent of the heather; "songs possessed of souls caught from living lips"; the Scotch mist, even, which served to remind him "of the mysterious ways of Providence."

And yet he was not servile to his ancestry, the strain of whose thoughts had run through the "radical breasts" (a phrase he has himself used) of his parents. In his love for the voice of the organ, for example, he doubtless shocked many of his psalm-singing compatriots as did David when he danced before the ark of the Lord. And how pleased Mr. Carnegie would be with the program of this afternoon, dominated by music and crowned by an oratorio, of which he expressed such discerning appreciation in his delightful story of his travels in Great Britain, for he once said that those who thought music an unworthy intruder in the domain of sacred dogma "should remember that the Bible tells us that in Heaven music is the principal source of happiness—the sermon seems nowhere—and it may go hard with such as fail to give it the first place on earth."

He has unwittingly, no doubt, made the best characterization of himself in the definition of every Scotchman, who is "two Scotchmen":—

"As his land has the wild, barren, stern crags and mountain peaks around which the tempests blow, and also the smiling valleys below where the wild rose, the foxglove and the bluebell blossom, so the Scotchman, with his rugged and hard intellect in his head above, has a heart below capable of being touched to the finest issues. . . . Poetry and Song are a part of his nature. Touch his head and he will begin and argue with you to the last; touch his heart and he falls upon your breast."

These two men did not struggle against each other in the one energetic, restless body, but helped each other. The poet enhanced the deed (for as Mr. Carnegie said, "to do things is only one-half the battle; to be able to tell the world what you have done—that is the greater accomplishment"). And the hard-headed man put the poetry into everyday life, with an enchanting book, or the celestial voice of an organ, or an illuminating statistic, or an eternal truth for the first time discovered, or a telescope revealing the differing glory of the stars, or the stirring voice of the bagpipes making the day, or a symphony ending it.

The Scotch minister whom I heard preach this morning referred to a little shop in Edinburgh in whose window little figures of kings and queens and princes and others were displayed, with the sign (which has given title to one of Robert Louis Stevenson's essays), "A Penny Plain, Twopence Colored." Mr. Carnegie's figures were all colored—colored by his generous, warm heart.

The two Scotchmen in him were held together in happy partnership by an American tolerance, a New World breadth of generosity (which is not usually associated with the Scotch) and a Western humor which had, however, a tang of the moors in it, and was over-conscious of the ethics of the golf links. I have a vivid memory of one characteristic bit of his kindly, quiet wit at my own expense. We had played a few holes in my first game of golf with him, when my conscience, beginning to trouble me, provoked me to question whether I ought to be out in the country away from my work playing golf with him. "Oh," he said, quick as a flash, "Pritchett and I will both certify that you are not playing golf."

And when we played our last game together, it was out by the Dornoch Firth, in the first days of the Great War in August of 1914. After he had finished the game, which he must have divined would be the last, he gave me his putter with this inscription in his own hand: "A very close game: couldn't have been closer so equally and badly we play."

Ah! If we could all but play the game of life as manfully and cheerfully, as eagerly, as fearlessly, as hopefully, and with as kind a heart as he, we might be proud of our score, even though he, a Scotchman, would go no farther than to admit of his own "it micht ha' bin waur."

★ ★ ★

Beyond the dark Brook of the Shadow he's gone
On over the hills and the moors toward the dawn,
This Laird o' the castle by Dornoch's gray Firth
To find the Great Peace he had sought for the earth.

ALBERT EINSTEIN (1879–1955)

by Ernst Straus (1955)

Albert Einstein was a German-born physicist who is widely considered to be one of the most influential scientists of the twentieth century. Best remembered for his theories of general and special relativity, Einstein won the Nobel Prize in Physics in 1921 for his explanation of the photoelectric event. The following eulogy was delivered by German-American mathematician Ernst Straus, who was Albert Einstein's former assistant and longtime friend.

WHEN I WAS told of this memorial, I was informed that we were to divide his memory into that of Einstein the man, the scientist, the humanitarian, and the Jew. This is in a sense an impossible task, for he was a man of a single mold and there was no dividing line between his various aspects. I shall try therefore to tell you of the Einstein in his daily association rather than the public figure manifest in his discoveries, his thoughts and actions. It is fortunate that over the years I jotted down some of his remarks that seemed significant or characteristic, so that where my words would be feeble I'll be able to speak with his.

Einstein often referred to himself as a lonely man—he would call it that loneliness that is so hard on the young, but so sweet to the old—and in a sense that is true. He always preserved a certain emotional detachment, yet even if he was not deeply involved, he had a genuine liking and respect for people. Often on our way to work someone would waylay him, tell him how much he had looked forward to meeting the great Einstein. Einstein would pose with the waylayer's wife, children, or grandchildren as desired and exchange a few good-natured words. Then he would go on shaking his head, saying, "Well, the old elephant has gone through his tricks again."

He was very fond of small children and animals. With children he would go through various tricks, making funny noises with his hands and wiggling his ears. In fact, his ability to wiggle his ears was the only accomplishment of which he would boast shamelessly and which he was quite eager to show off.

Tiger, his old tomcat, was mainly the pet of the ladies of the house, but in an emergency he would come to the master. Whenever it rained he would complain bitterly. Einstein would be quite apologetic; he'd say, "I know what's wrong, my dear, but I really don't know how to turn it off."

Our own cat would make it a habit to walk over to the institute and cry under our office window until we let her in. Or if we proved hard-hearted, she would wait at the front door, slip in with the first comer, and then scratch at our office door for admission. Then she would sit perfectly quietly on the chalk tray or the bookcase and watch us work. Einstein grew quite fond of her, and later most of his letters to us in California would end with "regards to your dear cat." When the cat had kittens, he was quite eager to see them and came home with us in a detour on his walk home. He was dismayed when he saw that our neighbors were all people from the institute and said, "Let's walk quickly. There are so many people here whose invitations I've declined. I hope they don't find out that I came to visit your kittens."

While he hated all competitive games, he loved little puzzles of all kinds and was very fond of gadgets—not the kind that reduce the labor in some chore by thirty seconds but the kind that are based on some clever design. Once we were at his house for dinner when he had just received a little mechanical bird that would dip into a glass of water and keep this up as long as its head stayed moist. He watched it delightedly all through dinner and stroked its head gently to start it off again. When we saw him last, another bird—one that walked up walls on suction-cup feet—had just become popular, and my wife said, "I'll bet Einstein has one." Sure enough, after dinner he said, "I have a treat for you." First he brought a big umbrella, then he wound up the bird and started it up the wall. Then he opened the umbrella upside down "so it won't fall so hard," and caught it gently as the suction gave out.

Let us now speak of Einstein the enthusiastic, indefatigable seeker, thinker, and worker. Among my notes I find the following quotes:

"Two things are needed for our kind of work: One is indefatigable persistence; the other is the ability to discard something in which one has invested great labor and many ideas."

"God is inexorable in the way in which he has distributed his gifts. To me he has given the stubbornness of a mule and nothing else—on second thought he has also given me intuition."

"When we think for ourselves but not for publication, we dismount from our logical steed and sniff the ground. Afterward we cover our tracks in order to enhance our godlike stature."

I might mention here a good anecdote he told about himself. We were looking for a paper clip for a manuscript and finally found one too badly bent to be usable, so we looked for a tool to straighten it. In doing so we found a drawer full of perfectly good paper clips, and Einstein was just about to bend one out of shape when I asked him what he was doing. "If you hadn't been here, I should certainly have ruined this clip in order to straighten the bent one. This always happens to me when I get stuck on a problem."

I cannot recall a single moment that Einstein was not thinking about some great problem that he had posed for himself; even when he was talking with people or engaged in another activity, part of his mind would always stay on the task.

The first theory on which we worked when I came to be his assistant he had worked on alone for over a year, and we continued working on it for about nine months more. Then one evening I found a class of solutions to the field equations which in the light of the next morning seemed to show that the theory could not have physical significance. We turned it over and over all morning but the conclusion was inevitable. So we left for home one half hour early. I must say that I was quite dejected. If the pick-and-shovel man feels so badly about the collapse of his edifice, how badly must the architect feel! But when I came to work the next morning, Einstein was eager and excited: "You know, I've been thinking last night, and the proper approach seems to be . . ." This was the start of an entirely new theory, also relegated to the trash heap after half a year's work and mourned no longer than its predecessor.

He would allow himself some wry remarks on the failure of a theory, such as: "It is already a success if you can force nature to stick out its tongue at you." "In this nature is truly satanic—that she makes one think one is on the way to the greatest triumph when one has gone completely astray." "Mathematics is the only perfect method to lead yourself around by the nose."

The last theory on which we worked was his last. He knew this, saying, "If nothing comes of this theory, then I will not find the right one, for I am too old for a fundamentally new idea." However, he had great and growing confidence in his theory. Often when he noted a satisfactory feature he would exult: "This is so simple God could not have passed it up." The fact that the mathematical difficulties were tremendous did not surprise him. "The further we advance, the simpler logically and the more complicated mathematically things become. We are like children who have found a giant hammer. They can't even lift it." His greatest sorrow was that, as he would say, "I'll have to bite the dust before finding out whether this theory is the right one." I do not believe that he ever seriously entertained the thought that there might be no such perfect theory as the one he was seeking. . . .

It may be appropriate here to say a few words about Einstein the political figure. He had been described as naive, a babe in the woods of politics, by those who disagree with his views, and as a social and political thinker of a stature that rivals his stature as a scientist by those who agree. Neither of these extremes would be his own appraisal. He kept himself very well informed on political issues and brought the same lucid and dispassionate mind, the same courage and forthright-ness to bear on them. Yet he did not have the same sense of involvement and feeling of destiny that he had in his scientific thinking. He would speak out courageously to prevent a wrong or to promote a right, but he did not often express himself publicly on the laws that govern social and political life.

Once after a meeting of his Committee of Atomic Scientists, he said, "Thus one is forced to divide one's time between politics and our equations, but these equations are ever so much more important. Political problems are problems of the moment but such an equation is a matter for eternity." He would often express his regret about his role in bringing the atomic bomb to the world. That is, he regretted the fact that an overestimate of Germany's atomic research had prompted his letter to President Roosevelt. I never heard him express regret about the role his scientific discoveries had played.

Einstein did not like to shock people. On many occasions when he did, he did so unintentionally because he simply did not expect their emotions. He told me that when he was a little boy in Munich he was taken to see a parade of the Royal Guards in their splendid uniforms. He cried bitterly because he felt so sorry for those poor people who were made to strut about in this ridiculous fashion and in those silly outfits. He had since learned that some people like to march, but in his heart he never believed it. As he would put it: "Often evidence convicts you of the validity of a statement but it doesn't convince you." In a similar vein he would never be convinced that Americans really enjoy the ownership of all those shiny cars and household appliances. He felt that they were foisted on people in order to keep the economy going, diverting them from what they would really like to do—such as play music or hike in the woods.

He liked to stand alone on his own two feet and never lean on anyone or anything, nor did he have much sympathy for the feelings of those who needed something to lean on. "Nothing is so hateful to me as to belong in any group, be it a nation or a party, an academy or an institute. One always has the responsibility for actions on which one has no influence. My only refuge is not to take it too seriously."

This same feeling of independence made any plea of a personal god or an immortal soul quite unacceptable to him. When he was invited to speak on his faith at an anniversary of the Jewish Theological Seminary of New York, he said this, and was quite bewildered by the result: "Never did I get so much mail, and such vituperations! What concern is it of theirs what I believe?" After this he would reply to public questions concerning his faith that his god was the god of Spinoza, who manifests himself in the order of his universe only.

As a matter of fact, this did not give a completely accurate picture of his faith, for he judged the order of the universe to be a matter of logical simplicity alone and not a creation of any being, personal or otherwise. This is the way he put it: "What really interests me is whether God had any choice in the creation of the world; that is to say, whether the demand of logical simplicity leaves any alternative. One must admit after all that this logical simplicity determines the universe far more precisely than one would have thought fifty years ago." I think that in this remark he expressed both the fundamental goal of his scientific work and his estimate of his success.

Let me close with this thought and challenge that was so typical of him: "Greatness in the world of ideas is basically a question of character. The main thing is never compromise."

JOHN F. KENNEDY (1917–1963)

by Mike Mansfield, Earl Warren, and John W. McCormack (1963)

John F. Kennedy served as the 35th President of the United States, during which time he presided over a number of foreign crises, including the Cuban Missile Crisis and the Bay of Pigs Invasion. Credited for achievements such as the Nuclear Test-Ban Treaty, the Alliance for Progress, and the furthering of the Space Race, Kennedy was assassinated on November 22, 1963. The following eulogies were delivered at the Rotunda of the United States Capitol by Mike Mansfield, Majority Leader of the United States Senate; Earl Warren, Chief Justice of the United States Supreme Court; and John W. McCormack, Speaker of the House of Representatives.

MIKE MANSFIELD, Majority Leader of the United States Senate

THERE WAS A sound of laughter; in a moment, it was no more. And so she took a ring from her finger and placed it in his hands.

There was a wit in a man neither young nor old, but a wit full of an old man's wisdom and of a child's wisdom, and then, in a moment it was no more. And so she took a ring from her finger and placed it in his hands.

There was a man marked with the scars of his love of country, a body active with the surge of a life far, far from spent and, in a moment, it was no more. And so she took a ring from her finger and placed it in his hands.

There was a father with a little boy, a little girl and a joy of each in the other. In a moment it was no more, and so she took a ring from her finger and placed it in his hands.

There was a husband who asked much and gave much, and out of the giving and the asking wove with a woman what could not be broken in life, and in a moment it was no more. And so she took a ring from her finger and placed it in his hands, and kissed him and closed the lid of a coffin.

A piece of each of us died at that moment. Yet, in death he gave of himself to us. He gave us of a good heart from which the laughter came. He gave us of a profound wit, from which a great leadership emerged. He gave us of a kindness and a strength fused into a human courage to seek peace without fear.

He gave us of his love that we, too, in turn, might give. He gave that we might give of ourselves, that we might give to one another until there would be no room, no room at all, for the bigotry, the hatred, prejudice, and the arrogance which converged in that moment of horror to strike him down.

In leaving us these gifts, John Fitzgerald Kennedy, President of the United States, leaves with us. Will we take them, Mr. President? Will we have, now, the sense and the responsibility and the courage to take them?

I pray to God that we shall and under God we will.

EARL WARREN, Chief Justice of the United States

THERE ARE FEW events in our national life that unite Americans and so touch the hearts of all of us as the passing of a President of the United States.

There is nothing that adds shock to our sadness as the assassination of our leader, chosen as he is to embody the ideals of our people, the faith we have in our institutions and our belief in the fatherhood of god and the brotherhood of man.

Such misfortunes have befallen the Nation on other occasions, but never more shockingly than 2 days ago.

We are saddened; we are stunned; we are perplexed.

John Fitzgerald Kennedy, a great and good President, the friend of all men of good will, a believer in the dignity and equality of all human beings, a fighter for justice, an apostle of peace, has been snatched from our midst by the bullet of an assassin.

What moved some misguided wretch to do this horrible deed may never be known to us, but we do know that such acts are commonly stimulated by forces of hatred and malevolence, such as today are eating their way into the bloodstream of American life. What a price we pay for this fanaticism.

It has been said that the only thing we learn from history is that we do not learn. But surely we can learn if we have the will to do so. Surely there is a lesson to be learned from this tragic event.

If we really love this country, if we truly love justice and mercy, if we fervently want to make this Nation better for those who are to follow us, we can at least abjure the hatred that consumes people, the false accusations that divide us, and the bitterness that begets violence. Is it too much to hope that the martyrdom of our beloved President might even soften the hearts of those who would themselves recoil from assassination, but who do not shrink from spreading the venom which kindles thoughts of it in others?

Our Nation is bereaved. The whole world is poorer because of his loss. But we can all be better Americans because John Fitzgerald Kennedy has passed our way, because he has been our chosen leader at a time in history when his character, his vision, and his quiet courage have enabled him to chart for us a safe course through the shoals of treacherous seas that encompass the world.

And now that he is relieved of the almost superhuman burdens we imposed on him, may he rest in peace.

JOHN W. McCORMACK, Speaker of the House of Representatives

As WE GATHER here today bowed in grief, the heartfelt sympathy of Members of the Congress and of our people are extended to Mrs. Jacqueline Kennedy and to Ambassador and Mrs. Joseph P. Kennedy and their loved ones. Their deep grief is also self-shared by countless millions of persons throughout the world, considered a personal tragedy, as if one had lost a loved member of his own immediate family.

Any citizen of our beloved country who looks back over its history cannot fail to see that we have been blessed with God's favor beyond most other peoples. At each great crisis in our history we have found a leader able to grasp the helm of state and guide the country through the troubles which beset it. In our earliest days, when our strength and wealth were so limited and our problems so great, Washington and Jefferson appeared to lead our people. Two generations later, when our country was torn in two by a fratricidal war, Abraham Lincoln appeared from the mass of the people as a leader able to reunite the Nation.

In more recent times, in the critical days of the depression and the great war forced upon us by Fascist aggression, Franklin Delano Roosevelt—later, Harry S. Truman—appeared on the scene to reorganize the country and lead its revived citizens to victory. Finally, only recently, when the cold war was building up the supreme crisis of a threatened nuclear war capable of destroying everything—and everybody—that our predecessors had so carefully built, and which a liberty-loving world wanted, once again a strong and courageous man appeared ready to lead us.

No country need despair so long as God, in His infinite goodness, continues to provide the Nation with leaders able to guide it through the successive crises which seem to be the inevitable fate of any great nation.

Surely no country ever faced more gigantic problems than ours in the last few years, and surely no country could have obtained a more able leader in a time of such crises. President John Fitzgerald Kennedy possessed all the qualities of greatness. He had deep faith, complete confidence, human sympathy, and broad vision which recognized the true values of freedom, equality, and the brotherhood which have always been the marks of the American political dreams.

He had the bravery and a sense of personal duty which made him willing to face up to the great task of being President in these trying times. He had the warmth and the sense of humanity which made the burden of the task bearable for himself and for his associates, and which made all kinds of diverse peoples and races eager to be associated with him in his task. He had the tenacity and determination to carry each stage of his great work through to its successful conclusion.

Now that our great leader has been taken from us in a cruel death, we are bound to feel shattered and helpless in the face of our loss. This is but natural, but as the first bitter pangs of our incredulous grief begins to pass we must thank God that we were privileged, however briefly, to have had this great man for our President. For he has now taken his place among the great figures of world history.

While this is an occasion of deep sorrow it should be also one of dedication. We must have the determination to unite and carry on the spirit of John Fitzgerald Kennedy for a strengthened America and a future world of peace.

T. S. ELIOT (1888–1965)

by Sir Rupert Hart-Davis (1965)

*T. S. Eliot was an American-born English poet, playwright,
publisher, and critic. A leader of the modernist movement,
Eliot's seminal work* The Waste Land *is generally regarded
as one of the most influential poems of the twentieth century.
The following address was delivered at a memorial service
on September 26, 1965, which would have been Eliot's
seventy-seventh birthday, by the notable publisher Sir Rupert
Hart-Davis, a close friend and colleague of Eliot.*

I DO NOT propose to say much about his works. His poems, his plays,
and his essays are all in print and can be got from any bookshop or
library. There are at least two excellent long-playing records of him
reading his own poems, so that you can hear his voice. Many books
have been written about him and many more will be written in the
future.

But it is not of the great poet and critic that I want to talk to you,
but of the man who wrote those poems and that criticism, the warm,
affectionate human being whom his many friends loved and will
forever mourn. . . .

In appearance he was the opposite of the romantic idea of what a
poet should look like, as exemplified by his lifelong friend Ezra
Pound. No long hair, Byronic collars, or unusual clothes for him.
He was always neatly and inconspicuously dressed—elegantly, and
always suitably, for he had a great sense of fittingness and tradition—
his lined face usually grave, almost solemn, but in private, laughter
kept breaking through. When you were with him you knew for
certain that he was a great man, even though you might not be able
to explain exactly why. I suspect that it had something to do with

his obvious goodness. A younger poet, W. H. Auden, wrote of him after his death: "To me the proof of a man's goodness is the effect he has upon others. So long as one was in Eliot's presence, one felt it was impossible to say or do anything base."

That remark is completely true, but to someone who did not know Eliot it might suggest a rather priggish or forbidding person, a spoil-sport, whereas in fact he was one of the most amusing and entertaining companions you could imagine. He had a lovely sense of fun. He loved jokes of all kinds—in his younger days, even practical jokes—and was a superb teller of amusing stories, which were made all the funnier by his precise diction and deadpan expression.

He had a great love of cats, as you can see if you read his delightful book of light poems about them, *Old Possum's Book of Practical Cats*. Later he became very fond of Yorkshire terriers. One day when he was being driven somewhere, he and the chauffeur passed the time by discussing the merits of their respective dogs. Eventually the chauffeur thought that perhaps he had overpraised his own dog, and said, "But, sir, he isn't really what you'd call a consequential dog." Eliot always said that he must write *A Book of Consequential Dogs*, but alas, he never did. . . .

He was also humble, in a way that perhaps only the great can be humble. In "East Coker" he wrote:

> *The only wisdom we can hope to acquire*
> *Is the wisdom of humility: humility is endless.*

And he lived up to this belief. He could, and did, talk about himself, his past life, and his achievements with complete simplicity and humility, as though it had all happened to someone else.

He was mild and gentle, courteous and polite, but he could quickly be roused to passionate indignation and speech by injustice or bad manners. Once, when he had agreed to give evidence in a court of law on behalf of the London Library, he was so apprehensive that he couldn't sleep the night before, and began his evidence quietly and with hesitation. Then, luckily, one of the opposing counsel made a remark to which he took exception. His eyes flashed, and he spoke with vehemence and passion, until finally he had almost to be dragged from the witness box.

I knew him best during the last eight years of his life, the years of his blessed second marriage. Until then his personal life had been for the most part lonely and unhappy. And then, as he approached old age, he found the perfect peace, understanding, companionship, and happiness which he had despaired of ever knowing. Just to see him and his wife together, holding hands simply in a roomful of people, was a moving and heartening sight. He expressed some of his feelings in the beautiful poem called "A Dedication to My Wife," which is printed at the end of the latest edition of his *Collected Poems*. It is the only one of his poems that is wholly composed of love and joy and gratitude. For several years before his death the doctors had given him up, and they could explain his survival only by his immense will to live. And he wanted to live because he was so happy. . . .

. . . However ill or disinclined he might be feeling, he insisted on appearing or speaking or writing on behalf of causes or institutions in which he believed. The London Library was one of these, and there were many others. Once in America, when he had read some poems at a party for such a cause, and signed all the copies of his books that were brought up to him, his admirers would not be satisfied until he had autographed the labels on all the empty wine bottles, which the exhausted poet obligingly did.

In small matters, as in great, his kindness was absolute. He discovered that I enjoyed smoking corncob pipes, and told me that the best ones in the world were made in his birthplace, St. Louis. He promised to bring me some next time he went there, and this promise he fulfilled, not once but three times, carrying these tiresomely fragile parcels half across the world and triumphantly handing them over.

The last words of the poem "East Coker" are "In my end is my beginning." Now the end and the beginning are one, and as you pass this tablet on the wall, say a prayer, by all means, for the great poet it commemorates, but, above all, say a prayer for the great and good man whom we remember today, on his birthday, with joy, with gratitude, and with love.

MARTIN LUTHER KING JR. (1929–1968)

by Benjamin E. Mays (1968)

> *Martin Luther King Jr. was a Baptist minister, social activist, and leader of the American Civil Rights Movement. One of the most influential figures in American history, King played a pivotal role in putting an end to legal segregation, as well as the passing of the Civil Rights Act of 1964 and the Voting Rights Act of 1965. The following eulogy was delivered by fellow activist and minister Benjamin E. Mays at a memorial service at Morehouse College in Atlanta on April 9, 1968.*

TO BE HONORED by being requested to give the eulogy at the funeral of Dr. Martin Luther King Jr. is like asking one to eulogize his deceased son, so close and so precious was he to me. Our friendship goes back to his student days here at Morehouse. It is not an easy task. Nevertheless, I accept it with a sad heart and with full knowledge of my inadequacy to do justice to this good man. It was my desire that if I predeceased Dr. King, he would pay tribute to me on my final day. It was his wish that if he predeceased me, I would deliver the homily at *his* funeral. Fate has decreed that I eulogize him. I wish it might have been otherwise, for after all. I am three score years and ten, and Martin Luther is dead at thirty-nine. How strange.

God called the grandson of a slave on his father's side, and the grandson of a man born during the Civil War on his mother's side, and said to him, "Martin Luther, speak to America about war and peace. Speak to America about social justice and racial discrimination. Speak to America about its obligation to the poor. And speak to America about nonviolence."

Let it be thoroughly understood that our deceased brother did not embrace nonviolence out of fear or cowardice. Moral courage was one of his noblest virtues. As Mahatma Gandhi challenged the British Empire without a sword and won, Martin Luther King Jr. challenged the interracial injustice of his country without a gun. And he had faith to believe that he would win the battle for social justice. I make bold to assert that it took more courage for Martin Luther to practice nonviolence than it took his assassin to fire the fatal shot. The assassin is a coward. He committed his dastardly deed and fled. When Martin Luther disobeyed an unjust law, he accepted the consequences of his actions. He never ran away and he never begged for mercy. He returned to Birmingham jail to serve his time.

Perhaps he was more courageous than soldiers who fight and die on the battlefield. There is an element of compulsion in their dying. But when Martin Luther faced death, again and again, and finally embraced it, there was no external pressure. He was acting on an inner urge that drove him on. More courageous than those who advocate violence as a way out, for they carry weapons of destruction for defense. But Martin Luther faced the dogs, the police, jail, heavy criticism, and finally death. And he never carried a gun, not even a pocketknife to defend himself. He had only his faith in a just God to rely on, and his belief that "thrice is he armed who has his quarrels just." The faith that Browning writes about when he says:

> One who never turned his back but marched abreast forward,
> Never doubted the clouds would break,
> Never dreamed, though right were worsted, wrong would triumph,
> Held we fall to rise, are baffled to fight better,
> Sleep to wake.

Coupled with moral courage was Martin Luther King Jr.'s capacity to love people. Though deeply committed to a program of freedom for Negroes, he had a love and concern for all kinds of people. He drew no distinction between the high and the low. None between the rich and the poor. He believed, especially, that he was sent to champion the cause of the man farthest down. He would probably say, "If death had to come, I am sure there was no greater cause to die for than fighting to get a just wage for garbage collectors." This man was supra-race, supra-nation, supra-denomination, supra-class, and supra-culture. He belonged to the world and to mankind. Now he belongs to posterity.

But there is a dichotomy in all this. This man was loved by some and hated by others. If any man knew the meaning of suffering, King knew. House bombed. Living day-by-day for thirteen years under constant threats of death. Maliciously accused of being a communist. Falsely accused of being insincere and seeking limelight for his own glory. Stabbed by a member of his own race. Slugged in a hotel lobby. Jailed thirty times. Occasionally deeply hurt because his friends betrayed him. And yet this man had no bitterness in his heart, no rancor in his soul, no revenge in his mind. And he went up and down the length and breadth of this world preaching nonviolence and the redemptive power of love.

He believed in all of his heart, mind, and soul that the way to peace and brotherhood is through nonviolence, love, and suffering. He was severely criticized for his opposition to the war in Vietnam. It must be said, however, that one could hardly expect a prophet of King's commitment to advocate nonviolence at home and violence in Vietnam. Nonviolence to King was total commitment, not only in solving the problems of race in the United States but in solving the problems of the world.

Surely, surely this man was called of God to his work. If Amos and Micah were prophets in the eighth century B.C., Martin Luther King Jr. was a prophet in the twentieth century. If Isaiah was called of God to prophesy in his day, Martin Luther was called of God to prophesy in his day. If Hosea was sent to preach love and forgiveness centuries ago, Martin Luther was sent to expound the doctrine of nonviolence and forgiveness in the third quarter of the twentieth century. If Jesus was called to preach the Gospel to the poor, Martin Luther was called to bring dignity to the common man. If a prophet is one who interprets in clear and intelligible language the will of God, Martin Luther King Jr. fits that designation. If a prophet is one who does not seek popular causes to espouse, but rather the causes which he thinks are right, Martin Luther qualifies on that score.

No, he was not ahead of his time. No man is ahead of his time. Every man is within his star. Each man must respond to the call of God in his lifetime and not somebody else's time. Jesus had to respond to the call of God in the first century A.D., and not in the twentieth century. He had but one life to live. Jesus couldn't wait. How long do you think Jesus would have had to wait for the constituted authorities to accept him? Twenty-five years? A hundred years? A thousand? Never? He died at thirty-three. He couldn't wait.

Paul, Copernicus, Martin Luther the Protestant reformer, Gandhi, and Nehru couldn't wait for another time. They had to act in their lifetime. No man is ahead of his time. Abraham, leaving his country in obedience to God's call. Moses leading a rebellious people to the Promised Land. Jesus dying on a cross. Galileo on his knees recanting at seventy. Lincoln dying of an assassin's bullet. Woodrow Wilson crusading for a League of Nations. Martin Luther King Jr. fighting for justice for garbage collectors. None of these men were ahead of their time. With them, the time is always ripe to do that which is right [*Amen*] and that which needs to be done. [*That's right*]

Too bad, you say, Martin Luther Jr. died so young. I feel that way too. But as I have said many times before, it isn't how long one lives, but how well. Jesus died at thirty-three. Joan of Arc at nineteen. Byron and Burns at thirty-six. Keats and Marlowe at twenty-nine. And Shelley at thirty. Dunbar before thirty-five. John Fitzgerald Kennedy at forty-six. [*Yes*] William Rainey Harper at forty-nine. And Martin Luther King Jr. at thirty-nine. It isn't how long, but how well.

We all pray that the assassin will be apprehended and brought to justice. But make no mistake, the American people are, in part, responsible for Martin Luther King's death. [*That's right*] The assassin heard enough condemnation of King and Negroes to feel that he had public support. [*Tell it, yes sir*] He, he knew that there were millions of people in the United States who wished that King was dead. [*That's right*] He had support. [*Yes sir*]

The Memphis officials must bear some of the guilt for Martin Luther King's assassination. [*Yes sir, applause*] The strike should have been settled [*Yes sir*] several weeks ago. [*Yes*] The lowest-paid men in our society should not have to strike to get a decent wage. A century after Emancipation [*Speak, sir*], and after the enactment of the Thirteenth, Fourteenth, and Fifteenth Amendments [*Yes sir*], it should not have been necessary for Martin Luther King Jr. to stage marches in Montgomery, Birmingham, [*Yeah*] Selma, and go to jail thirty times, trying to achieve for his people those rights which people of lighter hue get by virtue of the fact that they are born white. [*Yes sir*]

We, too, are guilty of murder. [*Speak, sir*] It is a time for the American people to repent and make democracy equally, equally applicable to all Americans. What can we do? We and not the assassin, we and not the prejudiced, we and not the apostles of hate, we represent, here today, America at its best. [*All right*] We have the power to make democracy function so that Martin Luther King and his kind will not have to march.

What can we do? If we love Martin Luther King, and respect him, as this crowd surely testifies, let us see to it that he did not die in vain. [*Yes sir, amen,* applause] Let us see to it that we do not dishonor his name by trying to solve our problems through rioting in the streets. [*Amen*] Violence was foreign to his nature. [*Yes sir, that's right*] He warned that continued riots could produce a fascist state. But let us see to it, also, that the conditions that cause riots are promptly removed, as the president of the United States is trying to get us to do. Let black and white alike search their hearts. And if there be any prejudice in our hearts against any racial or ethnic group, let us exterminate it, and let us pray, as Martin Luther would pray if he could, "Father, forgive them, for they know not what they do." [*Amen, preach it*]

If we do this, Martin Luther King Jr. will have died a redemptive death for which all mankind will benefit. Morehouse will never be the same because Martin Luther came by here. And the nation and the world will be indebted to him for centuries to come. It is natural, therefore, that we here at Morehouse, and Doctor Gloster, would want to memorialize him to serve as an inspiration to all students who study in this center. I close by saying to you what Martin Luther King Jr. believed. If physical death was the price he had to pay to rid America of prejudice and injustice, nothing could be more redemptive. And, to paraphrase the words of the immortal John Fitzgerald Kennedy, permit me to say that Martin Luther King Jr.'s unfinished work on earth must truly be our own. [*Amen,* applause]

W. H. AUDEN (1907–1973)

by Stephen Spender (1974)

W. H. Auden was a Pulitzer Prize–winning British poet, widely considered one of the twentieth century's most influential literary figures. Stephen Spender, Auden's close friend and contemporary, was an English poet and novelist who was appointed the 17th Poet Laureate Consultant in Poetry to the United States Library of Congress. Spender delivered the following remembrance on October 2, 1974, when Auden's name was added to the famous Poets' Corner in Westminster Abbey.

WYSTAN HUGH AUDEN is received within these walls, *in diesen heiligen Hallen.* I am sure that to him this ceremony would seem Mozartian: like being transported into the music of *The Magic Flute,* of which he and his friend Chester Kallmann wrote their version of the libretto. . . .

As both man and poet, for him this would seem homecoming: or perhaps I should say going home. For Auden, like Herman Melville, whom he so much admired, was one of those who arrive home by a circuitous route. As a citizen, he considered himself a New Yorker; as a colleague, his first and last home was Oxford: in early days among his fellow poets, Louis MacNeice, Cecil Day-Lewis, Rex Warner, and Sir John Betjeman, and towards the end of his life at the high table of Christ Church, his old college. As a poet whose first love, even before poetry, was music, the village of Kirchstetten near the Vienna of great composers was home. He is buried in Kirchstetten and another monument bears his name. But all these homes return to the England of the limestone Northern landscape of his childhood

171

in the green and river-running countryside, which he always regarded as the Garden of Eden.

And his first and last home was the Church of England. He would feel the utmost fulfillment is being received within these sacred walls, the body of the English Church, for his religion was to him more important even than poetry or music. However, it is as a poet that his name is spelled out in the Poets' Corner, here in the centre of London, where the stones and skies are mostly grey and where the pigeons outside are like grey stones flying between grey walls. I mention birds designedly because Auden's feelings about home are made particularly vivid for me by an anecdote recorded by his friend Dr. Oliver Sacks, who recalls being with him in New York:

Once we saw a bird fly to its nest atop a sooty lamp-post in St. Mark's Place: "Look!" exclaimed Wystan, "It's gone home to its nest. Think how cozy it must be in its nest!"

This anecdote brings Wystan idly to me. I see him turning to his companion with that clarifying entertained sideways glance which would accompany such a very exposed comment: "just think of him flying to his nest!"

And if the recollection glashes to you a somewhat grotesque vision of Auden appearing in the precincts of Westminster or Trafalgar Square in the likeness of a somewhat bulky pigeon, flying not with-out difficulty and perching on a lamp-post, that is just as it should be: with him the grotesque or absurd stands close to the appropriate and serious. The shocking, the outrageous had for him an awakening touch. The joking word pointed to the highest reality was the bait that drew poetry to it, and was incongruous with his religion.

When, as happened once within these sacred walls, he preached a sermon, he usually managed to smuggle into it at least one phrase which, if it had not been partly muffled by the ambiguities of his collided Oxford and New York vowels and consonants, might have stunned some of the more conventional members of his audience. They were perhaps fortunate on such occasions to be able to go away not believing that they had heard what he had only mumbled.

Although he himself, if he were here, might feel nothing but gratitude that his poetic fame had provided him with a passport which enabled his name to become so literally a part of the body of the Abbey, it is as a poet that we think of him today. We think of his name on the stone near to those of colleagues belonging to this company of poets before he was born and near to that of one who was his contemporary—T. S. Eliot, whom he and all our generation of slightly younger poets admired this side of idolatry.

I should like then to say something about the nature of that poetry which justifies us in honouring Auden as he is now honoured.

Auden did not attach to poetry the immense pretensions which fill many poets at once with a sense of their transcendent personal superiority and with a sense of the near-unattainability of their objective aims in their work. He thought of a poem as a verbal object made by a craftsman who was to be judged to a great extent, though not entirely, by his technical competence in shaping language. At the same time he knew well that the modern poet, by taking many untamed, seemingly unpoetic, and even abstruse complex objects and naming them in diverse poetic forms, could make them familiar, accessible, capable of being handled like stones or bits of wood, could also make them, on occasion, sacred objects . . . He broke down great areas of contemporary experience into objects controlled by wit, crackling in jokes or transformed into objects of terrifying beauty. . . .

. . . He had also the strongest sense that poets should be modest in their claims on truth, that they should not indulge in the rhetorical lies which come so easily even to the greatest poets. When, with his wisdom, sense of beauty, and wit he directed his gaze upon the centre of the stage of our modern world, he was able to portray us in our situation, in poetry that combines accuracy of analysed experience with an authority of the imagination that shows our world to us as it is, while contrasting it with a vision of a life based on acceptance of a humanity which, despite its limitations, can still retain a certain innocence of nature: a glimpse of that Garden of Eden which the poet had first found in the green landscape of the England of his childhood.

ANAÏS NIN (1903–1977)

by Henry Miller (1977)

Anaïs Nin was a French-born author and essayist, most remembered for her published diaries, which won her great literary acclaim throughout the 1930s and 1940s. Many of these diaries centered around her long and tumultuous relationship with American author Henry Miller, who delivered the following eulogy at her funeral.

IT IS ONLY once or so each century that our sorry sublunary world is graced by the passage of a spirit as rare and courageous as was that of Anaïs Nin. In the realm of literature, I can think of few feminine figures who could hold a candle to Anaïs for artistic inventiveness and sheer personal radiance. Among these I would surely include Sappho, Emily Dickinson, Marie Corelli, Anna Akhmatova, and possibly the still-youthful Erica Jong. But few others seem to me to have possessed that special combination of toughness and magic, of power and elegance, which Anaïs and her counterparts so rarely and so perfectly embodied, both as writers and as women.

In a recent letter, Lawrence Durrell wrote that Anaïs had taught in her life and writings that women must put a high price on themselves and demand the right to be free, but that in so doing they should not lose their femininity—for, as Durrell put it,

> *...the whole civilized world of good values upon which our children will depend for their growth and mental well-being is precisely the work of the feminine element. And a world without real women in it to guide and nourish and inform its values will fall apart.*

Of the many women I have known in the course of my life, few could come close to Anaïs in beauty and feminine grace. She was both an enchantress and an aristocrat, a tireless helper of those in need and a fiercely private person. But she was also a writer of undeniable genius. And for all these reasons put together she now is the possession of the whole world, as it were.

I have repeated often before that her Diary ranks among the genuinely great and genuinely life-enhancing works of literature of all time. Now that her childhood diaries have been translated from the French and are about to be published, it will become even more obvious to her readers—the ones who have eyes and ears, bien entendu—how impressive has been the achievement of this lonely child whose only weapons, in the face of an unusually cruel fate, were pen and paper and the ink étoilique in which she very early taught herself to dip her pen.

Those who have humanly—all-too-humanly—criticized the work of Anaïs Nin in recent years have tended to accuse her of dwelling too much on "private" concerns. The writer of one current article in a widely read ladies' magazine, for example, says that "Anaïs' apolitical nature was self-indulgent and escapist; her analyses of poverty, struggle, and political realities were romantic constructs useful to very few." Such charges have a familiar ring. They would have sounded familiar to Plotinus, Boehme, Swedenborg, William Blake, Berdiaev, the Balzac of Seraphita, the Rimbaud of A Season in Hell, whom Anaïs loved so much, as well as to Sappho and Emily Dickinson.

But who would deny that these figures have done more to initiate the inevitable task of "changing life" (in Rimbaud's phrase) than all the ones with the "correct" analyses of poverty put together? Who would deny that the whole sorry lot of orthodox commentators on "political realities" have a much less vital message to offer us than these so-called otherworldly spirits? Anaïs Nin, to my mind, belongs in this "celestial" company. Like them, she continues to speak to us. Like them, she will live forever.

THE *CHALLENGER* ASTRONAUTS

by President Ronald Reagan (1986)

On January 28, 1986, the NASA Space Shuttle Challenger *broke apart shortly after takeoff, killing all seven crew members aboard. The seven astronauts who died in the* Challenger *disaster included Commander Francis (Dick) Scobee, Pilot Michael Smith, Mission Specialist Ronald McNair, Mission Specialist Ellison Onizuka, Mission Specialist Judith Resnik, Payload Specialist Gregory Jarvis, and Payload Specialist Christa McAuliffe. The following eulogy was delivered by President Ronald Reagan at a memorial service for the crew members at the Johnson Space Center in Houston on February 1, 1986.*

WE COME TOGETHER today to mourn the loss of seven brave Americans, to share the grief that we all feel and, perhaps in that sharing, to find the strength to bear our sorrow and the courage to look for the seeds of hope.

Our nation's loss is first a profound personal loss to the family and the friends and loved ones of our shuttle astronauts. To those they have left behind—the mothers, the fathers, the husbands and wives, brothers and sisters—yes and especially the children—all of America stands beside you in your time of sorrow.

What we say today is only an inadequate expression of what we carry in our hearts. Words pale in the shadow of grief; they seem insufficient even to measure the brave sacrifice of those you loved and we so admired. Their truest testimony will not be in the words we speak but in the way they led their lives and in the way they lost their lives—with dedication, honor and an unquenchable desire to explore this mysterious and beautiful universe.

The best we can do is remember our seven astronauts—our *Challenger* Seven—remember them as they lived, bringing life and love and joy to those who knew them and pride to a nation.

They came from all parts of this great country—from South Carolina to Washington State; Ohio to Mohawk, New York; Hawaii to North Carolina to Concord, New Hampshire. They were so different, yet in their mission, their quest, they held so much in common.

We remember Dick Scobee, the commander who spoke the last words we heard from the space shuttle *Challenger*. He served as a fighter pilot in Vietnam, earning many medals for bravery; later as a test pilot of advanced aircraft, before joining the space program. Danger was a familiar companion to Commander Scobee.

We remember Michael Smith, who earned enough medals as a combat pilot to cover his chest, including the Navy Distinguished Flying Cross, three Air Medals and the Vietnamese Cross of Gallantry with Silver Star, in gratitude from a nation he fought to keep free.

We remember Judith Resnik, known as J.R. to her friends, always smiling, always eager to make a contribution, finding beauty in the music she played on her piano in her off-hours.

We remember Ellison Onizuka, who, as a child running barefoot through the coffee fields and macadamia groves of Hawaii, dreamed of someday traveling to the moon. Being an Eagle Scout, he said, had helped him soar to the impressive achievements of his career.

We remember Ronald McNair, who said that he learned perseverance in the cotton fields of South Carolina. His dream was to live aboard the space station, performing experiments and playing his saxophone in the weightlessness of space. Well, Ron, we will miss your saxophone; and we will build your space station.

We remember Gregory Jarvis. On that ill-fated flight he was carrying with him a flag of his university in Buffalo, New York—a small token, he said, to the people who unlocked his future.

We remember Christa McAuliffe, who captured the imagination of the entire nation, inspiring us with her pluck, her restless spirit of discovery; a teacher, not just to her students but to an entire people, instilling us all with the excitement of this journey we ride into the future.

We will always remember them, these skilled professionals, scientists, and adventurers, these artists and teachers and family men and women, and we will cherish each of their stories—stories of triumph and bravery, stories of true American heroes.

On the day of the disaster, our nation held a vigil by our television sets. In one cruel moment, our exhilaration turned to horror; we waited and watched and tried to make sense of what we had seen. That night, I listened to a call-in program on the radio. People of every age spoke of their sadness and the pride they felt in "our astronauts." Across America, we are reaching out, holding hands, and finding comfort in one another.

The sacrifice of your loved ones has stirred the soul of our nation and, through the pain, our hearts have been opened to a profound truth: the future is not free, the story of all human progress is one of a struggle against all odds. We learned again that this America, which Abraham Lincoln called the last best hope of man on Earth, was built on heroism and noble sacrifice. It was built by men and women like our seven star voyagers, who answered a call beyond duty, who gave more than was expected or required, and who gave it with little thought to worldly reward.

We think back to the pioneers of an earlier century, the sturdy souls who took their families and their belongings and set out into the frontier of the American West. Often, they met with terrible hardship. Along the Oregon Trail you can still see the grave markers of those who fell on the way. But grief only steeled them to the journey ahead.

Today, the frontier is space and the boundaries of human knowledge. Sometimes, when we reach for the stars, we fall short. But we must pick ourselves up again and press on despite the pain. Our nation is indeed fortunate that we can still draw on immense reservoirs of courage, character, and fortitude—that we are still blessed with heroes like those of the space shuttle *Challenger.*

Dick Scobee knew that every launching of a space shuttle is a technological miracle. And he said, if something ever does go wrong, I hope that doesn't mean the end to the space shuttle program. Every family member I talked to asked specifically that we continue the program, that that is what their departed loved one would want above all else. We will not disappoint them.

Today, we promise Dick Scobee and his crew that their dream lives on; that the future they worked so hard to build will become reality. The dedicated men and women of NASA have lost seven members of their family. Still, they, too, must forge ahead with a space program that is effective, safe, and efficient but bold and committed.

Man will continue his conquest of space, to reach out for new goals and ever greater achievements. That is the way we shall commemorate our seven *Challenger* heroes.

Dick, Mike, Judy, El, Ron, Greg and Christa, your families and your country mourn your passing. We bid you goodbye. We will never forget you. For those who knew you well and loved you, the pain will be deep and enduring. The nation, too, will long feel the loss of her seven sons and daughters, her seven good friends. We can find consolation only in faith for we know in our hearts that you who flew so high and so proud now make your home beyond the stars, safe in God's promise of eternal life.

May God bless you all and give you comfort in this difficult time.

MICKEY MANTLE (1931–1995)

by Bob Costas (1995)

Mickey Mantle was a professional American baseball player whose 18-year career with the New York Yankees saw him hit 536 home runs and finish three seasons as the American League's Most Valuable Player. The following eulogy was delivered by renowned American sportscaster Bob Costas at Mickey Mantle's funeral on August 15, 1995.

YOU KNOW, IT occurs to me as we're all sitting here thinking of Mickey, he's probably somewhere getting an earful from Casey Stengel, and no doubt quite confused by now.

One of Mickey's fondest wishes was that he be remembered as a great teammate, to know that the men he played with thought well of him.

But it was more than that. Moose and Whitey and Tony and Yogi and Bobby and Hank, what a remarkable team you were. And the stories of the visits you guys made to Mickey's bedside the last few days were heartbreakingly tender. It meant everything to Mickey, as would the presence of so many baseball figures past and present here today.

I was honored to be asked to speak by the Mantle family today. I am not standing here as a broadcaster. Mel Allen is the eternal voice of the Yankees and that would be his place. And there are others here with a longer and deeper association with Mickey than mine.

But I guess I'm here, not so much to speak for myself, as to simply represent the millions of baseball-loving kids who grew up in the fifties and sixties and for whom Mickey Mantle was baseball.

And more than that, he was a presence in our lives—a fragile hero to whom we had an emotional attachment so strong and lasting that it defied logic. Mickey often said he didn't understand it, this enduring connection and affection—the men now in their forties and fifties, otherwise perfectly sensible, who went dry in the mouth and stammered like schoolboys in the presence of Mickey Mantle.

Maybe Mickey was uncomfortable with it, not just because of his basic shyness, but because he was always too honest to regard himself as some kind of deity.

But that was never really the point. In a very different time than today, the first baseball commissioner, Kenesaw Mountain Landis, said, "Every boy builds a shrine to some baseball hero, and before that shrine, a candle always burns."

For a huge portion of my generation, Mickey Mantle was that baseball hero. And for reasons that no statistics, no dry recitation of facts can possibly capture, he was the most compelling baseball hero of our lifetime. And he was our symbol of baseball at a time when the game meant something to us that perhaps it no longer does.

Mickey Mantle had those dual qualities so seldom seen—exuding dynamism and excitement, but at the same time touching your heart—flawed, wounded. We knew there was something poignant about Mickey Mantle before we knew what poignant meant. We didn't just root for him, we felt for him.

Long before many of us ever cracked a serious book, we knew something about mythology as we watched Mickey Mantle run out a home run through the lengthening shadows of a late Sunday afternoon at Yankee Stadium.

There was greatness in him, but vulnerability, too.

He was our guy. When he was hot, we felt great. When he slumped or got hurt, we sagged a bit, too. We tried to crease our caps like him; kneel in an imaginary on-deck circle like him; run like him, heads down, elbows up.

Billy Crystal is here today. Billy says that at his bar mitzvah he spoke in an Oklahoma drawl. Billy's here today because he loved Mickey Mantle, and millions more who felt like him are here today in spirit as well.

It has been said that the truth is never pure and rarely simple.

Mickey Mantle was too humble and honest to believe that the whole truth about him could be found on a Wheaties box or a baseball card. But the emotional truths of childhood have a power that transcends objective fact. They stay with us through all the years, withstanding the ambivalence that so often accompanies the experience of adults.

That's why we can still recall the immediate tingle in that instant of recognition when a Mickey Mantle popped up in a pack of Topps bubble gum cards—a treasure lodged between an Eli Grba and a Pumpsie Green.

That's why we smile today, recalling those October afternoons when we'd sneak a transistor radio into school to follow Mickey and the Yankees in the World Series.

Or when I think of Mr. Tomasi, a very wise sixth-grade teacher who understood that the World Series was more important, at least for one day, than any school lesson could be. So he brought his black-and-white TV from home, plugged it in and let us watch it right there in school through the flicker and the static. It was richer and more compelling than anything I've seen on a high-resolution, big-screen TV.

Of course, the bad part, Bobby, was that Koufax struck fifteen of you guys out that day.

My phone's been ringing the past few weeks as Mickey fought for his life. I've heard from people I hadn't seen or talked to in years—guys I played stickball with, even some guys who took Willie's side in those endless Mantle-Mays arguments. They're grown up now. They have their families. They're not even necessarily big baseball fans anymore. But they felt something hearing about Mickey, and they figured I did, too.

In the last year, Mickey Mantle, always so hard on himself, finally came to accept and appreciate that distinction between a role model and a hero. The first he often was not, the second he always will be.

And, in the end, people got it. And Mickey Mantle got from America something other than misplaced and mindless celebrity worship. He got something far more meaningful. He got love—love for what he had been, love for what he made us feel, love for the humanity and sweetness that was always there mixed in with the flaws and all the pain that wracked his body and his soul.

We wanted to tell him that it was OK, that what he had been was enough. We hoped he felt that Mutt Mantle would have understood and that Merlyn and the boys loved him.

And then in the end, something remarkable happened—the way it does for champions. Mickey Mantle rallied. His heart took over, and he had some innings as fine as any in 1956 or with his buddy, Roger, in 1961.

But this time, he did it in the harsh and trying summer of '95. And what he did was stunning. The sheer grace of that ninth inning—the humility, the sense of humor, the total absence of self-pity, the simple eloquence and honesty of his pleas to others to take heed of his mistakes.

All of America watched in admiration. His doctors said he was, in many ways, the most remarkable patient they'd ever seen. His bravery, so stark and real, that even those used to seeing people in dire circumstances were moved by his example.

Because of that example, organ donations are up dramatically all across America. A cautionary tale has been honestly told and perhaps will affect some lives for the better.

And our last memories of Mickey Mantle are as heroic as the first.

None of us, Mickey included, would want to be held to account for every moment of our lives. But how many of us could say that our best moments were as magnificent as his?

This is the cartoon from this morning's *Dallas Morning News*. Maybe some of you saw it. It got torn a little bit on the way from the hotel to here. There's a figure here, St. Peter I take it to be, with his arm around Mickey, that broad back and the number seven. He's holding his book of admissions. He says "Kid, that was the most courageous ninth inning I've ever seen."

It brings to mind a story Mickey liked to tell on himself and maybe some of you have heard it. He pictured himself at the pearly gates, met by St. Peter, who shook his head and said, "Mick, we checked the record. We know some of what went on. Sorry, we can't let you in, but before you go, God wants to know if you'd sign these six dozen baseballs."

Well, there were days when Mickey Mantle was so darn good that we kids would bet that even God would want his autograph. But like the cartoon says, I don't think Mick needed to worry much about the other part.

I just hope God has a place for him where he can run again. Where he can play practical jokes on his teammates and smile that boyish smile, 'cause God knows, no one's perfect. And God knows there's something special about heroes.

So long, Mick. Thanks.

CORETTA SCOTT KING (1927–2006)

by Maya Angelou (2006)

*Coretta Scott King was an American civil rights leader who,
along with her husband, Martin Luther King Jr., played a
pivotal role in the African American Civil Rights movement
of the 1960s. Maya Angelou was an American poet and
author, best remembered for her 1969 autobiography,* I Know
Why the Caged Bird Sings. *Angelou delivered the following eulogy for Coretta Scott King on February 7, 2006.*

IN THE MIDST of national tumult, in the medium of international
violent uproar, Coretta Scott King's face remained a study in serenity. In times of interior violent storms she sat, her hands resting in
her lap calmly, like good children sleeping.

Her passion was never spent in public display. She offered her
industry and her energies to action, toward righting ancient and
current wrongs in this world.

She believed religiously in non-violent protest.

She believed it could heal a nation mired in a history of slavery
and all its excesses.

She believed non-violent protest religiously could lift up a nation
rife with racial prejudices and racial bias.

She was a quintessential African-American woman, born in the
small town repressive South, born of flesh and destined to become
iron, born—born a cornflower and destined to become a steel
magnolia.

She loved her church fervently. She loved and adored her husband
and her children. She cherished her race. She cherished women. She
cared for the conditions of human beings, of native Americans and
Latin—Latinos and Asian Americans. She cared for gay and straight

people. She was concerned for the struggles in Ireland, and she prayed nightly for Palestine and equally for Israel.

I speak as a—a sister of a sister. Dr. Martin Luther King was assassinated on my birthday. And for over 30 years, Coretta Scott King and I have telephoned, or sent cards to each other, or flowers to each other, or met each other somewhere in the world.

We called ourselves "chosen sisters" and when we traveled to South Africa or to the Caribbean or when she came to visit me in North Carolina or in New York, we sat into the late evening hours, calling each other "girl." It's a black woman thing, you know. And even as we reached well into our 70th decade, we still said "girl."

I stand here today for her family—which is my family—and for my family and all the other families in the world who would want to be here, but could not be here. I have beside me up here millions of people who are living and standing straight and erect, and knowing something about dignity without being cold and aloof, knowing something about being contained without being unapproachable—people who have learned something from Coretta Scott King.

I stand here for Eleanor Traylor and for Harry Belafonte, and I stand here for Winnie Mandela. I stand here for women and men who loved her—[Constancia] "Dinky" Romilly. On those late nights when Coretta and I would talk, I would make her laugh. And she said that Martin King used to tell her, "You don't laugh enough." And there's a recent book out about sisters in which she spoke about her blood sister. But at the end of her essay, she said, I did have—"I do have a chosen sister, Maya Angelou, who makes me laugh even when I don't want to." And it's true. I told her some jokes only for no-mixed company.

Many times on those late after-evenings she would say to me, "Sister, it shouldn't be an 'either-or,' should it? Peace and justice should belong to all people, everywhere, all the time. Isn't that right?" And I said then and I say now, "Coretta Scott King, you're absolutely right. I do believe that peace and justice should belong to every person, everywhere, all the time."

And those of us who gather here, principalities, presidents, senators, those of us who run great companies, who know something about being parents, who know something about being preachers and teachers—those of us, we owe something from this minute on; so that this gathering is not just another footnote on the pages of history. We owe something.

I pledge to you, my sister, I will never cease.
I mean to say I want to see a better world.
I mean to say I want to see some peace somewhere.
I mean to say I want to see some honesty, some fair play.
I want to see kindness and justice. This is what I want to see and I want to see it through my eyes and through your eyes, Coretta Scott King.

[Sings: "I open my mouth to the Lord and I won't turn back, no. I will go, I shall go. I'll see what the end is gonna be."]

NELSON MANDELA (1918–2013)

by President Barack Obama (2013)

Nelson Mandela was a South African activist and statesman who helped lead the anti-apartheid movement and played a pivotal role in ending the nation's racial segregation. In 1993, Mandela was awarded the Nobel Prize for Peace, before going on to become South Africa's first black president in 1994. The following eulogy was delivered by U.S. President Barack Obama at a memorial service in Mandela's honor on December 10, 2013.

TO GRAÇA MACHEL and the Mandela family; to President Zuma and members of the government; to heads of states and government, past and present; distinguished guests—it is a singular honor to be with you today, to celebrate a life like no other. To the people of South Africa—people of every race and walk of life—the world thanks you for sharing Nelson Mandela with us. His struggle was your struggle. His triumph was your triumph. Your dignity and your hope found expression in his life. And your freedom, your democracy is his cherished legacy.

It is hard to eulogize any man—to capture in words not just the facts and the dates that make a life, but the essential truth of a person—their private joys and sorrows; the quiet moments and unique qualities that illuminate someone's soul. How much harder to do so for a giant of history, who moved a nation toward justice, and in the process moved billions around the world.

Born during World War I, far from the corridors of power, a boy raised herding cattle and tutored by the elders of his Thembu tribe, Madiba would emerge as the last great liberator of the 20th century. Like Gandhi, he would lead a resistance movement—a movement that at its start had little prospect for success. Like Dr. King, he would give potent voice to the claims of the oppressed and the moral necessity of racial justice. He would endure a brutal imprisonment that began in the time of Kennedy and Khrushchev, and reached the final days of the Cold War. Emerging from prison, without the force of arms, he would—like Abraham Lincoln—hold his country together when it threatened to break apart. And like America's Founding Fathers, he would erect a constitutional order to preserve freedom for future generations—a commitment to democracy and rule of law ratified not only by his election, but by his willingness to step down from power after only one term.

Given the sweep of his life, the scope of his accomplishments, the adoration that he so rightly earned, it's tempting I think to remember Nelson Mandela as an icon, smiling and serene, detached from the tawdry affairs of lesser men. But Madiba himself strongly resisted such a lifeless portrait. Instead, Madiba insisted on sharing with us his doubts and his fears; his miscalculations along with his victories. "I am not a saint," he said, "unless you think of a saint as a sinner who keeps on trying."

It was precisely because he could admit to imperfection—because he could be so full of good humor, even mischief, despite the heavy burdens he carried—that we loved him so. He was not a bust made of marble; he was a man of flesh and blood—a son and a husband, a father and a friend. And that's why we learned so much from him, and that's why we can learn from him still. For nothing he achieved was inevitable. In the arc of his life, we see a man who earned his place in history through struggle and shrewdness, and persistence and faith. He tells us what is possible not just in the pages of history books, but in our own lives as well.

Mandela showed us the power of action; of taking risks on behalf of our ideals. Perhaps Madiba was right that he inherited, "a proud rebelliousness, a stubborn sense of fairness" from his father. And we know he shared with millions of black and colored South Africans the anger born of, "a thousand slights, a thousand indignities, a thousand unremembered moments...a desire to fight the system that imprisoned my people," he said.

But like other early giants of the ANC—the Sisulus and Tambos—Madiba disciplined his anger and channeled his desire to fight into organization, and platforms, and strategies for action, so men and women could stand up for their God-given dignity. Moreover, he accepted the consequences of his actions, knowing that standing up to powerful interests and injustice carries a price. "I have fought against white domination and I have fought against black domination. I've cherished the ideal of a democratic and free society in which all persons live together in harmony and [with] equal opportunities. It is an ideal which I hope to live for and to achieve. But if needs be, it is an ideal for which I am prepared to die."

Mandela taught us the power of action, but he also taught us the power of ideas; the importance of reason and arguments; the need to study not only those who you agree with, but also those who you don't agree with. He understood that ideas cannot be contained by prison walls, or extinguished by a sniper's bullet. He turned his trial into an indictment of apartheid because of his eloquence and his passion, but also because of his training as an advocate. He used decades in prison to sharpen his arguments, but also to spread his thirst for knowledge to others in the movement. And he learned the language and the customs of his oppressor so that one day he might better convey to them how their own freedom depends upon his.

Mandela demonstrated that action and ideas are not enough. No matter how right, they must be chiseled into law and institutions. He was practical, testing his beliefs against the hard surface of circumstance and history. On core principles he was unyielding, which is why he could rebuff offers of unconditional release, reminding the Apartheid regime that "prisoners cannot enter into contracts."

But as he showed in painstaking negotiations to transfer power and draft new laws, he was not afraid to compromise for the sake of a larger goal. And because he was not only a leader of a movement but a skillful politician, the Constitution that emerged was worthy of this multiracial democracy, true to his vision of laws that protect minority as well as majority rights, and the precious freedoms of every South African.

And finally, Mandela understood the ties that bind the human spirit. There is a word in South Africa—Ubuntu—a word that captures Mandela's greatest gift: his recognition that we are all bound together in ways that are invisible to the eye; that there is a oneness to humanity; that we achieve ourselves by sharing ourselves with others, and caring for those around us.

We can never know how much of this sense was innate in him, or how much was shaped in a dark and solitary cell. But we remember the gestures, large and small—introducing his jailers as honored guests at his inauguration; taking a pitch in a Springbok uniform;

turning his family's heartbreak into a call to confront HIV/AIDS—that revealed the depth of his empathy and his understanding. He not only embodied Ubuntu, he taught millions to find that truth within themselves.

It took a man like Madiba to free not just the prisoner, but the jailer as well—to show that you must trust others so that they may trust you; to teach that reconciliation is not a matter of ignoring a cruel past, but a means of confronting it with inclusion and generosity and truth. He changed laws, but he also changed hearts.

For the people of South Africa, for those he inspired around the globe, Madiba's passing is rightly a time of mourning, and a time to celebrate a heroic life. But I believe it should also prompt in each of us a time for self-reflection. With honesty, regardless of our station or our circumstance, we must ask: How well have I applied his lessons in my own life? It's a question I ask myself, as a man and as a President.

We know that, like South Africa, the United States had to overcome centuries of racial subjugation. As was true here, it took sacrifice—the sacrifice of countless people, known and unknown, to see the dawn of a new day. Michelle and I are beneficiaries of that struggle. But in America, and in South Africa, and in countries all around the globe, we cannot allow our progress to cloud the fact that our work is not yet done.

The struggles that follow the victory of formal equality or universal franchise may not be as filled with drama and moral clarity as those that came before, but they are no less important. For around the world today, we still see children suffering from hunger and disease. We still see run-down schools. We still see young people without prospects for the future. Around the world today, men and women are still imprisoned for their political beliefs, and are still persecuted for what they look like, and how they worship, and who they love. That is happening today.

And so we, too, must act on behalf of justice. We, too, must act on behalf of peace. There are too many people who happily embrace Madiba's legacy of racial reconciliation, but passionately resist even modest reforms that would challenge chronic poverty and growing inequality. There are too many leaders who claim solidarity with Madiba's struggle for freedom, but do not tolerate dissent from their own people. And there are too many of us on the sidelines, comfortable in complacency or cynicism when our voices must be heard.

The questions we face today—how to promote equality and justice; how to uphold freedom and human rights; how to end conflict and sectarian war—these things do not have easy answers. But there were no easy answers in front of that child born in World War I. Nelson Mandela reminds us that it always seems impossible until it is done. South Africa shows that is true. South Africa shows we can change, that we can choose a world defined not by our differences, but by our common hopes. We can choose a world defined not by conflict, but by peace and justice and opportunity.

We will never see the likes of Nelson Mandela again. But let me say to the young people of Africa and the young people around the world—you, too, can make his life's work your own. Over 30 years ago, while still a student, I learned of Nelson Mandela and the struggles taking place in this beautiful land, and it stirred something in me. It woke me up to my responsibilities to others and to myself, and it set me on an improbable journey that finds me here today. And while I will always fall short of Madiba's example, he makes me want to be a better man. He speaks to what's best inside us.

After this great liberator is laid to rest, and when we have returned to our cities and villages and rejoined our daily routines, let us search for his strength. Let us search for his largeness of spirit somewhere inside of ourselves. And when the night grows dark, when injustice weighs heavy on our hearts, when our best-laid plans seem beyond our reach, let us think of Madiba and the words that brought him comfort within the four walls of his cell: "It matters not how strait the gate, how charged with punishments the scroll, I am the master of my fate: I am the captain of my soul."

What a magnificent soul it was. We will miss him deeply. May God bless the memory of Nelson Mandela. May God bless the people of South Africa.

A CATALOG OF SELECTED DOVER
BOOKS IN ALL FIELDS OF INTEREST

100 BEST-LOVED POEMS, Edited by Philip Smith. "The Passionate Shepherd to His Love," "Shall I compare thee to a summer's day?" "Death, be not proud," "The Raven," "The Road Not Taken," plus works by Blake, Wordsworth, Byron, Shelley, Keats, many others. 96pp. 5³⁄₁₆ x 8¼. 0-486-28553-7

100 SMALL HOUSES OF THE THIRTIES, Brown-Blodgett Company. Exterior photographs and floor plans for 100 charming structures. Illustrations of models accompanied by descriptions of interiors, color schemes, closet space, and other amenities. 200 illustrations. 112pp. 8⅜ x 11. 0-486-44131-8

1000 TURN-OF-THE-CENTURY HOUSES: With Illustrations and Floor Plans, Herbert C. Chivers. Reproduced from a rare edition, this showcase of homes ranges from cottages and bungalows to sprawling mansions. Each house is meticulously illustrated and accompanied by complete floor plans. 256pp. 9⅜ x 12¼.
0-486-45596-3

101 GREAT AMERICAN POEMS, Edited by The American Poetry & Literacy Project. Rich treasury of verse from the 19th and 20th centuries includes works by Edgar Allan Poe, Robert Frost, Walt Whitman, Langston Hughes, Emily Dickinson, T. S. Eliot, other notables. 96pp. 5³⁄₁₆ x 8¼. 0-486-40158-8

101 GREAT SAMURAI PRINTS, Utagawa Kuniyoshi. Kuniyoshi was a master of the warrior woodblock print — and these 18th-century illustrations represent the pinnacle of his craft. Full-color portraits of renowned Japanese samurais pulse with movement, passion, and remarkably fine detail. 112pp. 8⅜ x 11. 0-486-46523-3

ABC OF BALLET, Janet Grosser. Clearly worded, abundantly illustrated little guide defines basic ballet-related terms: arabesque, battement, pas de chat, relevé, sissonne, many others. Pronunciation guide included. Excellent primer. 48pp. 4³⁄₁₆ x 5¾.
0-486-40871-X

ACCESSORIES OF DRESS: An Illustrated Encyclopedia, Katherine Lester and Bess Viola Oerke. Illustrations of hats, veils, wigs, cravats, shawls, shoes, gloves, and other accessories enhance an engaging commentary that reveals the humor and charm of the many-sided story of accessorized apparel. 644 figures and 59 plates. 608pp. 6 ⅛ x 9¼.
0-486-43378-1

ADVENTURES OF HUCKLEBERRY FINN, Mark Twain. Join Huck and Jim as their boyhood adventures along the Mississippi River lead them into a world of excitement, danger, and self-discovery. Humorous narrative, lyrical descriptions of the Mississippi valley, and memorable characters. 224pp. 5³⁄₁₆ x 8¼. 0-486-28061-6

ALICE STARMORE'S BOOK OF FAIR ISLE KNITTING, Alice Starmore. A noted designer from the region of Scotland's Fair Isle explores the history and techniques of this distinctive, stranded-color knitting style and provides copious illustrated instructions for 14 original knitwear designs. 208pp. 8⅜ x 10⅞. 0-486-47218-3

Browse over 9,000 books at www.doverpublications.com

THE BATTLES THAT CHANGED HISTORY, Fletcher Pratt. Historian profiles 16 crucial conflicts, ancient to modern, that changed the course of Western civilization. Gripping accounts of battles led by Alexander the Great, Joan of Arc, Ulysses S. Grant, other commanders. 27 maps. 352pp. 5⅜ x 8½. 0-486-41129-X

BEETHOVEN'S LETTERS, Ludwig van Beethoven. Edited by Dr. A. C. Kalischer. Features 457 letters to fellow musicians, friends, greats, patrons, and literary men. Reveals musical thoughts, quirks of personality, insights, and daily events. Includes 15 plates. 410pp. 5⅜ x 8½. 0-486-22769-3

BERNICE BOBS HER HAIR AND OTHER STORIES, F. Scott Fitzgerald. This brilliant anthology includes 6 of Fitzgerald's most popular stories: "The Diamond as Big as the Ritz," the title tale, "The Offshore Pirate," "The Ice Palace," "The Jelly Bean," and "May Day." 176pp. 5⅜ x 8½. 0-486-47049-0

BESLER'S BOOK OF FLOWERS AND PLANTS: 73 Full-Color Plates from Hortus Eystettensis, 1613, Basilius Besler. Here is a selection of magnificent plates from the *Hortus Eystettensis,* which vividly illustrated and identified the plants, flowers, and trees that thrived in the legendary German garden at Eichstätt. 80pp. 8⅜ x 11.
0-486-46005-3

THE BOOK OF KELLS, Edited by Blanche Cirker. Painstakingly reproduced from a rare facsimile edition, this volume contains full-page decorations, portraits, illustrations, plus a sampling of textual leaves with exquisite calligraphy and ornamentation. 32 full-color illustrations. 32pp. 9⅜ x 12¼. 0-486-24345-1

THE BOOK OF THE CROSSBOW: With an Additional Section on Catapults and Other Siege Engines, Ralph Payne-Gallwey. Fascinating study traces history and use of crossbow as military and sporting weapon, from Middle Ages to modern times. Also covers related weapons: balistas, catapults, Turkish bows, more. Over 240 illustrations. 400pp. 7¼ x 10¼. 0-486-28720-3

THE BUNGALOW BOOK: Floor Plans and Photos of 112 Houses, 1910, Henry L. Wilson. Here are 112 of the most popular and economic blueprints of the early 20th century — plus an illustration or photograph of each completed house. A wonderful time capsule that still offers a wealth of valuable insights. 160pp. 8⅜ x 11.
0-486-45104-6

THE CALL OF THE WILD, Jack London. A classic novel of adventure, drawn from London's own experiences as a Klondike adventurer, relating the story of a heroic dog caught in the brutal life of the Alaska Gold Rush. Note. 64pp. 5³⁄₁₆ x 8¼.
0-486-26472-6

CANDIDE, Voltaire. Edited by Francois-Marie Arouet. One of the world's great satires since its first publication in 1759. Witty, caustic skewering of romance, science, philosophy, religion, government — nearly all human ideals and institutions. 112pp. 5³⁄₁₆ x 8¼. 0-486-26689-3

CELEBRATED IN THEIR TIME: Photographic Portraits from the George Grantham Bain Collection, Edited by Amy Pastan. With an Introduction by Michael Carlebach. Remarkable portrait gallery features 112 rare images of Albert Einstein, Charlie Chaplin, the Wright Brothers, Henry Ford, and other luminaries from the worlds of politics, art, entertainment, and industry. 128pp. 8⅜ x 11. 0-486-46754-6

CHARIOTS FOR APOLLO: The NASA History of Manned Lunar Spacecraft to 1969, Courtney G. Brooks, James M. Grimwood, and Loyd S. Swenson, Jr. This illustrated history by a trio of experts is the definitive reference on the Apollo spacecraft and lunar modules. It traces the vehicles' design, development, and operation in space. More than 100 photographs and illustrations. 576pp. 6¾ x 9¼. 0-486-46756-2

DOOMED SHIPS: Great Ocean Liner Disasters, William H. Miller, Jr. Nearly 200 photographs, many from private collections, highlight tales of some of the vessels whose pleasure cruises ended in catastrophe: the *Morro Castle, Normandie, Andrea Doria, Europa,* and many others. 128pp. 8⅞ x 11¾. 0-486-45366-9

THE DORÉ BIBLE ILLUSTRATIONS, Gustave Doré. Detailed plates from the Bible: the Creation scenes, Adam and Eve, horrifying visions of the Flood, the battle sequences with their monumental crowds, depictions of the life of Jesus, 241 plates in all. 241pp. 9 x 12. 0-486-23004-X

DRAWING DRAPERY FROM HEAD TO TOE, Cliff Young. Expert guidance on how to draw shirts, pants, skirts, gloves, hats, and coats on the human figure, including folds in relation to the body, pull and crush, action folds, creases, more. Over 200 drawings. 48pp. 8¼ x 11. 0-486-45591-2

DUBLINERS, James Joyce. A fine and accessible introduction to the work of one of the 20th century's most influential writers, this collection features 15 tales, including a masterpiece of the short-story genre, "The Dead." 160pp. 5³⁄₁₆ x 8¼. 0-486-26870-5

EASY-TO-MAKE POP-UPS, Joan Irvine. Illustrated by Barbara Reid. Dozens of wonderful ideas for three-dimensional paper fun — from holiday greeting cards with moving parts to a pop-up menagerie. Easy-to-follow, illustrated instructions for more than 30 projects. 299 black-and-white illustrations. 96pp. 8⅜ x 11. 0-486-44622-0

EASY-TO-MAKE STORYBOOK DOLLS: A "Novel" Approach to Cloth Dollmaking, Sherralyn St. Clair. Favorite fictional characters come alive in this unique beginner's dollmaking guide. Includes patterns for Pollyanna, Dorothy from *The Wonderful Wizard of Oz,* Mary of *The Secret Garden,* plus easy-to-follow instructions, 263 black-and-white illustrations, and an 8-page color insert. 112pp. 8¼ x 11. 0-486-47360-0

EINSTEIN'S ESSAYS IN SCIENCE, Albert Einstein. Speeches and essays in accessible, everyday language profile influential physicists such as Niels Bohr and Isaac Newton. They also explore areas of physics to which the author made major contributions. 128pp. 5 x 8. 0-486-47011-3

EL DORADO: Further Adventures of the Scarlet Pimpernel, Baroness Orczy. A popular sequel to *The Scarlet Pimpernel,* this suspenseful story recounts the Pimpernel's attempts to rescue the Dauphin from imprisonment during the French Revolution. An irresistible blend of intrigue, period detail, and vibrant characterizations. 352pp. 5³⁄₁₆ x 8¼. 0-486-44026-5

ELEGANT SMALL HOMES OF THE TWENTIES: 99 Designs from a Competition, Chicago Tribune. Nearly 100 designs for five- and six-room houses feature New England and Southern colonials, Normandy cottages, stately Italianate dwellings, and other fascinating snapshots of American domestic architecture of the 1920s. 112pp. 9 x 12. 0-486-46910-7

THE ELEMENTS OF STYLE: The Original Edition, William Strunk, Jr. This is the book that generations of writers have relied upon for timeless advice on grammar, diction, syntax, and other essentials. In concise terms, it identifies the principal requirements of proper style and common errors. 64pp. 5⅜ x 8½. 0-486-44798-7

THE ELUSIVE PIMPERNEL, Baroness Orczy. Robespierre's revolutionaries find their wicked schemes thwarted by the heroic Pimpernel — Sir Percival Blakeney. In this thrilling sequel, Chauvelin devises a plot to eliminate the Pimpernel and his wife. 272pp. 5³⁄₁₆ x 8¼. 0-486-45464-9

FIVE ACRES AND INDEPENDENCE, Maurice G. Kains. Great back-to-the-land classic explains basics of self-sufficient farming. The one book to get. 95 illustrations. 397pp. 5⅜ x 8½. 0-486-20974-1

FLAGG'S SMALL HOUSES: Their Economic Design and Construction, 1922, Ernest Flagg. Although most famous for his skyscrapers, Flagg was also a proponent of the well-designed single-family dwelling. His classic treatise features innovations that save space, materials, and cost. 526 illustrations. 160pp. 9⅜ x 12¼.

0-486-45197-6

FLATLAND: A Romance of Many Dimensions, Edwin A. Abbott. Classic of science (and mathematical) fiction — charmingly illustrated by the author — describes the adventures of A. Square, a resident of Flatland, in Spaceland (three dimensions), Lineland (one dimension), and Pointland (no dimensions). 96pp. 5³⁄₁₆ x 8¼.

0-486-27263-X

FRANKENSTEIN, Mary Shelley. The story of Victor Frankenstein's monstrous creation and the havoc it caused has enthralled generations of readers and inspired countless writers of horror and suspense. With the author's own 1831 introduction. 176pp. 5³⁄₁₆ x 8¼. 0-486-28211-2

THE GARGOYLE BOOK: 572 Examples from Gothic Architecture, Lester Burbank Bridaham. Dispelling the conventional wisdom that French Gothic architectural flourishes were born of despair or gloom, Bridaham reveals the whimsical nature of these creations and the ingenious artisans who made them. 572 illustrations. 224pp. 8⅜ x 11. 0-486-44754-5

THE GIFT OF THE MAGI AND OTHER SHORT STORIES, O. Henry. Sixteen captivating stories by one of America's most popular storytellers. Included are such classics as "The Gift of the Magi," "The Last Leaf," and "The Ransom of Red Chief." Publisher's Note. 96pp. 5³⁄₁₆ x 8¼. 0-486-27061-0

THE GOETHE TREASURY: Selected Prose and Poetry, Johann Wolfgang von Goethe. Edited, Selected, and with an Introduction by Thomas Mann. In addition to his lyric poetry, Goethe wrote travel sketches, autobiographical studies, essays, letters, and proverbs in rhyme and prose. This collection presents outstanding examples from each genre. 368pp. 5⅜ x 8½. 0-486-44780-4

GREAT EXPECTATIONS, Charles Dickens. Orphaned Pip is apprenticed to the dirty work of the forge but dreams of becoming a gentleman — and one day finds himself in possession of "great expectations." Dickens' finest novel. 400pp. 5³⁄₁₆ x 8¼.

0-486-41586-4

GREAT WRITERS ON THE ART OF FICTION: From Mark Twain to Joyce Carol Oates, Edited by James Daley. An indispensable source of advice and inspiration, this anthology features essays by Henry James, Kate Chopin, Willa Cather, Sinclair Lewis, Jack London, Raymond Chandler, Raymond Carver, Eudora Welty, and Kurt Vonnegut, Jr. 192pp. 5⅜ x 8½. 0-486-45128-3

HAMLET, William Shakespeare. The quintessential Shakespearean tragedy, whose highly charged confrontations and anguished soliloquies probe depths of human feeling rarely sounded in any art. Reprinted from an authoritative British edition complete with illuminating footnotes. 128pp. 5³⁄₁₆ x 8¼. 0-486-27278-8

THE HAUNTED HOUSE, Charles Dickens. A Yuletide gathering in an eerie country retreat provides the backdrop for Dickens and his friends — including Elizabeth Gaskell and Wilkie Collins — who take turns spinning supernatural yarns. 144pp. 5⅜ x 8½. 0-486-46309-5